마르지 않는 우물(井): 남춘모론

NAM TCHUN-MO A Well That Never Dries

배 원 정 | 미술사학자
Bae Wonjung | Ph.D. in Art History

Hartmann Books

차 례

Contents

Ⅰ. 서문

남춘모(1961-)는 선의 구조적 힘과 물질의 감각적 특성을 탐구하며, 전통적 '골법(骨法)'의 현대적 해석과 반복적 행위에 따른 '카르마(業)'적 실천을 통해 자신만의 독창적인 작품 세계를 구축해 온 작가다.[1]

그의 회화는 어떤 단일한 양식적 계보에 국한되지 않는다. 전통과 현대, 감각과 구조, 수공(手工)적 물성 작업과 추상적 조형, 신체성과 정신성, 그리고 개인적인 추억과 공동체의 문화적 경험들을 유기적으로 관통하며, 독특한 예술 세계를 보인다.

그가 다루는 조형 요소 중 핵심은 '선(線)'이다. 그의 선은 단순한 윤곽선이나 추상적 제스처를 넘어, 밭고랑과 '우물 정(井)' 자, 창호의 창살과 서까래 같은 전통 건축에서 유래된 조형적 기억과 긴밀히 연결된다. 선은 반복과 리듬의 시간성을 담고 있으면서, 동시에 화면에서 시각적으로 질서와 공간감을 만들어내는 핵심 역할을 한다.

1 계명대학교 미술대학(1986) 및 동 대학원(1988)을 졸업. 1990년부터 시공갤러리, 조현화랑, 리안갤러리, 독일 Galerie Dorothea van der Koelen, 프랑스 Ceysson & Bénétière Gallery 등 국내외 주요 갤러리 및 국립현대미술관, 대구미술관, 파워롱미술관 상하이, 인당미술관, 독일 Ludwig Museum Koblenz 등에서 개인전 및 단체전에 참여했다. 그에 대한 자세한 사항은 작가 홈페이지 http://www.namtchunmo.com 참조.

Ⅰ. Preface

By exploring the structural power of lines and the sensory qualities of materials, artist Nam Tchun-Mo (b. 1961) has cultivated a distinct and highly original body of work.[1] Through repetitive actions, he engages in a karmic painting practice, offering a contemporary interpretation of "*golbeop*" (骨法, "bone methods and use of brush"), a classical principle of East Asian painting that emphasizes structural integrity through brushwork. Yet Nam's painting cannot be confined to any single stylistic lineage. He organically traverses tradition and contemporaneity, sense and structure, handcrafted materiality and abstract form, physicality and spirituality, as well as personal memories and collective cultural experience. These syntheses result in a unique and multifaceted artistic world.

The core formal element of Nam's practice is the line. Beyond simple contours or abstract gestures, his lines incorporate memories of furrowed fields, the Chinese character "井" (*jeong*, meaning "water well"), and elements of traditional architecture, such as lattice windows and rafters. His lines contain the temporality of his own repetition and rhythm, while also creating a sense of space and visual order within the painting.

1 Nam Tchun-Mo earned his bachelor's and master's degrees from the College of Fine Arts at Keimyung University in 1986 and 1988, respectively. Since 1990, he has held solo exhibitions and been featured in group exhibitions at many domestic and international venues, including Ci Gong Gallery, Johyun Gallery, Leeahn Gallery, Galerie Dorothea van der Koelen in Germany, and Ceysson & Bénétière Gallery in France, as well as major institutions such as the National Museum of Modern and Contemporary Art, Korea; Daegu Art Museum; Powerlong Museum, Shanghai; Indang Museum; and Ludwig Museum Koblenz in Germany. For details, please see the artist's website: http://www.namtchunmo.com.

이러한 선의 특성은 남춘모의 작품에서 감각적 구조를 형성한다. 여기서 '감각적 구조'란, 선과 색, 질감 등의 조형 요소들이 유기적으로 조직되어 감상자의 시각을 자극하고, 고유한 미적 경험을 유도하는 방식을 말한다. 남춘모의 작업에서 선은 단순한 시각적 표현을 넘어 리듬과 공간감을 형성하며, 물질과 시간, 기억과 감각이 교차하는 복합적인 체험을 감상자에게 이끄는 구조적 틀이다. 선을 구축해 나가는 반복적 작업은 시간의 누적을 화면에 각인시키고, 그의 캔버스는 삶의 궤적이자 감각의 지층으로 변모한다.

이러한 맥락에서 남춘모 회화는 단색화의 '무위(無爲)적 수행성'과는 구별되는 '유위(有爲)의 실천'으로 이해된다. 단색화가 주로 '하지 않음'이나 '비움'의 무위적 미학으로 해석되어 온것과 달리, 남춘모는 산업 재료인 폴리코트(플라스틱 합성수지)를 통해 전통 회화의 표현 방식과 미학적 가치를 재해석한다. 그리고 이를 반복과 구축의 방식으로 실행함으로써 '유위의 실천'을 보여준다. 남춘모는 전통의 외형을 그대로 모방하지 않는다. 대신 전통 건축의 서까래나 기와층, 문과 창살에서 발견되는 구조적 리듬과 '정(井)'자의 공간적 상징성을 폴리코트와 추상미술의 언어로 현대적으로 번안(飜案)한다. 이 과정에서 그는 전통의 구조적 사유와 감성을 전이시키고, 변환하며, 재구성한다.

These properties of the line form the "sensory structure" of Nam Tchun-Mo's work, organically organizing the formal elements—line, color, texture—to stimulate the viewer's vision and induce a distinctive aesthetic experience. Transcending mere visual expression, his lines generate their own rhythm and spatiality, drawing viewers into a complex realm where time and matter, memory and sensation intersect. His repetitive labor of accruing lines physically imprints the passage of time onto the surface, effectively transforming each canvas into a stratified layer of sensation that records the trajectory of a life.

Nam Tchun-Mo's paintings are best understood as the "practice of *yuwi*" (有爲, "action"), as opposed to the "performance of *muwi*" (無爲, "nonaction" or "not doing"), a concept often associated with Dansaekhwa (Korean monochrome). Whereas Dansaekhwa has generally been interpreted through the aesthetics of "not doing" or "emptying," Nam Tchun-Mo uses processes of repetition and construction to demonstrate a "practice of action," actively reinterpreting the expressive methods and aesthetic values of traditional painting through his use of polycoat (a synthetic industrial material). Beyond merely imitating the external appearance of tradition, he uses polycoat to modernize the structural elements of traditional architecture (e.g., rafters, roof tiles, doors, and lattice windows) and translate the spatial symbolism of the character "井" (*jeong*) into the language of abstraction. In doing so, he transforms and revitalizes the structural thought and sensibility of tradition.

기존의 선행 비평들은 그의 작업을 설치와 회화, 추상과 재현의 경계 해체나, 재료의 물성 등에 주목해 왔다.[2] 본 글은 보다 근본적인 회화론 및 미학적 관점에서 그의 작업을 조망하고자 한다. 특히 동아시아 회화 이론의 핵심인 사혁(謝赫)의 육법론(六法論)을 통해 남춘모 회화의 감각적 구조와 조형적 특성을 분석하고, 이것이 현대미술의 실천에서 갖는 의미를 탐구하고자 한다.

이러한 관점에서 본 글에서는 남춘모의 예술 세계를 다음의 다섯 장으로 나누어 분석한다. II장에서는 그의 작품에서 반복적으로 나타나는 선의 구조와 리듬이 동아시아 회화의 '골법(骨法)' 및 '기운생동(氣韻生動)'이라는 개념과 어떻게 연결되고 구축되는지를 살핀다. III장은 '밭고랑'이란 작가적 풍토와 '⊔자 유닛'이라는 모티프가 작가의 유년기 경험 및 기억 속에서 어떠한 정신지리학적 공간으로 재구성되는지를 다루며, 그의 창작 근원지와 이에 반응하는 신체성에 주목한다. IV장은 Beam과 Spring 시리즈 등에서 도출되는 격자 구조를 중심으로 회화가 어떻게 회화적 공간성을 이루며 감각적 구조이자 동시대적 기호의 상징으로 확장되는지를 검토한다. 마지막으로 V장에서는 반복과 노동, 생존의식이 예술가의 실존적 조건 및 유위(有爲)의 실천 윤리와 어떻게 연결되는지를 고찰하며 그의 회화를 단순한 추상의 계보가 아닌 '삶을 지속하는 업', 즉 '카르마'임을 이해한다.

2 남춘모에 대한 주요 선행 연구 및 비평으로는 유명진, 「남춘모_풍경이 된 선」, 『남춘모_풍경이 된 선』 (대구미술관, 2018), pp. 10-14; 베아테 라이펜샤이드, 「남춘모/제스처-공간-빛」, 앞의 책, pp. 19-26; 케이트 림, 「남춘모: 2.5차원의 입체선(線)과 빛이 그린 그림자」, 『남춘모: From Lines』 (대구보건대학교 인당뮤지엄, 2023), p. 15, pp. 18-19; 윤진섭, 「제3의 '질'을 향하여」, 『남춘모 개인전 도록』 (리안갤러리, 2016), pp. 7-11; Philippe Piguet, 「Nam Tchun-Mo, Colour and Light」, 『Nam Tchun-Mo Selected Works 1998-2009』 (Seok Gallery 외, 2010), pp. 18-22; 윤진섭, 「신체와 지각의 접점(接點)」, 앞의 책, p. 70, p. 72; 김미경, 「Nam Tchun-Mo; "Strokes" Breathing in the Space」, 『남춘모 개인전 도록』 (카이스 갤러리, 2007) 등이 있다. 이들 연구는 주로 남춘모 작품에 나타나는 '선', '공간', '빛', '재료'의 형식적 특징과 효과에 대한 분석에 초점을 맞추고 있다.

Previous discussion of Nam Tchun-Mo's work has often focused on the dissolution of boundaries between installation and painting or abstraction and representation, as well as the materiality of his chosen media.[2] However, this essay approaches his practice from a more fundamental perspective of painting theory and aesthetics. In particular, it analyzes the sensory structures and formal aesthetics of Nam Tchun-Mo's paintings through the framework of the "Six Principles of Painting" (六法論), a cornerstone of East Asian painting theory conceived by critic Xie He (active 500–535) of China's Southern Dynasties, and explores their significance in contemporary artistic practice.

For these purposes, Nam Tchun-Mo's artistic world has been divided into four primary themes, each of which is explored in a respective chapter of this essay. Following this introduction, Chapter II examines how the structural rhythms and repetitions of lines in Nam's works reflect the concepts of "*golbeop*" (骨法, "bone methods and use of brush") and "*giun saengdong*" (氣韻生動, "spiritual resonance and life's motion") from East Asian painting. Chapter III explores how motifs drawn from the artist's childhood memories and personal experiences, such as furrowed fields and "⊔-shaped units," are reconstituted as a psychogeographic space, highlighting the origins of Nam's creative work and the physicality that reflects those origins. Chapter IV analyzes how the motif of grid structures that Nam has developed in series such as *Beam* and

2 Prior research and criticism on Nam Tchun-Mo includes: Kim Mi-Gyeong, "Nam Tchun-Mo; 'Strokes' Breathing in the Space", in Nam Tchun-Mo Solo Exhibition Catalogue (CAIS Gallery, 2007); Philippe Piguet, "Nam Tchun-Mo, Colour and Light", in Nam Tchun-Mo Selected Works 1998–2009 (Seok Gallery et al., 2010), pp. 18–22; Yoon Jin sup, "The Interface of Body and Perception", in the same volume, pp. 70 and 72; Yoon Jin sup, "Toward a Third Quality", in Nam Tchun-Mo Solo Exhibition Catalogue (Leeahn Gallery, 2016), pp. 7–11; Yu Myungjin, "Nam Tchun-Mo: Line to Landscape", in Nam Tchun-Mo: Line to Landscape (Daegu Art Museum, 2018), pp. 10–14; Beate Reifenscheid, "Nam Tchun-Mo: Gesture–Space–Light", in the same volume, pp. 19–26; Kate Lim, "Nam Tchun-Mo: 2.5-Dimensional Linear Forms and Shadows Painted by Light", in Nam Tchun-Mo: From Lines (Indang Museum, Daegu Health College, 2023), p. 15, pp. 18–19. These studies have primarily focused on analyzing the formal characteristics and effects of line, space, light, and material in Nam Tchun-Mo's work.

이는 남춘모의 작업을 '물성-감각-철학-윤리'로 점층화 시켜 나가는 접근이다. 남춘모 회화의 내용과 형식을 분석하는데 있어 회화의 조형적 특성(선, 골법), 개인적인 배경(유년기 경험), 재료적 특성(폴리코트), 구조적 상징(정자살, 우물 정), 그리고 그의 작업 태도(반복, 노동) 등을 다각도로 검토하고자 했다.

이러한 논의는 남춘모의 작품을 단순히 특정 미술 사조나 경향으로 분류하기보다는, 전통과 현대가 만나고, 예술가의 존재와 창작 행위가 융합되는 독특한 예술세계로 읽어내기 위함이다. 이를 통해 한국 현대미술사에서 남춘모 작업이 갖는 독자적 위치와 그 미학적·역사적 의미를 새롭게 가늠해보고자 한다.

Spring form a pictorial spatiality that expands into both a sensory structure and a representation of contemporary signs. Finally, Chapter V considers how repetition, labor, and the consciousness of survival are connected to the ethics of "*yuwi*" (有爲, "action") and the existential state of the artist himself, understanding his painting not merely as part of an abstract lineage, but as an ongoing practice of karma that sustains life.

This approach successively layers Nam Tchun-Mo's art through the dimensions of "materiality," "sense," "philosophy," and "ethics," while analyzing the form and content of his paintings in terms of their pictorial elements (line, golbeop), personal background (childhood experiences), material characteristics (polycoat), structural symbolism (lattice patterns, "井"), and working process (repetition, labor). Rather than simply trying to assign Nam Tchun-Mo's paintings to a certain movement or trend, this essay instead contemplates the singular nature of his artistic world, where the traditional and contemporary converge through the unique integration of his existence and creative practice. By thus elucidating the aesthetic and historical significance of Nam Tchun-Mo's work, the essay ultimately seeks to reconsider his position within the history of contemporary Korean art.

II. 선으로부터

1. 선(線)으로 구축된 회화

동아시아에서는 선조(線條)의 아름다움은 작품의 표현력을 좌우하는 핵심 요소였다. 이러한 선조의 미는 서양 회화의 필촉(brush-touch)과는 구별되는 동양 회화만의 독특한 미적 조건이다. 심지어 "선이 없으면 그림이 아니"라고 할 만큼 선의 중요성이 강조되어 왔다. 이러한 전통적 맥락에서 볼 때, 남춘모 회화에서 '선(line)'은 단순한 시각적 표현이나 기호가 아니라, 회화를 구성하는 근본적인 구조, 즉 '골격(骨格)'이자 작가의 존재를 드러내는 행위의 시작점이다.

남춘모는 회화의 표면 위에 선을 '그리는 것'이 아니라, '구조를 짓는' 건축적 방법을 취한다. 이러한 방법을 통해 선은 평면 위에 머무르지 않고 화면 내부의 공간 구조를 구축해내며, 감상자로 하여금 다층적인 시간과 깊이를 체험하도록 유도한다. 그에게 있어 '선을 긋는 행위'는 단순한 표현 이상의 물질적·신체적 실천이며, 이를 통해 화면에 밀도와 리듬, 공간적 깊이를 형성한다.

그는 학창 시절, 선조들이 그려낸 동양화의 여백 속에 그어진 단 한 줄의 선이 만들어내는 공간의 힘에 주목했다. 서양의 유화가 물감을 쌓아 올리는 '페인팅(painting)'의 예술이라면, 동양의 수묵화는 선을 중심으로 이루어지는 '드로잉(drawing)'의 예술에 가깝다. 그에게 있어 선이란 단순한 외곽선이나 경계가 아니라, 공간을 구축하는 뼈대이자 사유의 근간이었다. 선은 면과 달리 방향성을 갖는다. 즉 전개하려는 운동감을 지니고 있는데, 이러한 경향성에 대한 고민이 그의 드로잉에 녹아있는 것이다.

II. From the Lines

1. Paintings Built by Lines

In East Asia, the "beauty of line" has always been regarded as a decisive element in determining the expressive power of an artwork. This aesthetic of line is unique to East Asian painting, distinguished from the "brush-touch" of Western painting. Indeed, it has often been said, "Without line, there is no painting." From this traditional perspective, lines are not simply a visual expression or sign in Nam Tchun-Mo's paintings; they are the fundamental structure that constitute the painting—its skeleton—and the starting point of the artist's act of existence.

Nam Tchun-Mo does not simply draw lines on the pictorial surface; rather, he employs an architectural method of building structure. Thus, his lines do not remain on the two-dimensional plane, instead building an internal spatial structure within the canvas, which guides the viewer into an experience of layered time and space. For him, the act of drawing a line is a physical and corporeal practice beyond mere expression, through which the surface is infused with density, rhythm, and depth.

As a student, Nam became attentive to the power of a single line inscribed within emptiness in a traditional ink wash painting, particularly its capacity to create a sense of space. If Western oil painting can be described as the art of painting, achieved by building up layers of pigment, then Eastern ink wash is closer to the art of drawing, structured around line. For him, the line was not a mere contour or boundary, but the framework that constructs space and the foundation of thought.

이러한 선에 대한 근본적 사유는 그의 작업이 단순한 드로잉에서 점차 회화적 붓질이 느껴지는 서체추상(calligraphic abstraction)의 회화로 발전하는 전 과정을 관통한다. 초기 목탄으로 작업한 Stroke Line 연작에서는 화면 아래에 그리드를 형성한 뒤 가로와 세로의 선들을 통해 선과 여백, 즉 '구조로서의 공간'에 대한 기초적 탐색을 시도했다Figs.1, 1-1. 이때의 선은 아직 단순한 구조적 실험으로서의 성격이 강했다.

Unlike a plane, a line possesses directionality, an inherent sense of movement that unfolds, which is precisely the tendency reflected in his drawing practice.

This fundamental reflection on line runs throughout the entire trajectory of his work, from simple drawings to paintings that approach calligraphic abstraction, resonating with the feel of painterly brushstrokes. In his early *Stroke Line* series, executed in charcoal, Nam used vertical and horizontal strokes to create an underlying grid, which he then drew diagonal lines on top of, exploring the relationship between line and blank space and investigating the notion of space as structure Figs.1, 1-1.

Fig. 1
Stroke-Lines 1997-3
Charcoal on paper, 57 x 76 cm, 1997

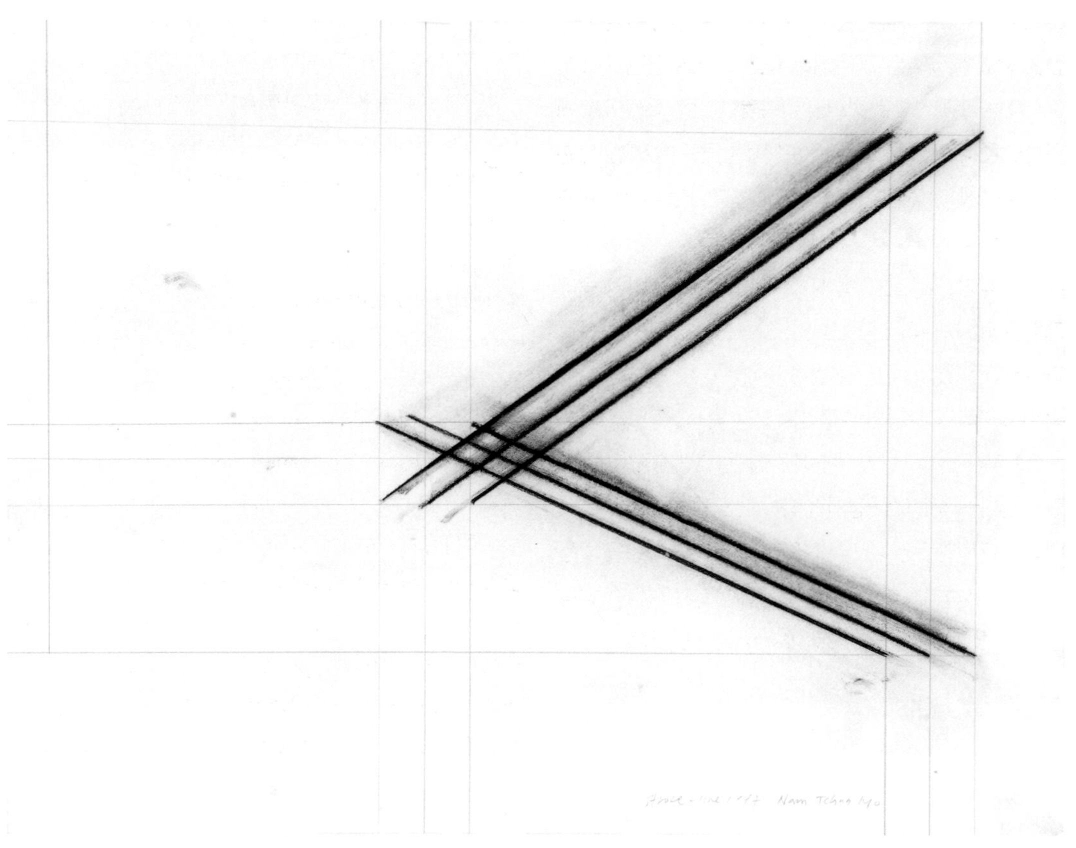

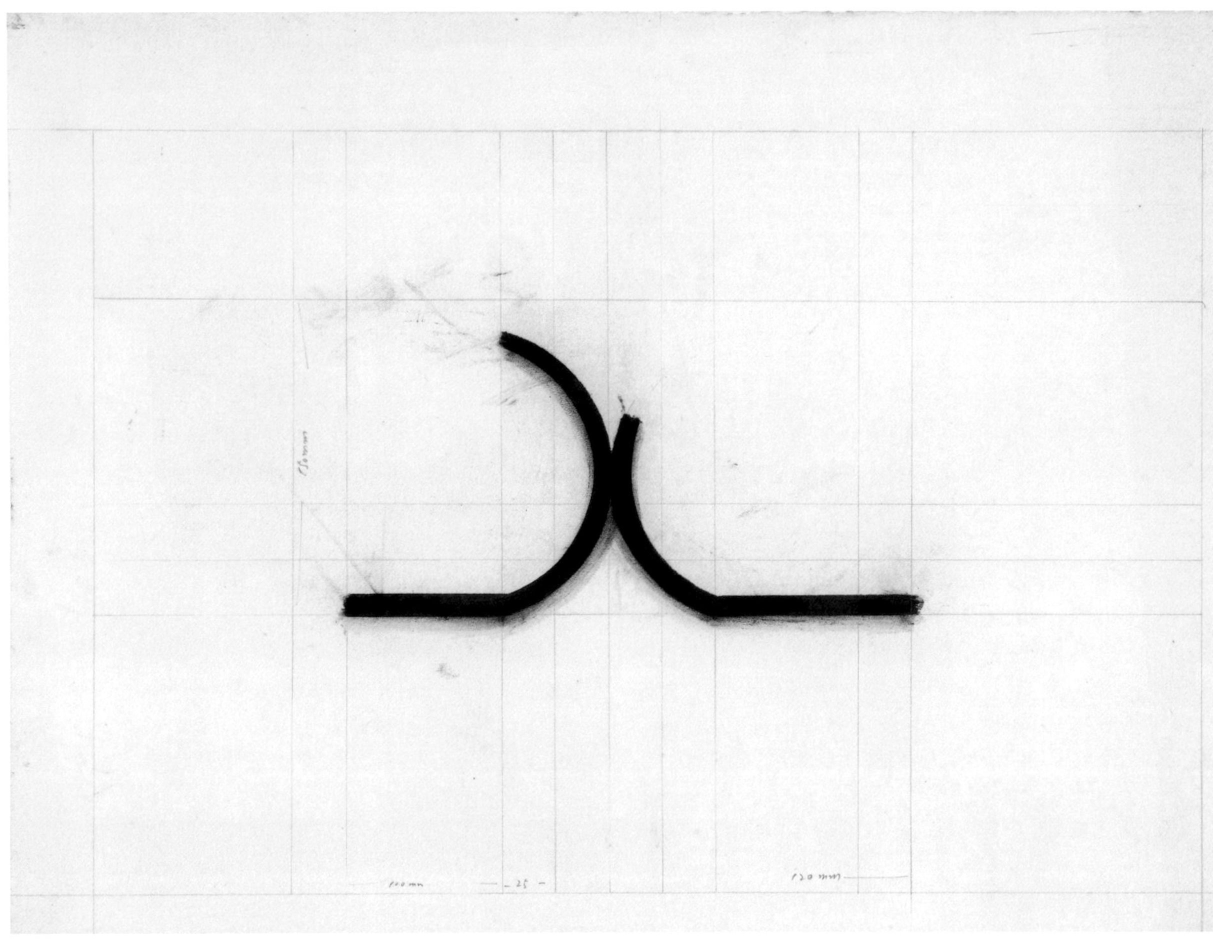

Fig. 1-1
Stroke-Lines 1997-3
Charcoal on paper, 57 x 76 cm, 1997

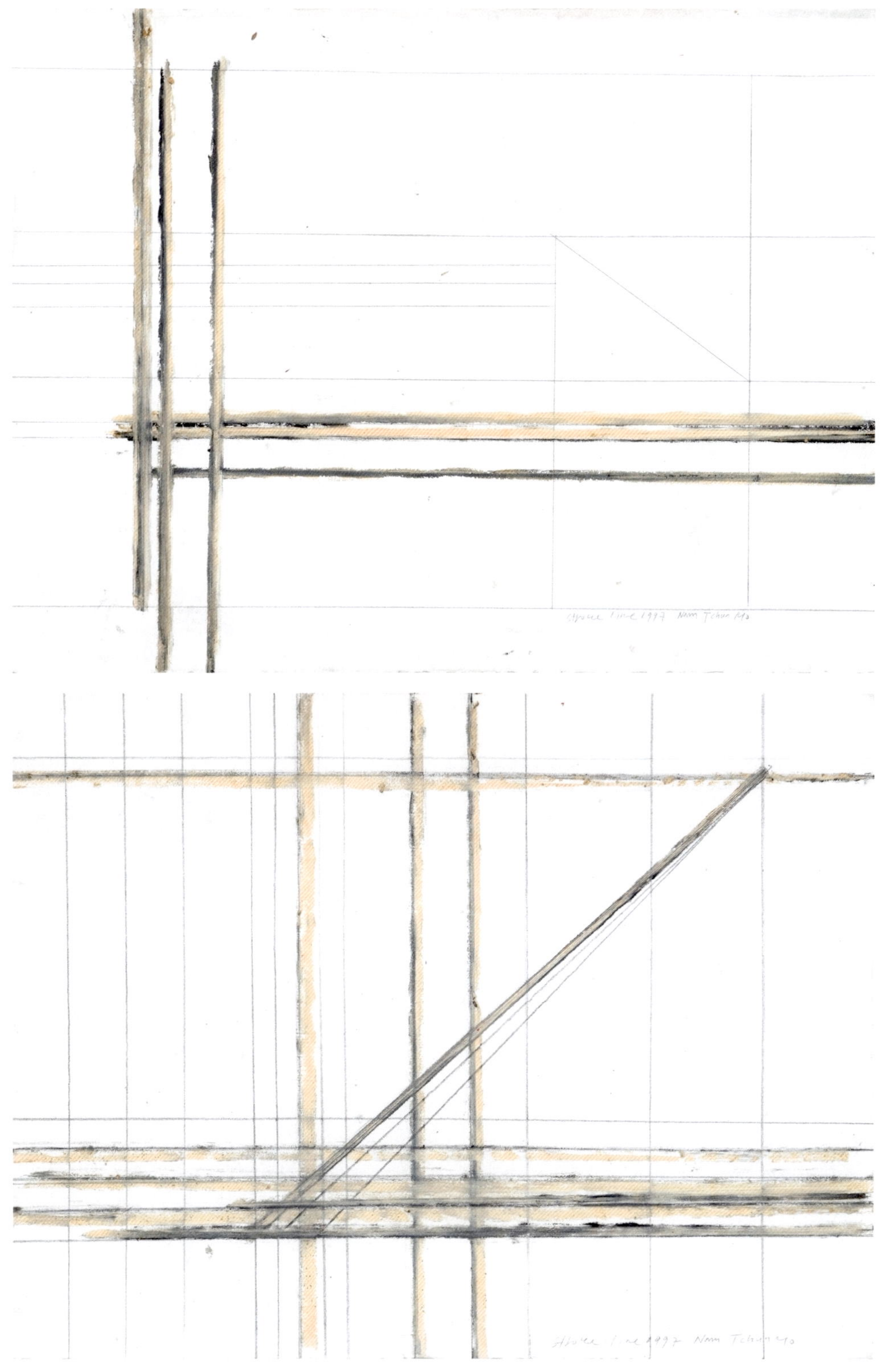

Fig. 2
Stroke-Lines 1997-7
Charcoal, oil on paper, 57 x 76 cm, 1997

Fig. 2-1
Stroke-Lines 1997-8
Charcoal, oil on paper, 57 x 76 cm, 1997

1997년 작업에서는 종이에 목탄을 사용하여 공간을 구획하고, 여기에 크레파스를 문질러 넣음으로써 먹선처럼 스며들고 번지는 감각을 구현해보기도 했다Figs.2, 2-1. 이는 동양화의 필획을 재해석하려는 시도로도 읽히는데, 선과 여백이 만들어내는 깊이와 감각적 공간을 실험하면서 선이 점차 회화적 표현력을 갖추어가는 모습을 보여준다.

이후 2019년, 2023년 등 최근까지 지속적으로 전개해온 Lines 작업에서는 짧은 선과 긴 선, 선의 굵기를 변화시키며 그림자를 함께 넣는 방식으로 발전한다Figs.3, 4, 5, 5-1. 여기서 선은 단순한 구조적 탐색을 넘어 보다 회화적인 표현 가능성을 모색하기 시작한다. 평면의 화면에 3차원적 깊이를 부여하려는 이러한 시도는 선이 점차 '골법(骨法)'의 개념으로 심화되는 과정을 보여준다. 즉 선이 단순한 형태적 요소에서 작품의 구조적 뼈대이자 회화적 생명력을 담는 그릇으로 진화하는 것이다.

이처럼 선에 대한 그의 탐구는 단순한 조형 실험을 넘어, 드로잉의 구조적 명료함에서 시작하여 서체추상의 회화적 표현력에 이르는 일관된 발전 과정을 보여준다. 이 과정에서 선은 점차 동양 미학의 핵심인 '골법'의 현대적 구현체로 자리잡게 된다.

At this stage, his lines still bore the character of a purely structural experiment. In works on paper from 1997, he used charcoal to divide the pictorial space before rubbing in crayon, yielding effects similar to the spread and seepage of ink linesFigs.2, 2-1. These works can also be read as an attempt to reinterpret the brushstrokes of Eastern ink wash painting. Through such experiments with the depth and sensory space generated by line and emptiness, Nam Tchun-Mo's lines gradually acquired painterly expressiveness.

He continued to develop his practice in various works entitled *Lines*, which he has returned to in recent years (2019 and 2023), varying the length and thickness of lines and incorporating shadowFigs.3, 4, 5, 5-1. Here the line begins to move beyond simple structural exploration toward painterly possibilities. These attempts to endow the pictorial plane with three-dimensional depth evince the traditional concept of *golbeop*, which refers to the use of brushwork to establish the skeletal framework of a painting. The line evolves from a mere formal element into a fundamental component of the work itself, the vessel that contains its expressive vitality. More than a simple formal experiment, Nam's exploration of line is a cohesive trajectory from the structural clarity of drawing to the painterly expressiveness of calligraphic abstraction. Through this process, line gradually takes its place as a contemporary embodiment of *golbeop*, the core of East Asian aesthetics.

Fig. 3
Lines 0401
Acrylic on paper, 105 x 75 cm, 2023

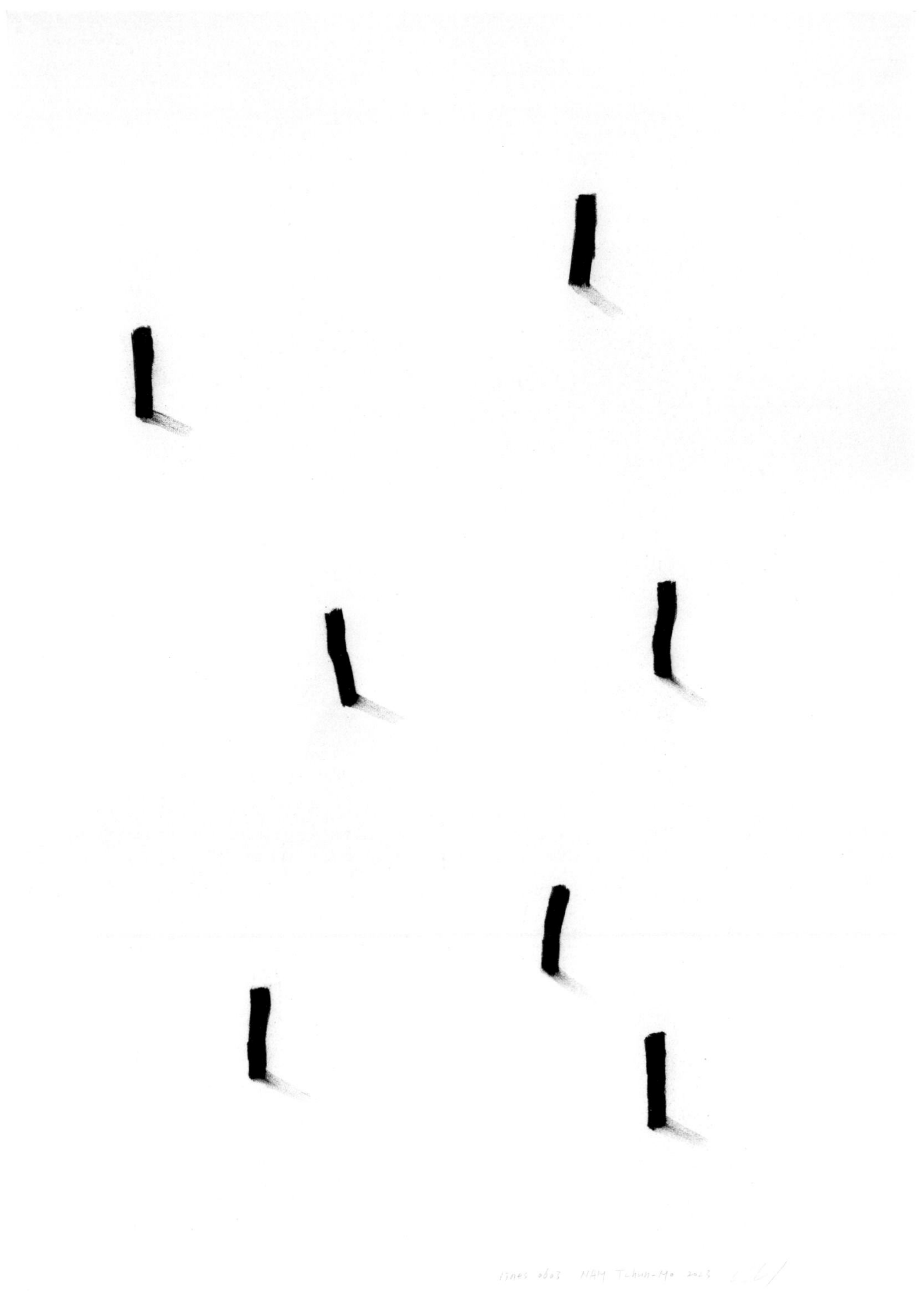

Fig. 4
Lines 0603
Charcoal on paper, 105 x 75 cm, 2023

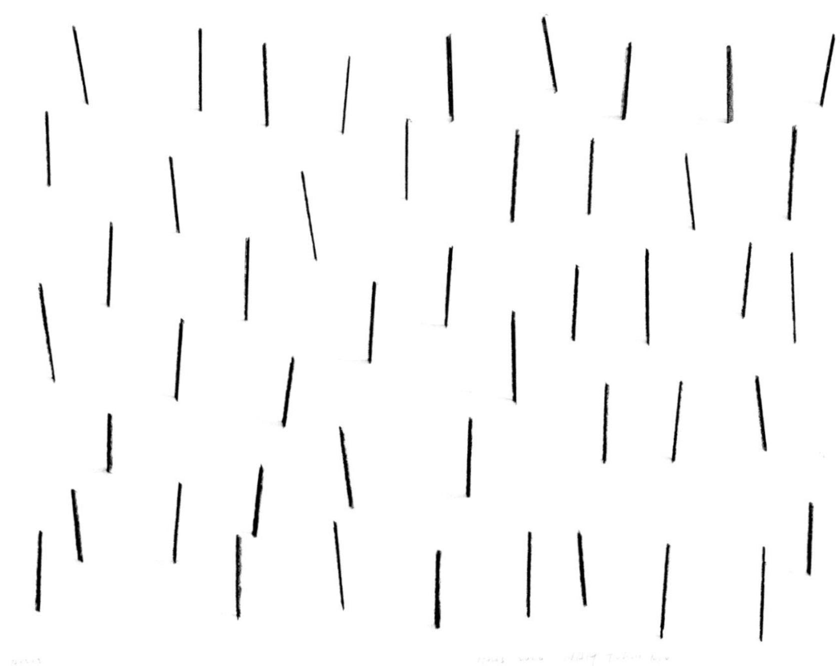

Fig. 5
Lines_A-203
Charcoal on paper, 75 x 105 cm, 2020

Fig. 5-1
Lines_A-213
Charcoal on paper, 75 x 105 cm, 2020

이러한 발전과정의 성과는 Strokes 연작에서 구체적으로 확인된다. 〈Stroke-Lines 20-09〉은 흑색 아크릴 물감이 중첩된 화면 위에 '井'자 형태의 굵은 선들이 교차하며 다층적 공간을 형성하고 있다Fig. 6, 6-1. 이 선들은 일정한 구조적 리듬과 강약의 변주를 보여주면서도, 미세한 떨림과 속도의 변화를 담고 있어 작가의 신체적 리듬과 호흡이 물질로 전이된 흔적처럼 느껴진다. 이러한 선들은 단순한 추상적 표현이 아닌, 공간을 조직하고 구조화하는 뼈대로 작용하며, 화면은 정적인 평면을 넘어 다양한 감각적 경험이 축적된 '체험적 구조체'로 변모한다.

그는 이러한 선을 즉흥적 표현이나 단순한 흔적으로 남기지 않고, 매 순간의 감각적 현존(presence)과 구조적 균형 속에서 체계적으로 구축해 나간다. 이 과정에서 붓질의 물리적 강도, 캔버스의 저항감, Beam, Spring 시리즈에서 볼 수 있는 폴리코트 처리된 표면의 물성 등은 모두 '선의 구조화'를 결정짓는 중요한 물질적 요소들이다Fig. 7. 남춘

The results of this development became more concrete in the *Strokes* series. In *Stroke-Lines 20-09*, for example, thick lines forming the Chinese character "井" (*jeong*, "well") intersect on a surface coated with black acrylic paint, creating a multi-layered spaceFig. 6, 6-1. While these lines display a steady structural tempo and variations in strength, they also convey subtle tremors and shifts in speed, which are materialized traces of the artist's bodily rhythms and breathing. As such, they transform the canvas from a static plane into an experiential structure where various sensory experiences are accumulated.

Rather than creating lines as spontaneous expressions or traces, Nam systematically builds them via the sensory presence and structural balance of each moment. The results of this process are evident in his *Beam* and *Spring* series, wherein the physical intensity of the brushstrokes, the resistance of the

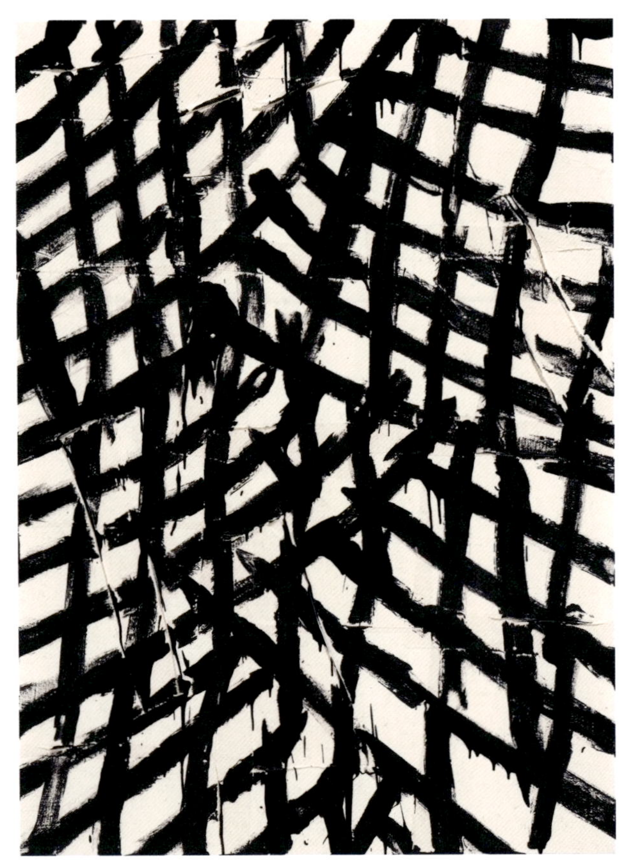

Fig. 6
Stroke-Lines 20-09
Acrylic on canvas, 162 x 120 cm, 2020

모의 선은 단순히 평면 위에 흐르는 자취가 아니다. 반복적으로 도포된 폴리코트로 구현된 선들은 점차 표면의 높낮이를 형성하고, 그 구조는 결국 '입체화된 평면', 즉 '부조회화(relief painting)'로 이행된다. 이는 그의 회화가 단순히 선의 구성에 머무르지 않고, 조형적 골격을 '짓는' 행위로 확장되고 있음을 보여준다.

이후 그의 구축적 선의 개념은 더욱 입체적인 방식으로 진화한다. Stroke-Beam 연작에서는 'ㅂ'자 모양의 유닛이 반복적으로 설치되며, 실제 공간 속에서 선을 더욱 구조적, 입체적으로 드러낸다Figs.8, 8-1, 8-2, 8-3. 이 선들은 더이상 평면 위의 흔적이 아니라, 공간을 가르고 관람자와 호흡하는 하나의 살아 있는 구조로서 과감히 작동해 나간다.

canvas, and the materiality of the polycoat-treated surfaces become core elements determining the structuring of lineFig. 7. Repeated applications of polycoat lines gradually bring depth to the flat surface, until the structure transitions into a three-dimensional plane or relief painting. In this way, Nam's works go beyond compositions of lines to become acts of constructing a formal framework.

The next evolutionary phase of this concept came with the *Stroke-Beam* series, in which Nam presented various assemblages of ㅂ -shaped units, further accentuating the formative and structural presence of lines in real spaceFigs.8, 8-1, 8-2, 8-3. No longer traces on a flat surface, lines are boldly realized as living structures that divide space and breathe together with the viewer.

Fig. 6-1
Stroke-Lines
Acrylic on canvas, 210 x 160 cm, 2020, each

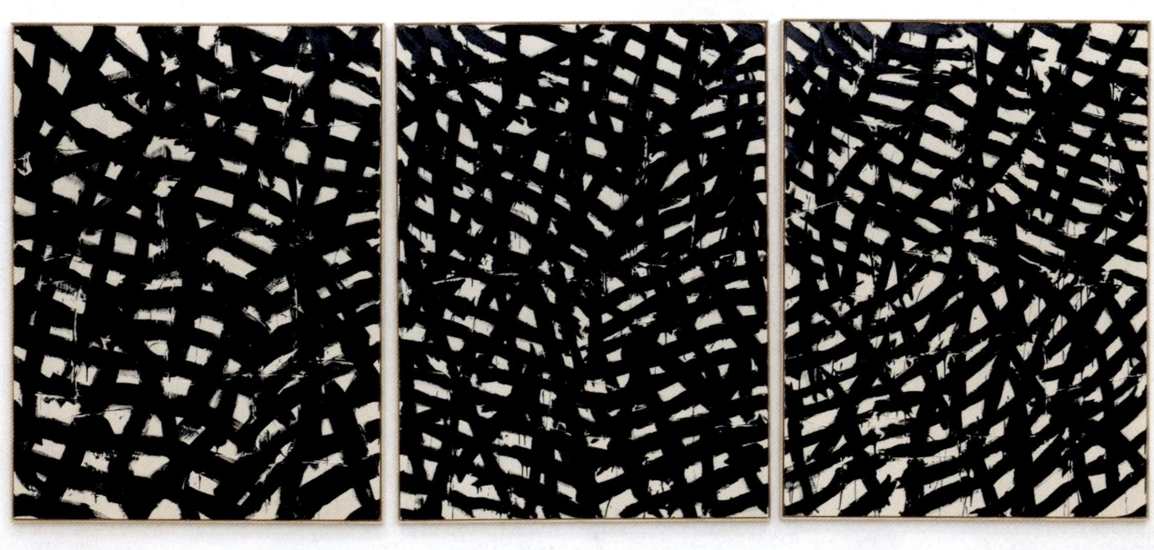

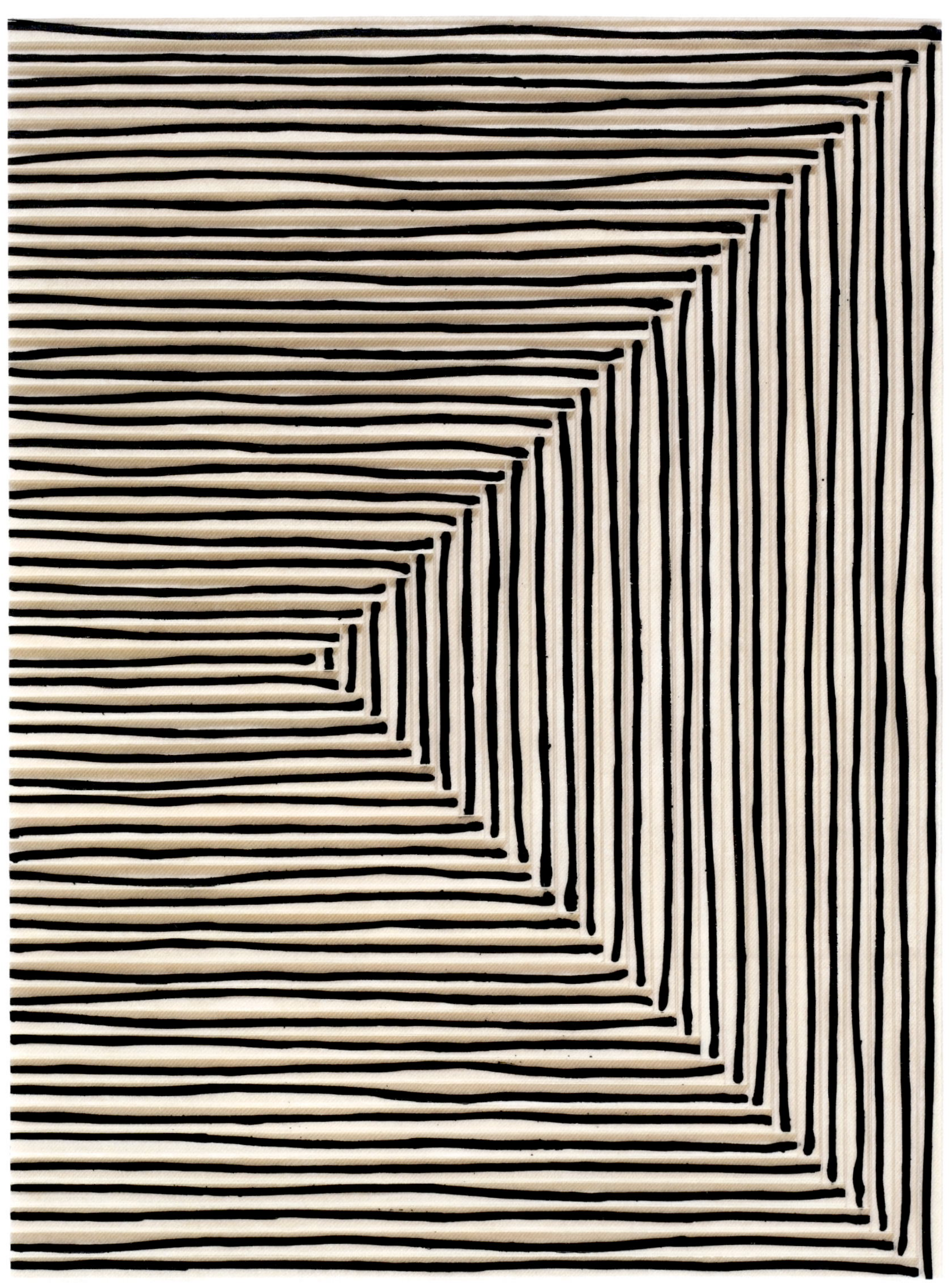

Fig. 7
Beam 17-143
Oil on coated fabric, 210 x 160 cm, 2017

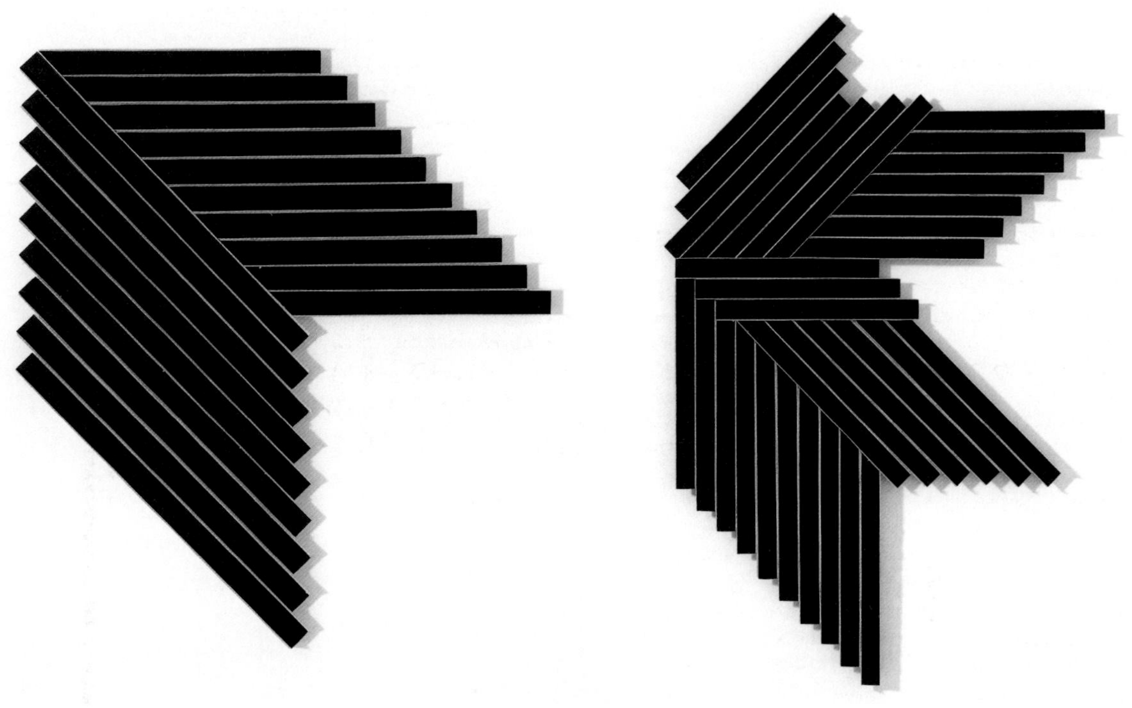

Fig. 8
Stroke-Beam
Oil on coated fabric, 143 x 123 x 7 cm, 2017

Fig. 8-1
Stroke-Beam
Oil on coated fabric, 198 x 134 x 6 cm, 2022

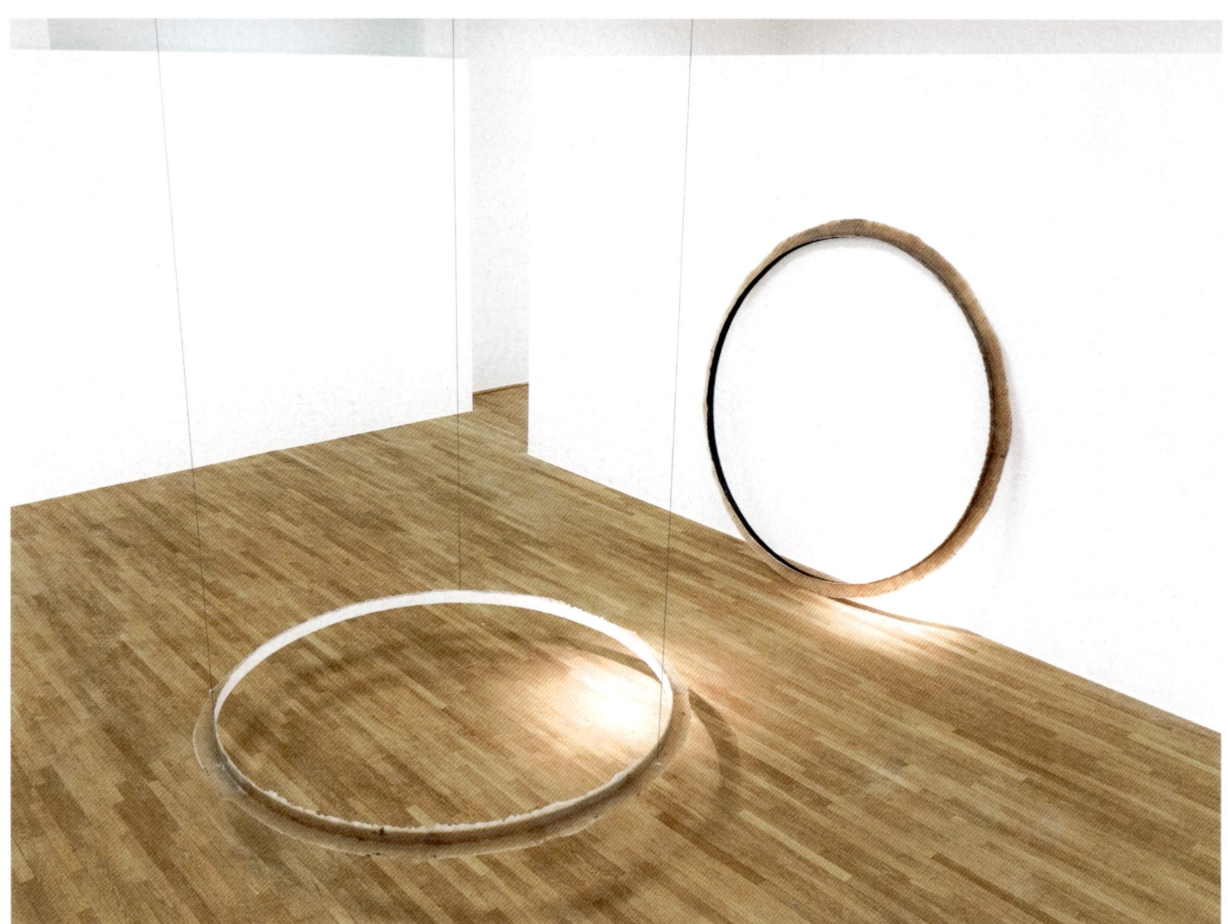

Fig. 8-2
Spring-Beam
Coated fabric, 280 x 10 cm, 2017

Installation
Ludwig Museum, Koblenz, Germany, 2019

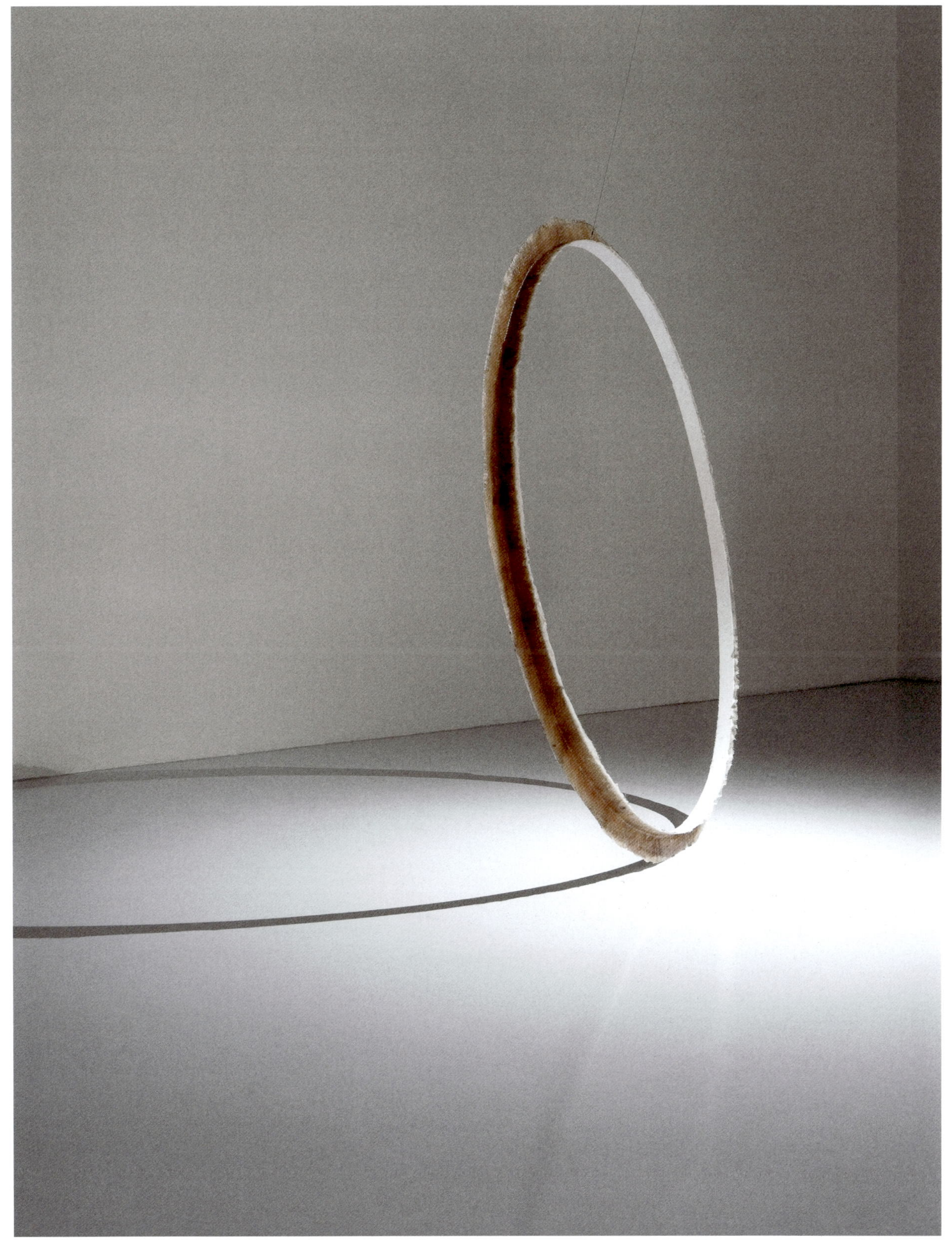

Fig. 8-3
Installation
Gyeongnam Art Museum, Korea 2018

2. 골법과 기운생동의 현대적 해석

남춘모의 작업에서 특히 주목할 만한 점은 동아시아 회화의 전통적 조형 원리인 '골법(骨法)'과 '기운생동(氣韻生動)' 개념이 현대적으로 재해석되는 양상이다. 중국 남북조 시대 화가이자 이론가인 사혁(謝赫)은 6세기경 《고화품록(古畫品錄)》에서 회화를 평가하고 실천하는 데 있어 여섯 가지 핵심 원칙인 육법론(六法論)을 제시하였다. 기운생동(氣韻生動), 골법용필(骨法用筆), 응물상형(應物象形), 수류부채(隨類賦彩), 경영위치(經營位置), 전이모사(傳移模寫)가 그것이다. 이 중 '골법용필'의 '골법'은 단순한 묘사 기술을 넘어, 그림의 구조를 세우고 생명력을 불어넣는 뼈대 같은 붓질을 의미한다. '골(骨)'은 기초 즉 뼈대라는 뜻으로, 구조와 필법으로 만들어지는 내적 힘의 감각이 골력(骨力)이다. 필선에 골력을 드러내어 예술작품의 맑고 굳세며 강인한 미학적 품격을 구현하는 것이 골법의 본질이다.[3]

3 주즈잉, 박성일 역, 『중국예술철학』(서울:동국대학교출판부, 2018) 참조.

2. Contemporary Interpretation of *Golbeop* and *Giun Saengdong*

Through his compelling use of line, structure, and space, Nam Tchun-Mo reinterprets traditional aesthetic principles of East Asian painting—such as *golbeop* ("bone methods and use of brush") and *giun saengdong* ("spiritual resonance and life's motion")—in a contemporary context. Around the sixth century, in his book *The Record of the Classification of Old* Painters (古畫品錄), the Chinese painter and theorist Xie He (謝赫) set forth the "Six Principles of Painting" as fundamental criteria for creating and evaluating paintings. The six principles are "*giun saengdong*" (氣韻生動, "spiritual resonance and life's motion"); "*golbeop yongpil*" (骨法用筆, "bone methods and use of brush"); "*eungmul sanghyeong*" (應物象形, "correspondence to the object in depicting forms"); "*suryu buchae*" (隨類賦彩, "appropriate application of color"); "*gyeongyeong wichi*" (經營位置, "proper arrangement and composition"); and "*jeoni mosa*" (傳移模寫, "transmission by copying the old masters").

Of particular interest here is "*golbeop yongpil*," which is the use of brushwork to infuse structure and texture, with an emphasis on imparting inner energy and vitality, beyond mere technical depiction. The term "*gol*" (骨, "bone") signifies foundation or framework, and the inner strength created through structure and brushwork is called "*gollyeok*" (骨力). The essence of *golbeop* lies in revealing *gollyeok* through the brushstroke, thus manifesting the clarity, firmness, and strength that define the aesthetic dignity of a work of art.[3]

3 Zhu Ziying, *Philosophy of Chinese Art*, trans. Park Seongil (Seoul: Dongguk University Press, 2018).

남춘모는 이러한 전통적 골법 개념을 단순히 차용하는 것을 넘어, 화면의 조형성을 확립하는 현대적 방법론으로 재정립한다. 그는 평면적 구성을 초월하여 입체적이고 촉각적인 선의 뼈대를 구축하는 방식으로 골법을 발전시킨다. 남춘모의 골법 실천이 가장 두드러지게 나타나는 작업으로는 Beam과 Spring 연작을 들 수 있다.Figs.9, 9-1, 10, 10-1 이들 작업에서 작가는 폴리코트(polycoate)로 처리된 'ㅁ'자 형태의 유닛을 화면에 부착함으로써 명확한 물리적 구조를 형성한다.

폴리코트는 합성수지로서 물감일 때는 액체 상태로 있다가 공기에 노출되면 중합 반응을 통해 고형화되어 단단한 도막을 형성한다. 남춘모는 이 재료의 특성을 활용하여 독특한 제작 과정을 개발했다. 먼저 생지(生紙)와 같은 광목천을 나무 목각에 입히고, 그 위에 폴리코트를 바르고 덧입혀 고형화시킴으로써 단단한 뼈대 골조를 구축한다. 이렇게 만들어진 구조체를 캔버스에 접착제로 붙인 후, 색을 입히거나 선을 그어 선의 골법을 완성한다. 이러한 과정은 반복적이면서도 신체적 노동을 전제로 하는 실천으로, 화면과 물질 사이의 긴장 관계를 구축한다. 폴리코트는 단지 표면을 코팅하는 기능에 그치지 않고, 선의 형상과 뼈대를 견고하게 지지하는 구조적 지지체가 된다.

골법이 선의 구조적 특성을 구현하는 방식이라면, 그 안에 담긴 생명력과 활력은 '기운생동'으로 이해할 수 있다. 사혁의 육법 중 최우선 원칙인 기운생동은 형식적 완결성을 넘어선 작품의 본질적 생명력과 활력을 의미한다. 골법용필이 형태를 구축하는 구조적 원리라면, 기운생동은 그 구조에 생명을 불어넣는 활력의 원리로 작용하는 것이다. 이 두 원리는 상호보완적 관계 속에서 회화의 총체적 조형성을 완성해 낸다.

Nam Tchun-Mo does not simply borrow this traditional concept of *golbeop*, but redefines it as a contemporary methodology for establishing the formal aesthetics of the pictorial plane. He expands upon *golbeop* by building skeletal frameworks of lines that are three-dimensional and tactile, transcending flat compositions. This practice is most prominently realized in Nam's two series *Beam and Spring*Figs.9, 9-1, 10, 10-1, in which he affixes hundreds of small ㅁ-shaped units, treated with polycoat, to the surface of the canvas, forming distinct physical structures.

As a synthetic resin, polycoat exists in a liquid state before application, but then solidifies into a hard film through polymerization when exposed to air. Nam Tchun-Mo has devised a unique production process that exploits these material properties. First, he covers a wooden frame with unprocessed cotton fabric, to which he then applies multiple layers of polycoat. As the substance hardens, it forms a rigid framework that adheres to the underlying canvas, after which colors are added or lines are drawn to enhance the *golbeop*. This repetitive process, which is inherently grounded in physical labor, generates a distinct tension between the surface and material. The polycoat is no longer merely a surface coating, but the structural support that secures and strengthens the form of line and the framework of the piece.

While *golbeop* represents the structural properties of line, the vitality and life force of line can be understood as "*giun saengdong*" ("spiritual resonance and life's motion"), the foremost of Xie He's "Six Principles of Painting." *Giun saengdong* is the essential life and energy of a work, surpassing technical mastery or formal completeness. If *golbeop yongpil* provides the structure and form of a work, then *giun saengdong* is the animating principle that breathes life into that structure. In their complementary relationship, these two concepts form the core of the formal aesthetics of painting.

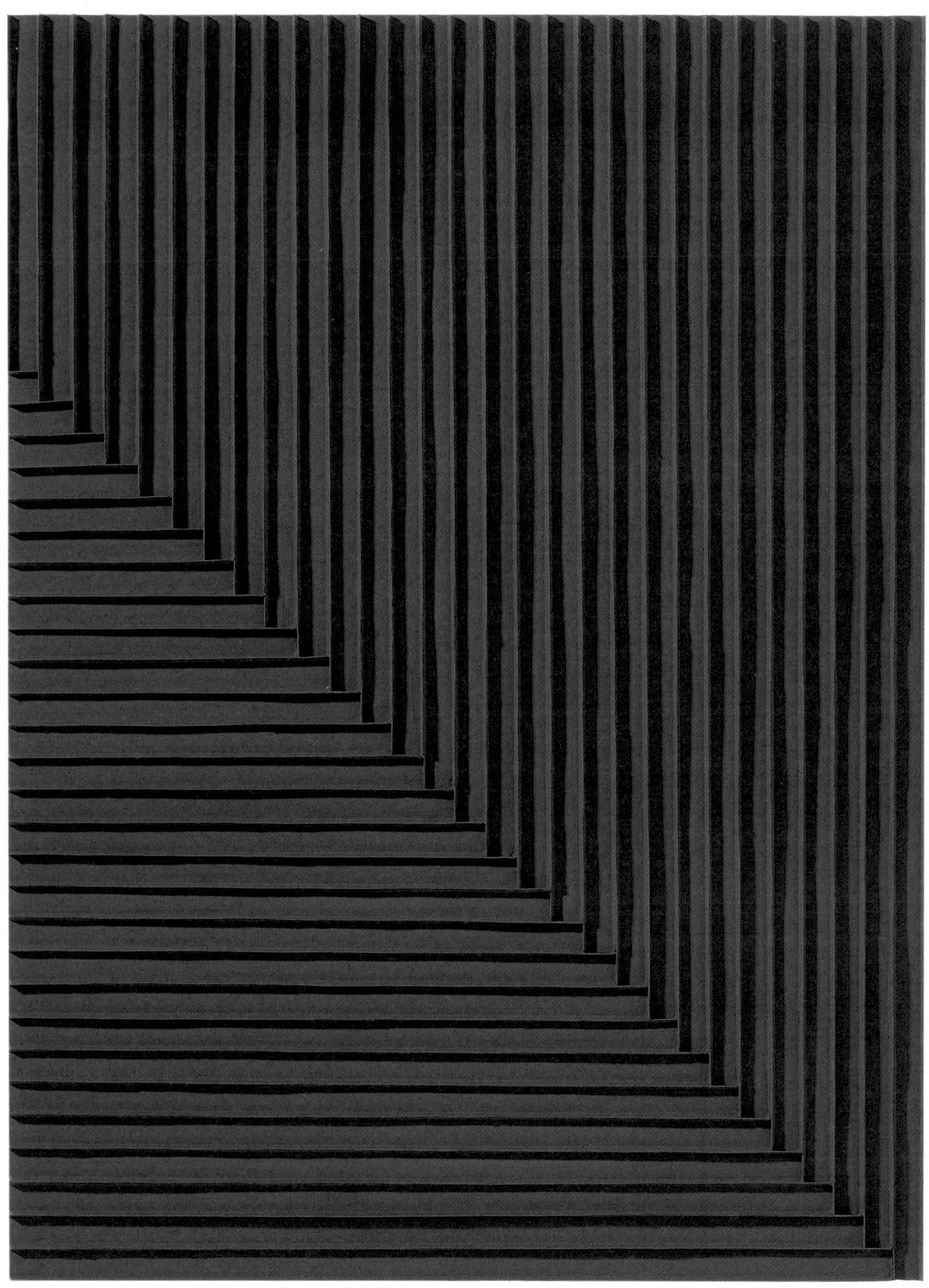

Fig. 9
Beam 17-01
Acrylic on coated fabric, 160 x 120 cm, 2017

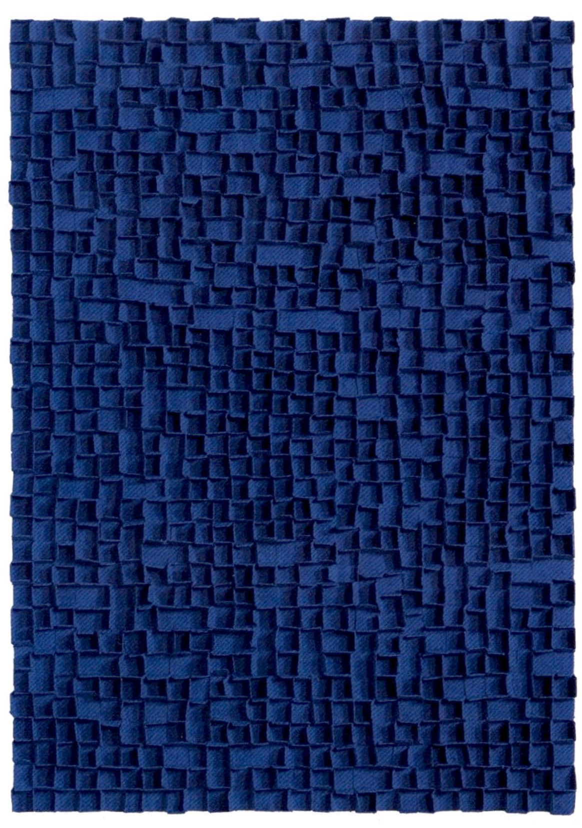

Fig. 9-1
Beam
Acrylic on coated fabric, 100 x 73 cm, 2013

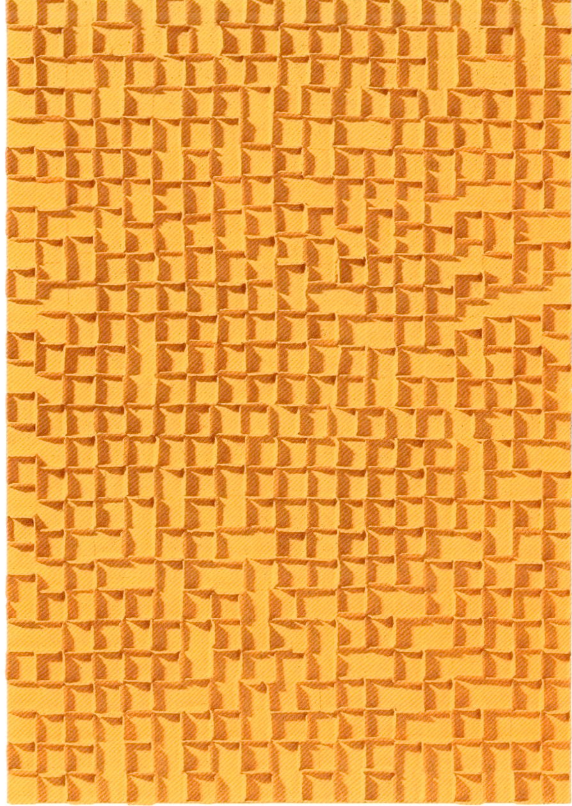

Fig. 9-2
Beam 17-74
Acrylic on coated fabric, 2017

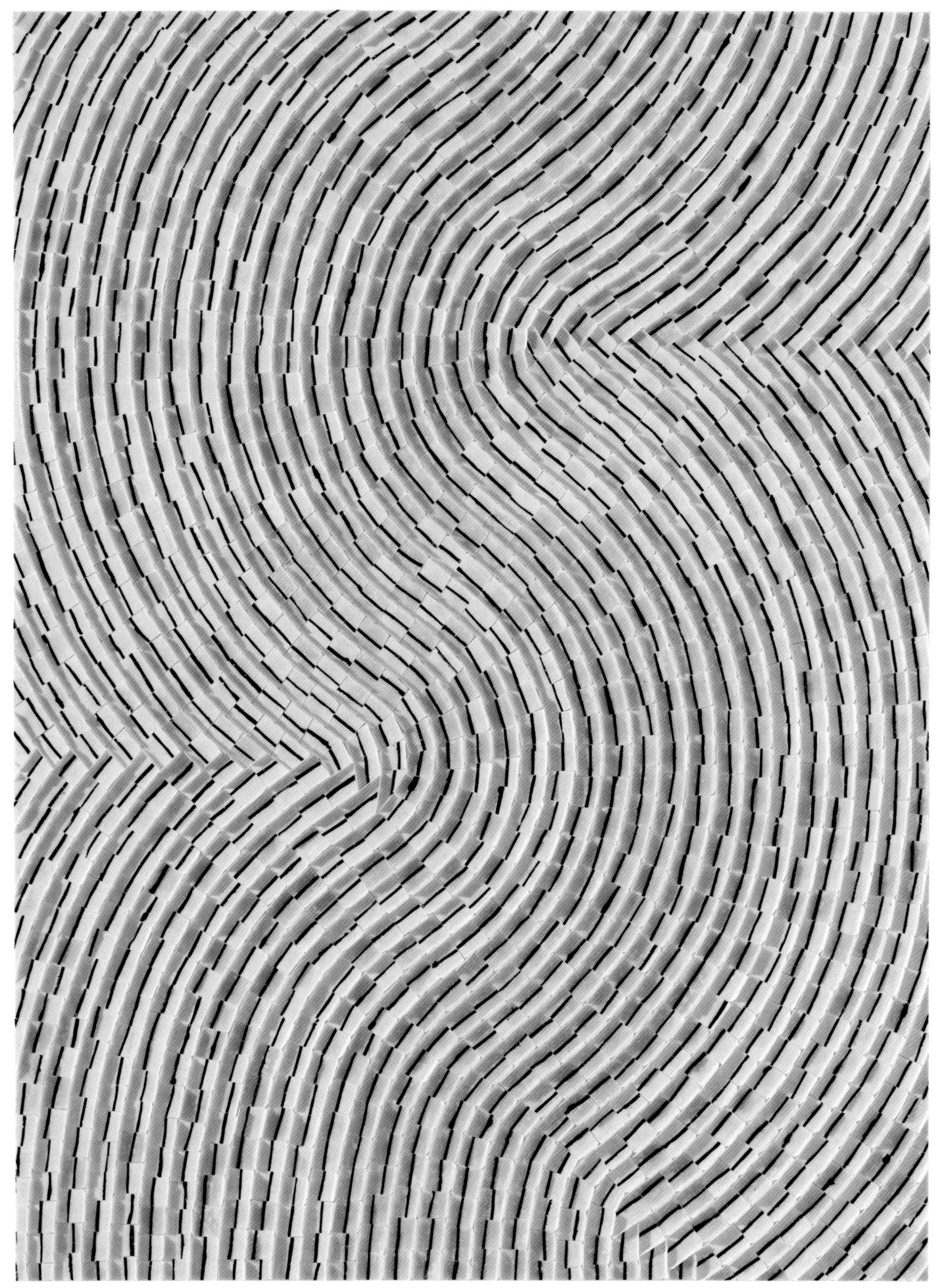

Fig. 10
Spring 22-59
Oil on coated fabric,160 x 120 cm, 2022

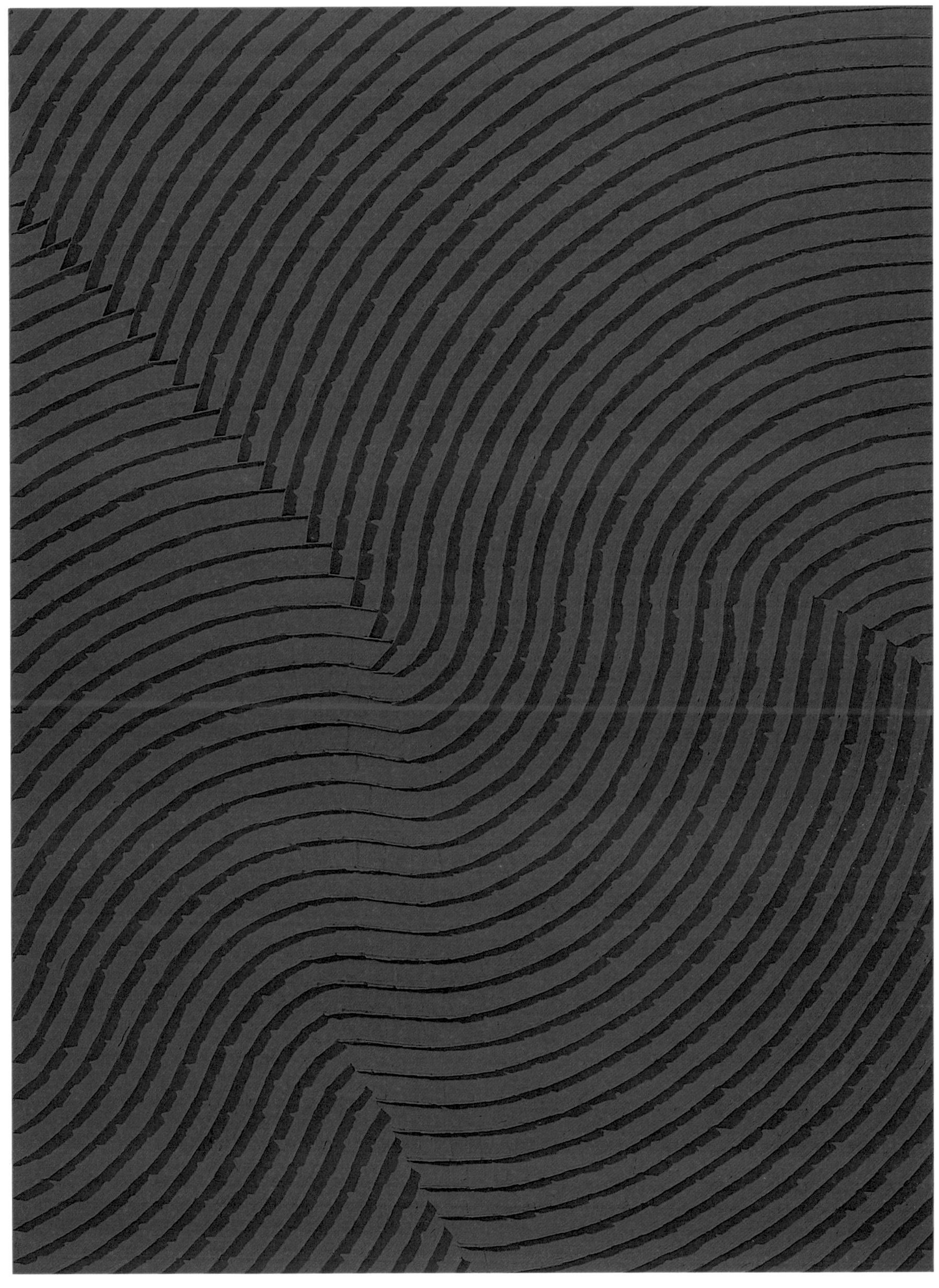

Fig. 10-1
Spring 22-59
Acrylic on coated fabric,160 x 120 cm, 2022

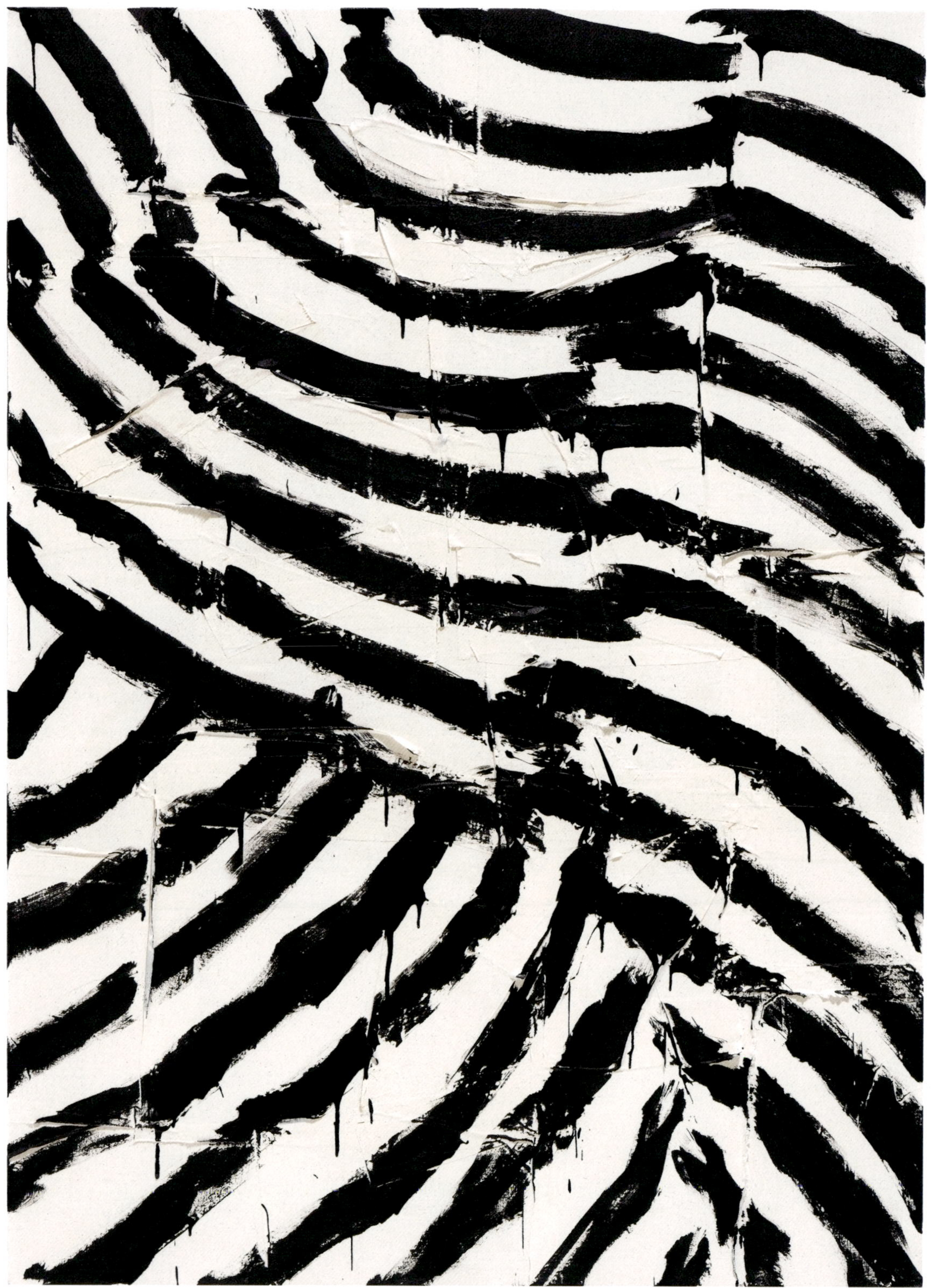

Fig. 11
Stroke-Lines 20-11
Acrylic on canvas, 162 x 120 cm, 2020

남춘모의 작업에서 이러한 기운생동은 단지 관념적 차원의 생명력이 아니라, 실제적인 공간 구성과 물질적 질감을 통해 구체화된다. Strokes 시리즈에서 나타나는 선의 역동적 흐름은 전통 문인화(文人畵)의 필선이 지닌 생명력을 연상시키지만, 이를 반복적 행위와 물리적 구축을 통해 현대적으로 재구성한다. 선의 두께와 강약, 밀도와 방향성의 변화는 화면에 리듬감과 운동성을 부여하며, 정적(靜的)인 평면이 아닌 진동하는 동적(動的)인 시각적 장(場)을 형성한다Figs.11, 11-1.

나아가 이러한 시각적 진동은 관람자의 신체적 움직임과 연동하여 실제적 공간 체험으로 확장된다. 관람자가 작품 앞에서 위치를 바꾸면 선들의 중첩과 교차가 만들어내는 시각적 깊이와 리듬이 지속적으로 변화한다. 이는 동양회화가 추구해 온 '이응(移應)', 즉 관람자의 시선 이동에 따른 공간 경험 변화의 현대적 구현이며, 전통적 '삼원법(三遠法)'의 다시점적 공간 체험을 선의 물리적 구축성과 시각적 중첩을 통해 현대적으로 물질화한 결과다.

남춘모의 작업에서 주목할 만한 또 다른 지점은 선의 구조적 배열이 만들어내는 '여백(餘白)'의 활성화이다. 동양회화에서 여백은 단순한 비어있음이 아니라 가장 적극적인 조형 요소로 기능해왔다. Strokes 시리즈에서 볼 수 있는 선들 사이의 여백은 마치 숨을 쉬는 듯한 리듬감을 형성하며, 화면 전체의 기운과 생동감을 결정짓는 중요한 요소가 된다Figs.12, 12-1. 이는 동양 미학의 '허실상생(虛實相生)', 즉 비어있음과 채워짐의 상호 생성적 관계 원리를 현대적 감각으로 재해석한 것이다.

In Nam Tchun-Mo's work, *giun saengdong* is not simply a conceptual vitality, but a physical force materialized through texture and spatial construction. The propulsive flow of lines in his *Strokes* series recalls the lifeforce of brushstrokes in traditional literati painting, but reconfigured in a contemporary mode through repetitive action and physical construction. Variations in the thickness, intensity, density, and direction of lines endow the canvas with rhythm and movement, creating not a static flat surface, but a vibrating, dynamic visual fieldFigs.11, 11-1.

Moreover, this visual vibration expands into a physical spatial experience through the bodily movements of the viewer. As the viewer changes position, the overlapping and intersecting lines of the work generate a continuously changing visual depth and rhythm. This phenomenon is a contemporary realization of the Eastern painting principle of "*ieung*" (移應, "corresponding change with movement"), in which the experience of space changes with the shifting gaze of the viewer. At the same time, the physical construction and visual layering of line invokes "*samwonbeop*" (三遠法, "three perspectives"), the traditional principle in which the viewer's spatial experience encompasses multiple perspectives.

Another notable element of Nam Tchun-Mo's work is his activation of blank space through the structural arrangement of lines. In Eastern ink wash painting, blank space is not mere emptiness, but an active component of the composition. Similarly, in Nam's *Strokes* series, the spaces between the lines induce a rhythm that seems to breathe, playing an essential role in amplifying the overall energy and vitality of the work Figs.12, 12-1. In this way, his works revisit the East Asian aesthetic principle of "*heosil sangsaeng*" (虛實相生), the generative interplay between emptiness and fullness.

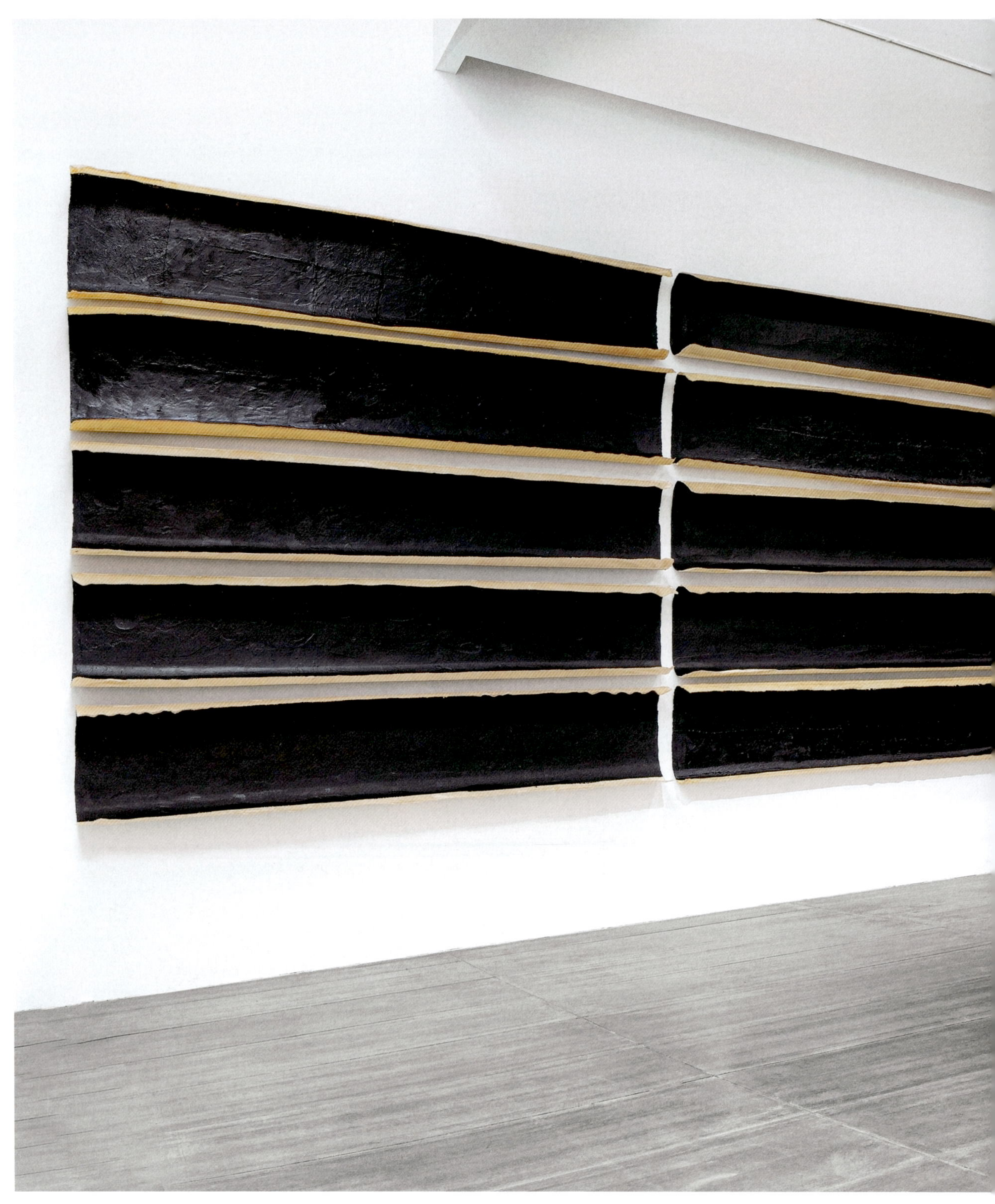

Fig. 11-1
Beam
55 x 320 x 15 cm, 2022-3, each, Installation, Indang Museum, Daegu, Korea 2023

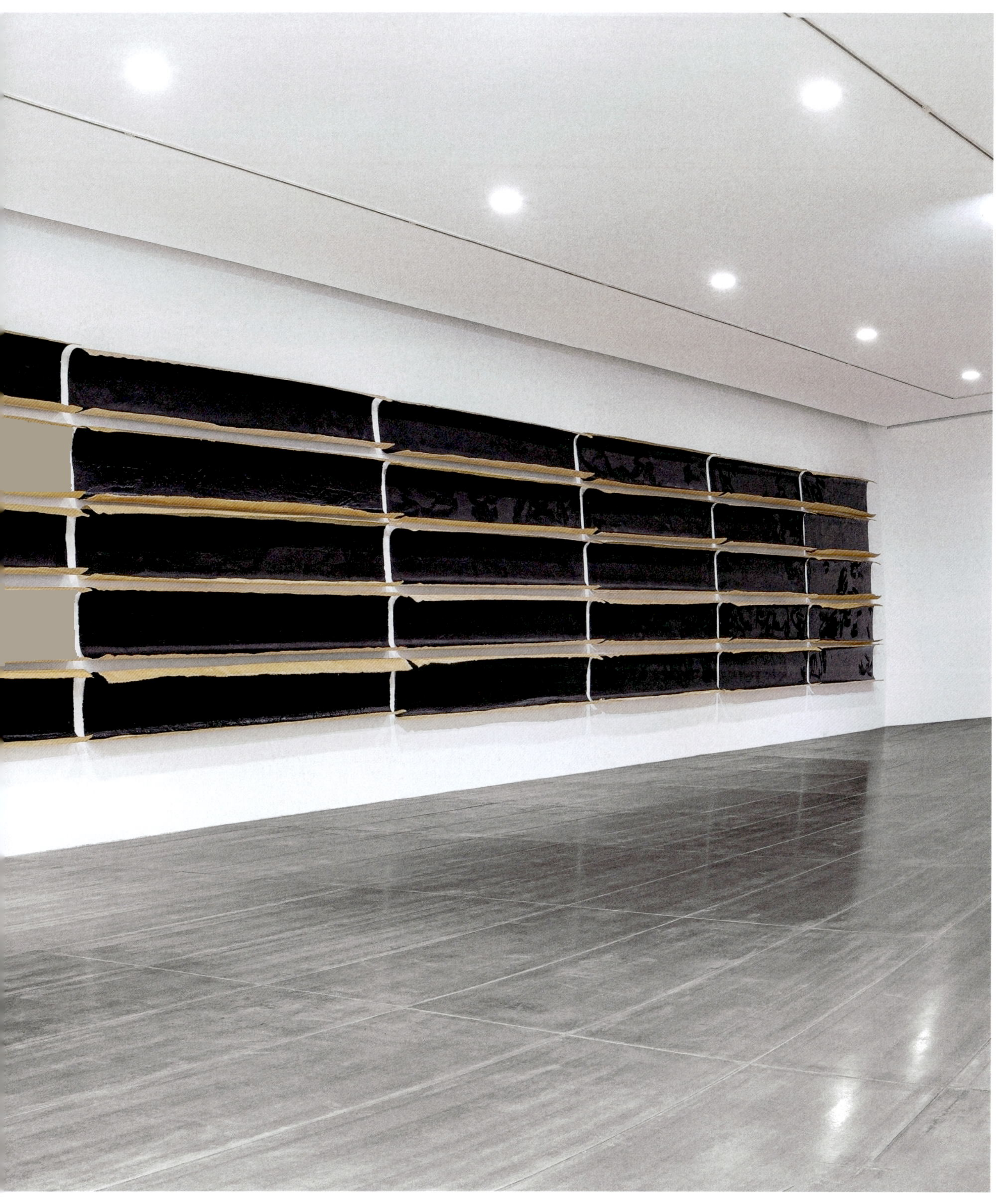

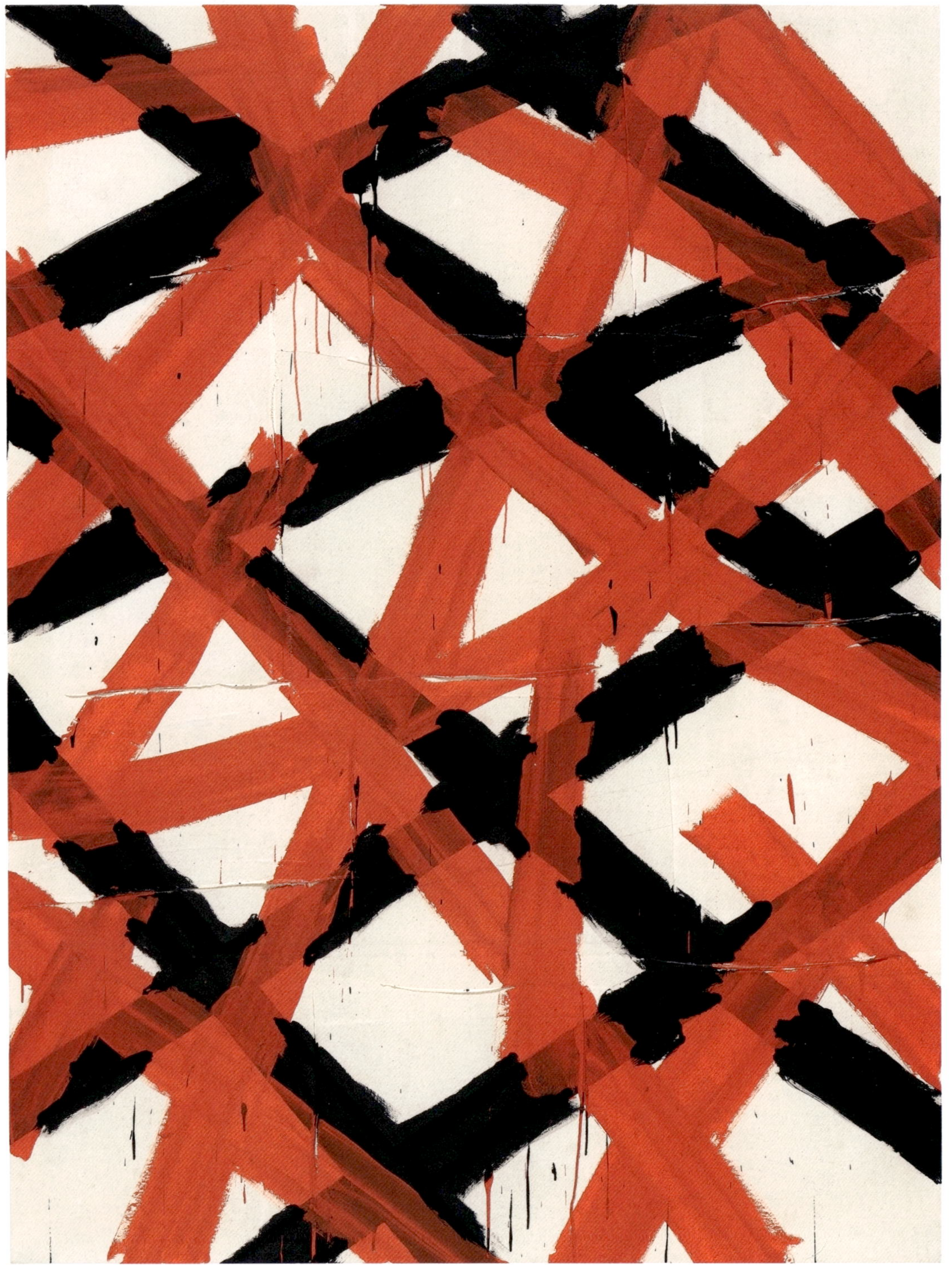

Fig. 12
Stroke-Lines 20-83
Acrylic on canvas, 210 x 160 cm, 2020

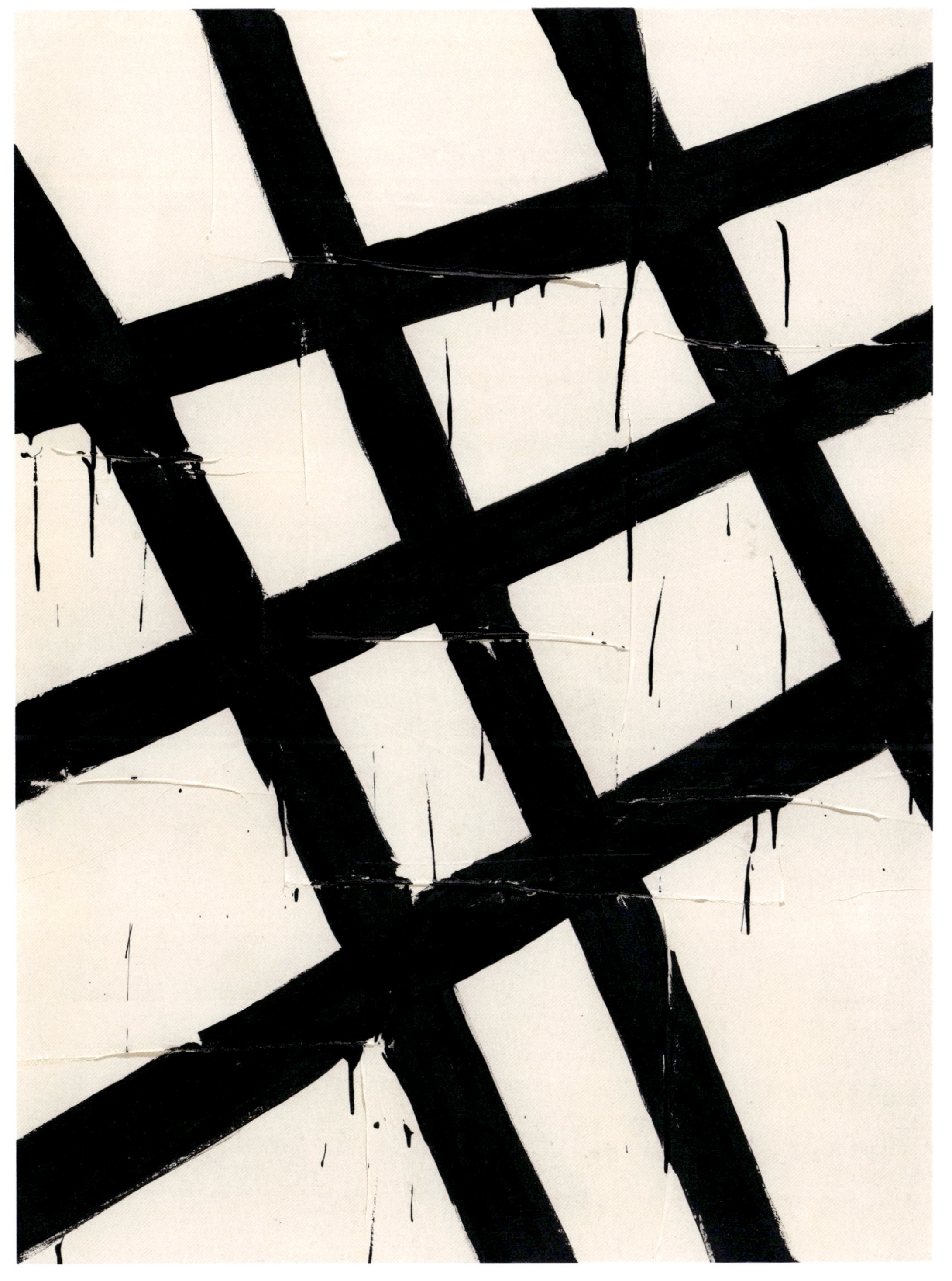

Fig. 12-1
Stroke-Lines 20-39
Acrylic on canvas, 160 x 120 cm, 2020

남춘모의 작업은 크게 두 가지 방향으로 골법과 기운생동을 실현한다. Stroke 시리즈를 위시한 드로잉과 페인팅 작업은 주로 평면 위에서 선의 중첩과 여백을 통해 시각적 깊이를 구현하며, 동양화의 전통적 공간 미학을 현대적으로 재해석한다Figs.13, 13-1, 13-2. 반면 Beam이나 Spring 시리즈, 조각, 설치 작업은 실제 공간 속에 입체적 구조를 형성하여 물리적 깊이를 창출하고 선을 통한 입체적 골격을 직접적으로 구축한다. 이러한 이중적 접근은 전통적 미학 원리가 현대 회화의 실천적 원리로 어떻게 확장될 수 있는지를 구체적으로 보여주는 중요한 실례이다Fig. 14.

결과적으로 남춘모의 작업은 선의 물리적 구축성을 통해 화면에 감각적 진동과 공간적 깊이를 부여하며, 단순한 시각적 대상에서 벗어나 총체적인 체험의 장으로 확장된다. 이는 동양 미학의 본질적 원리를 현대 미술의 물질성과 공간성 속에서 재발견하는 의미 있는 시도로 평가될 수 있다.

In his art, Nam Tchun-Mo realizes *golbeop* and *giun saengdong* through two different pathways. His drawings and paintings, including the *Strokes* series, primarily work through the pictorial plane, using overlapping lines and intersecting space to create a sense of visual depthFigs.13, 13-1, 13-2. Meanwhile, in his sculptures and installations, including the *Beam* and *Spring* series, he uses actual three-dimensional structures with physical size and depth to construct skeletal frameworks through line. This dual approach illustrates how traditional aesthetic principles can be expanded into operative principles of contemporary paintingFig. 14.

Through the physical construction of line, Nam Tchun-Mo imparts sensory vibration and spatial depth to the pictorial surface, eschewing a purely visual perception in favor of an immersive experiential field. In doing so, he rediscovers the essential principles of Eastern aesthetics within the materiality and spatiality of contemporary art.

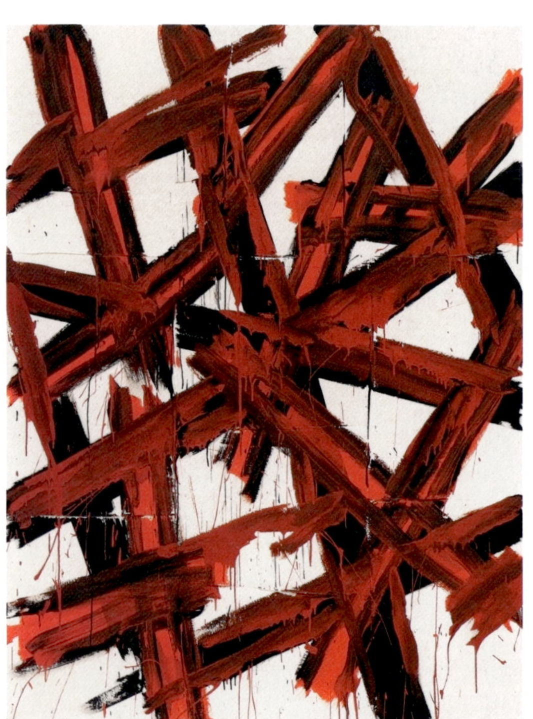

Fig. 13
Stroke-Lines 20-94
Acrylic on canvas, 210 x 160 cm, 2020

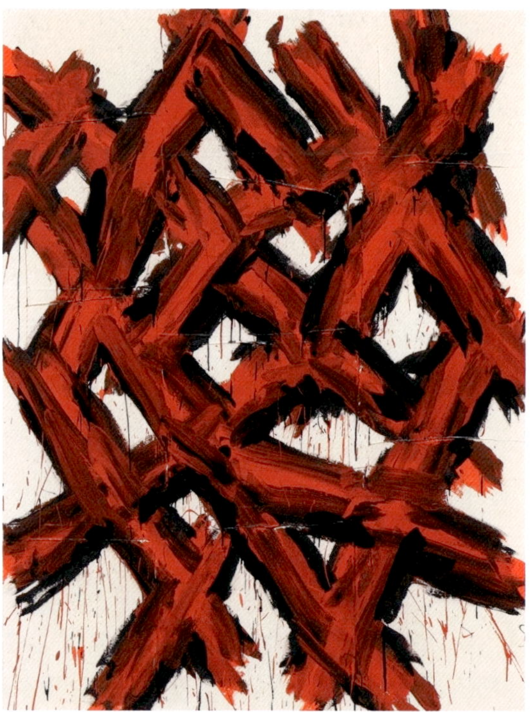

Fig. 13-1
Stroke-Lines 20-115
Acrylic on canvas, 210 x 160 cm, 2020

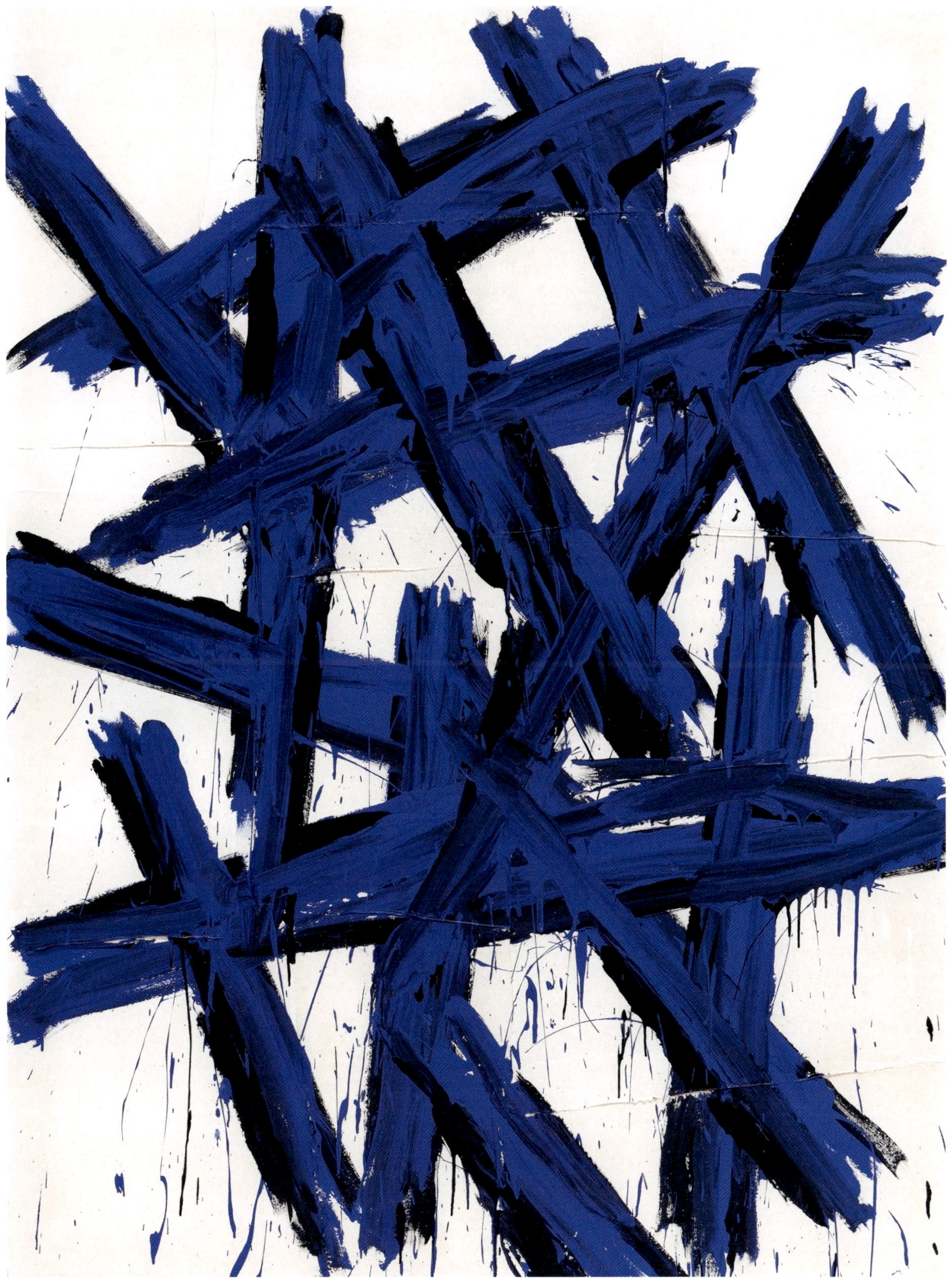

Fig. 13-2 Stroke-Lines 20-107 Acrylic on canvas, 210 x 160 cm, 2020

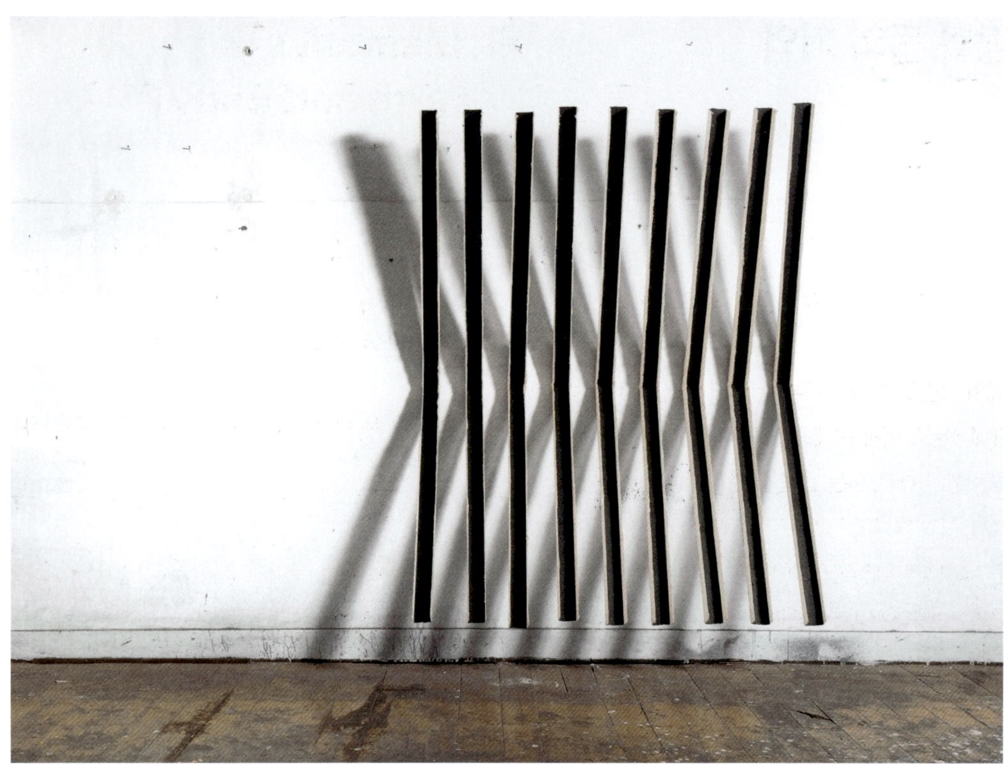

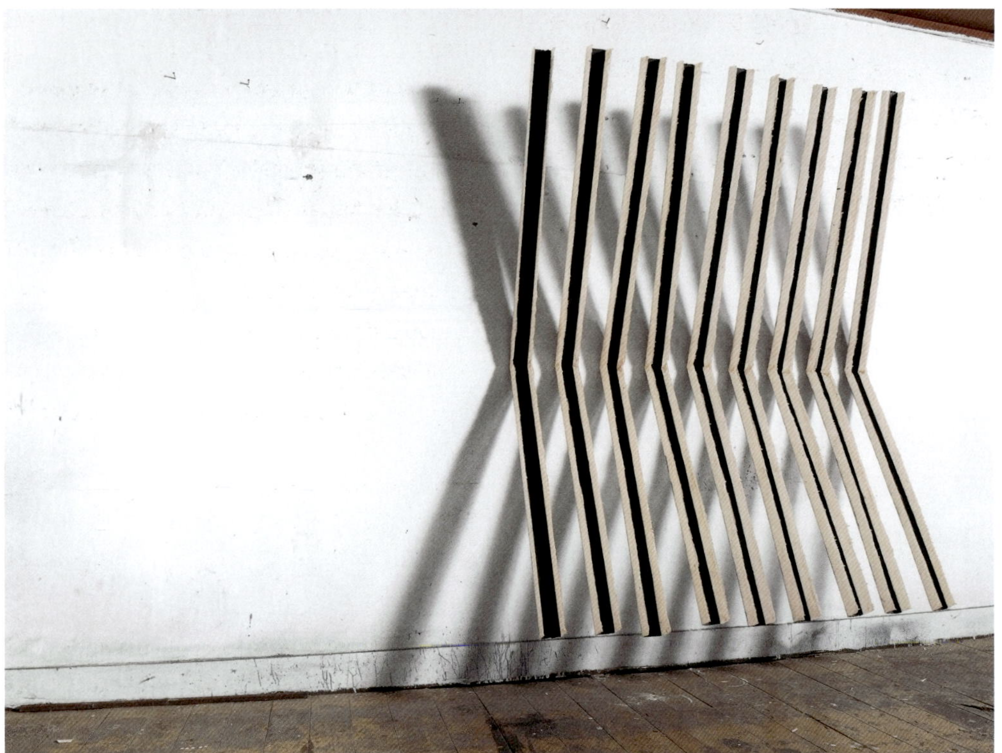

Fig. 14
Beam
Oil on coated fabric, 210 x 10 x 30 cm, 2016, each

III. 땅과 몸의 기억

III. Memories of Earth and Body

1. 기억의 지형학: 유년기 밭고랑의 시각적 원형

앞 장에서 남춘모 회화의 내부 논리에 대해 살펴보았다면, 본 장에서는 기억과 신체성을 통한 조형 행위의 근원을 탐색해보고자 한다. 이는 선과 골법의 개념적 구조에서 출발하여, 살결과 흙결의 감각 구조로 확장하려는 시도다. 회화가 단지 시각적 재현을 넘어 몸의 기억이 발현되는 감각적 실천임을 보이고, 삶의 기억과 신체 감각이 어떻게 조형 언어로 전환되는지 살핀다.

인간의 창작 행위는 특정한 장소와 시간의 흔적을 담는다Plate 1. 헤르더(Johann Gottfried Herder, 1744~1803)의 정신풍토학에서 '장소'는 단순한 물리적 배경이 아니라 인간의 소질과 창작력을 형성하는 정신적 토양으로 작용한다. 그는 인간이 각각의 '장소'에서 살아가며 그 땅과 생활방식에 따라 자신을 풍토화해가는 과정을 통해 고유한 성격과 창작력을 형성한다고 보았다.[4]

4 J.G.헤르더, 강성호 역, 『인류의 역사철학에 대한 이념』(서울:책세상, 2024) 참조.

1. Topography of Memory: The Visual Archetype of Furrowed Fields

While the previous chapter examined the internal logic of Nam Tchun-Mo's paintings, this chapter explores the origins of his creative acts through memory and corporeality, departing from the conceptual structure of line and *golbeop* and extending toward the tactile structure of skin and earth. For Nam, painting is not merely visual representation, but a sensory practice capable of manifesting the memories and sensations of the body, transforming them into a creative language.

Human creative activity embodies traces of specific places and times. In his theory of cultural climatologyPlate 1, Johann Gottfried Herder (1744–1803) argued that "place" is more than a physical backdrop for human dispositions and creative activities, also encompassing the spiritual soil that shapes them. Herder claimed that the experience of living in a particular place, adapting to the land and its incumbent lifestyle, is what causes people to form unique characteristics and creative power.[4]

4 J.G. Herder, *Ideas for the Philosophy of the History of Humanity*, trans. Kang Seongho (Seoul: Chaeksesang, 2024).

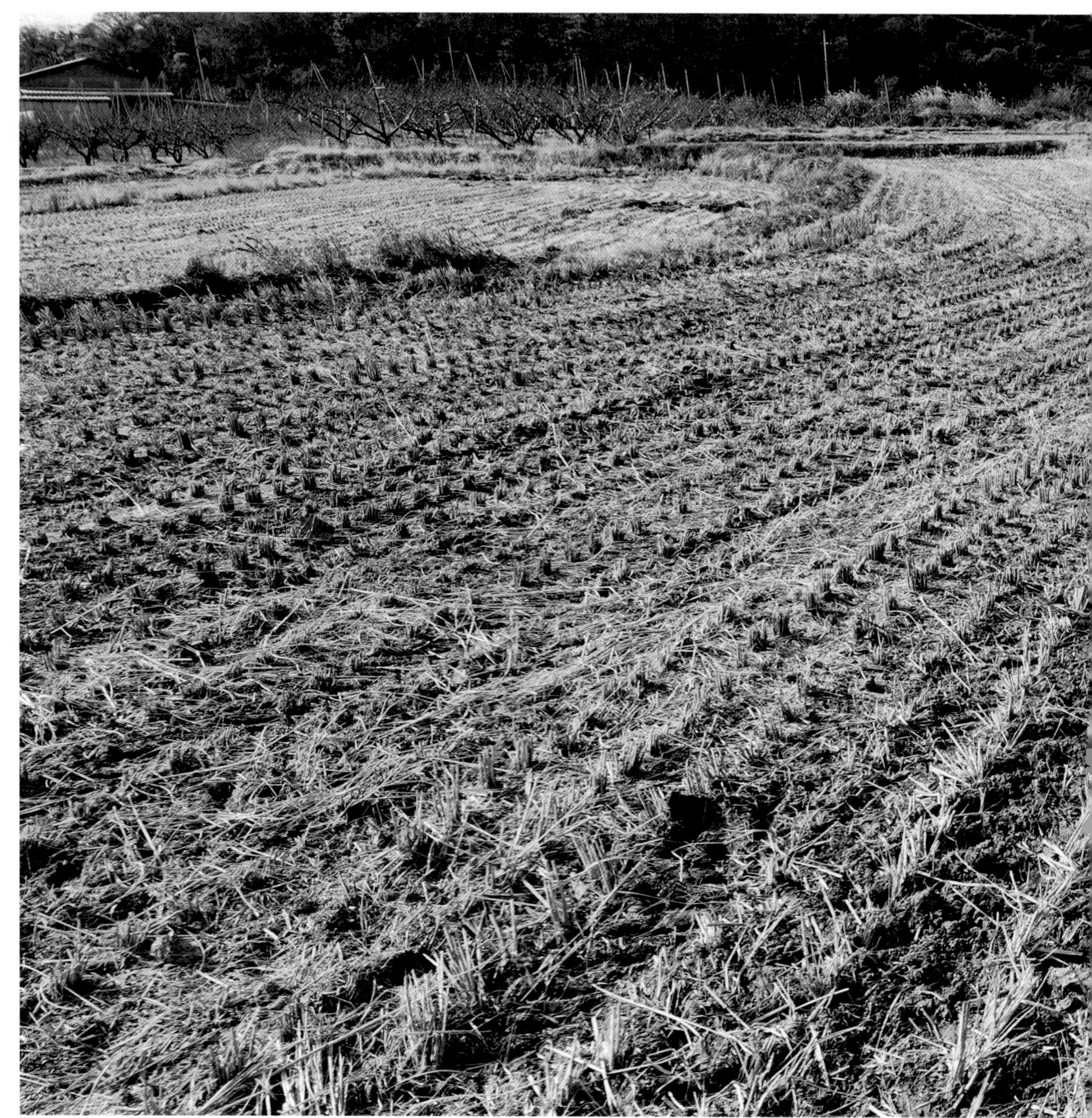

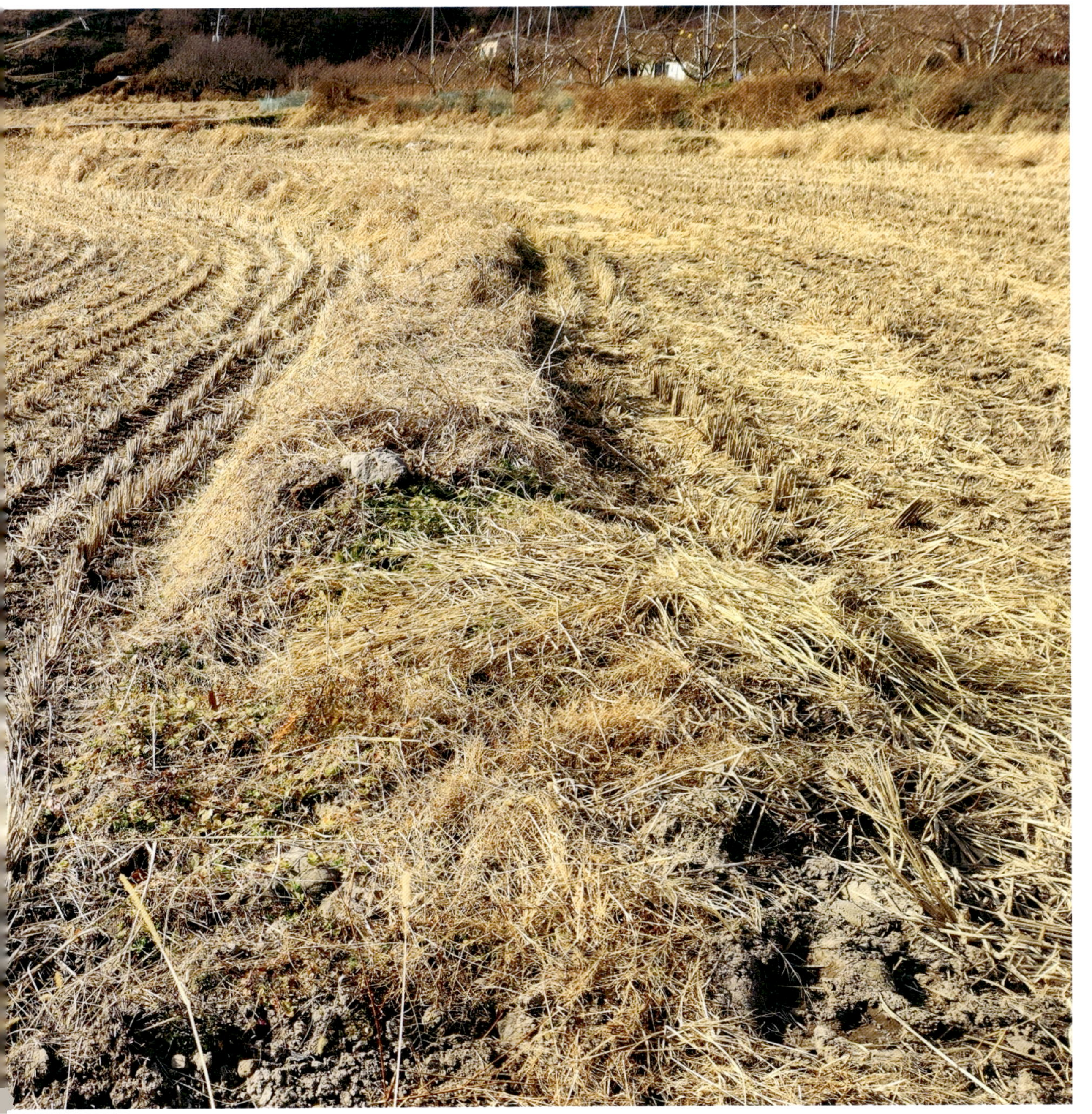

Plate 1
Furrowed fields of artist's hometown, Yeongyang, Korea 2025

바슐라르(Gaston Louis Pierre Bachelard, 1884~1962)는 이를 개인의 차원으로 심화시켜, 유년기의 공간적 경험이 어떻게 개인의 정신적 지형을 형성하는지 보여준다. 『공간의 시학』에서 그가 말한 '시적 공간'은 단순한 기억의 재현이 아니라, 현재의 창작 행위 속에서 되살아나는 감각적 실천이다.[5]

남춘모의 회화에서 '밭고랑'은 이 두 층위가 만나는 지점이다. 개인적 유년 기억이면서 동시에 한국의 농촌 풍토가 만들어낸 집단적 기억, 그것이 현재의 조형 언어로 전환되는 과정을 보여준다.

경북 영양의 산비탈에서 밭고랑을 매는 작업, 비닐로 멀칭하는 과정, 그것이 바람에 날리며 빛을 반사하는 풍경을 보고 자란 그의 경험은 어느 미술사조나 특정 작가의 영향이 아닌, 남춘모만이 할 수 있는 독특한 작업의 근원이 되었다Plate 2. 이는 극히 개인적인 유년기 기억에서 출발한 전체적 직관이 만들어낸 결과로서, 어떤 개념적 의도보다도 감각적 체험 자체가 조형적으로 표현된 것이라 말할 수 있다.

This notion was deepened and personalized by Gaston Bachelard (1884–1962), who explained how an individual's psyche is shaped by the spatial experiences of childhood. In *The Poetics of Space*, the "poetic space" that Bachelard describes is not simply a reproduction of memory, but a sensory practice that is revived within present acts of creation.[5]

In Nam Tchun-Mo's painting, these two dimensions converge in the form of soil furrows in agricultural fields, which are both a personal memory from the artist's childhood and a collective memory formed by the rural landscape of Korea. Nam's childhood experiences of working such fields on the mountain slopes of Yeongyang, North Gyeongsang Province, covering them with vinyl sheeting and watching the sheets blow in the wind and reflect light, became the fount of his artPlate 2. Hence, his paintings are not derived from any art movement or predecessor, but solely from the artist himself. An expansive intuition arose from personal childhood memories, through which sensory experience, transcending any conceptual intentions, was expressed in a pictorial language.

Plate 2

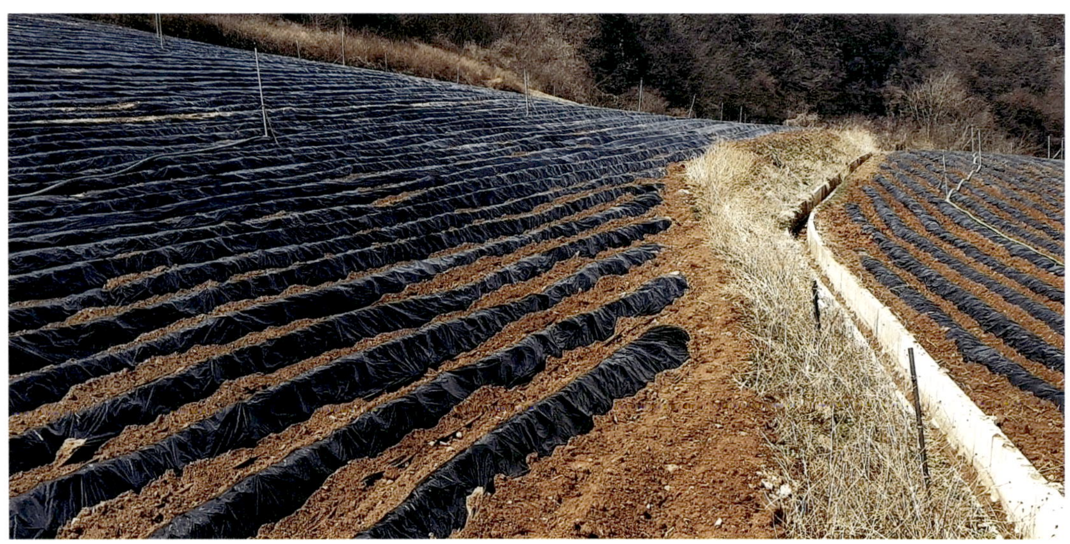

5 가스통 바슐라르, 곽광수 역, 『공간의 시학』(동문선, 2023) 참조.

5 Gaston Bachelard, *The Poetics of Space*, trans. Kwak Gwangsu (Seoul: Dongmunseon, 2023).

남춘모에게 밭고랑은 단순한 자연 풍경의 재현이 아니라, 작가의 내면 깊숙한 곳에서 발화되는 기억의 원형적 형상이다. 이는 생애 초기에 각인된 유년기의 시공간 경험이 조형 언어로 전환된 결과로서, 기억이 물질화된 지형이다.

“바람이 펄럭일 때, 흩뿌려지는 향토의 흙 색깔, 흰색과 검정색의 멀칭작업을 위한 비닐이 햇빛에 반짝이는 잔상들이 기억에 남아 있어요. 곡갱이와 소달구지로 큰 바위들은 피해가고, 그로 인해 자연스럽게 형성되어 가는 밭고랑의 전체적인 모습이 멀리서 바라보면 일률적이진 않아도 자연스런 모습에 마치 대지 아트처럼 멋져 보였죠”

(2025년 4월 작가인터뷰)

어린 시절 밭일을 하던 아버지와 함께 들판을 오가며 보았던 밭고랑은 반복되는 육체노동의 리듬, 땅의 물성, 빛과 그림자의 변화, 계절의 순환 등 감각의 복합체로 그에게 저장되었다. 이러한 풍토는 공기, 환경, 온습도, 바람 등 모든 것에 의해 결정된다. 작가는 이를 예민한 관찰을 통해 발견하고 ‘ㅛ’자형 유닛이라는 조형적 단위로 번역해 냈다. 이는 이후 작가의 조형 감각을 형성하는 심층적 기반이 되었으며, 그의 회화적 실천은 단순한 이미지의 반복이 아니라 헤르더적 의미에서 ‘풍토를 조형 언어로 번역하는 작업’이라 할 수 있다.

이러한 밭고랑 기억의 조형적 구현은 Beam 시리즈에서 그 초기 모습을 찾아볼 수 있다. 2014년에 제작한 Beam 시리즈들은 농작물 재배를 위해 지리적 환경에 따라 빛과 습도를 고려하여 만들어진 고랑과 이랑의 모습을 화면에 옮겨놓은 듯 보인다. 특히 실제 땅의 색채와 유사한 물감을 사용한 점은 작가가 어린 시절 감각적으로 체득한 기억을 회화적 언어로 구현하려는 적극적 시도로 읽힌다 Figs.15, 15-1.

For Nam Tchun-Mo, the furrowed fields are not simply a reproduction of natural scenery, but an archetypal memory of imprinted childhood experiences that surface from deep within, translated into a pictorial language:

“The mottled, earthy colors of the soil, and the lingering images of white and black vinyl sheets used for mulching, blowing in the wind and gleaming in the sunlight, remained in my memory. Using hoes and ox carts, we slightly veered to avoid large rocks, and through that process, the furrows naturally took shape. Even though they’re never perfectly uniform, the furrows still look beautiful from a distance, almost like some kind of land art.”

(Artist interview, April 2025)

The furrowed fields he saw while helping his father, who worked the land, were stored within a complex of sensory experiences: the rhythm of repeated physical labor, the materiality of the earth, the play of light and shadow, and the cycles of the seasons. Such a milieu encompasses every aspect of life—air, environment, temperature, humidity, wind, etc. Through keen observation, the artist nurtured his memories of the furrows, which eventually took the visual form of his ㅛ-shaped units. The memories became the foundation of Nam’s aesthetic sensibility, such that his painting can be understood not as a repetition of imagery, but a translation of place (in the Herderian sense) into a painterly language.

The first traces of these furrowed fields can be seen in the *Beam* series. In the works of the *Beam* series from 2014, it seems as if the ridges and furrows of earth made for growing crops, shaped in response to environmental conditions of light and humidity, have been transposed onto the canvas. This is particularly evident in the artist’s use of earthen tones resembling the colors of soil Figs.15, 15-1.

Fig. 15
Beam
Acrylic on coated fabric, 100 x 73 cm, 2014

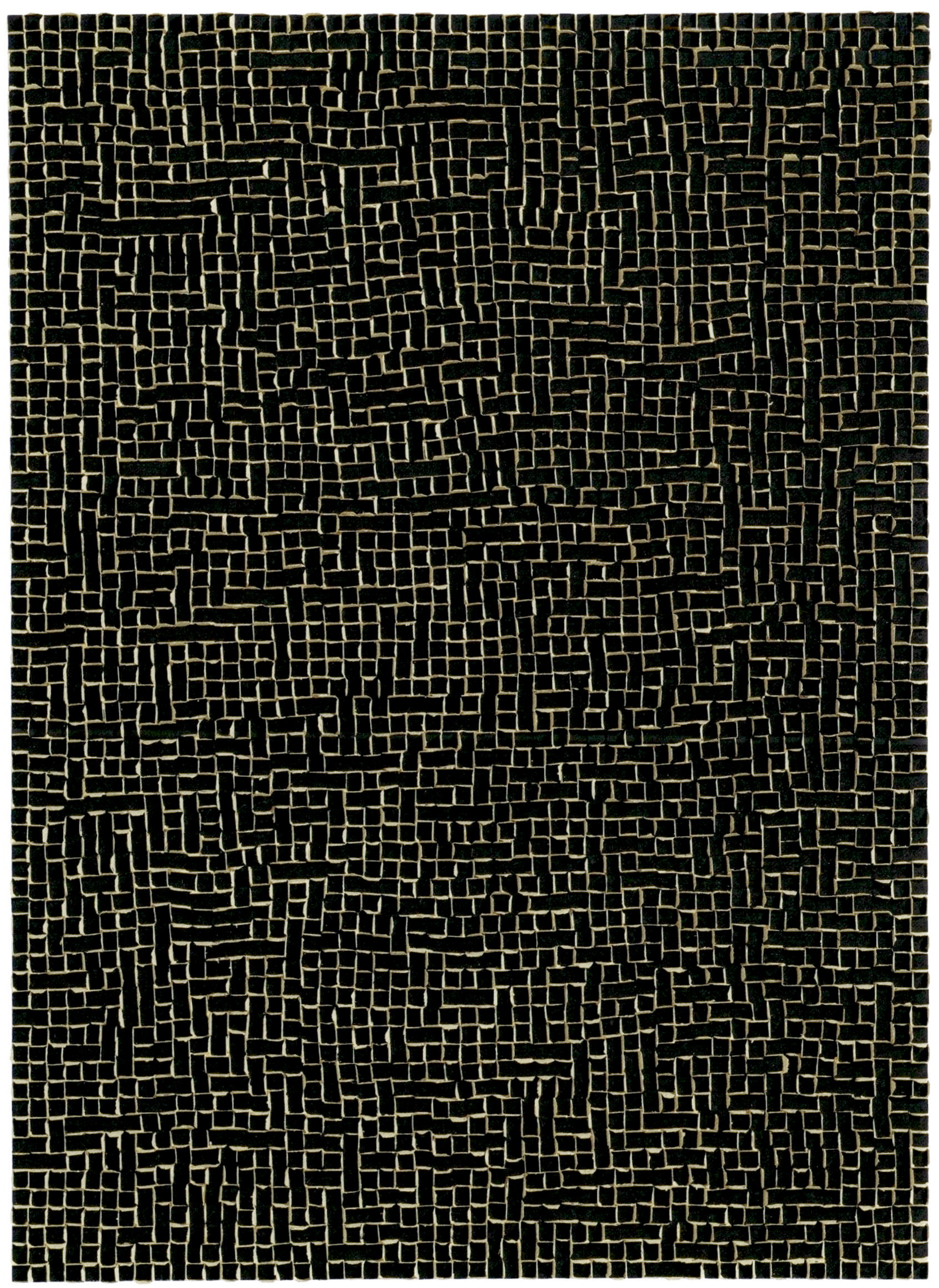

Fig. 15-1
Beam
Acrylic on coated fabric, 210 x 160 cm, 2014

Fig. 16
Beam 17-112
Oil on coated fabric, 210 x 160 cm, 2017

또한 2017년 작 〈Beam 17-112〉는 밭고랑에 씌운 비닐 멀칭의 모습 그 자체를 연상시킨다Fig. 16. 화면 상단과 하반부의 엇갈린 표현은 마치 바윗덩어리를 피해 경작한 그 모습과 닮아 있고, 유닛들의 오므라진 형태는 서구의 기하학적 추상이나 미니멀리즘에서 보이는 정확하게 그어진 엄격하고도 기계적인 선과는 확연한 차이가 있다. 화면 바깥으로 돌출된 부분의 정면으로 보이는 선들이 자연스럽게 삐뚤빼뚤한 선을 가시적으로 드러내며, 이는 경작기로 판 밭고랑이 아닌 직접 소달구지가 만들어낸 경작지의 모습과 더 유사하다.

이러한 밭고랑의 이미지는 선형 구조의 기본 형태이자, '⊔'자 혹은 'H빔' 형태로 반복되는 조형 유닛의 시각적·감각적 원형으로 작용한다. 남춘모의 회화에서 반복적으로 등장하는 구조적 단위는 단순히 미니멀한 형식 실험의 결과가 아니라, 유년기의 풍경과 신체적 경험이 농축된 기억의 구조다. 이는 곧 작가의 심리적 원형이자, 그의 작업이 단순한 조형 실험을 넘어 개인적 기억과 장소성이 결합된 회화의 영역으로 확장되는 중요한 지점이다.

작가가 이처럼 어린 시절을 소환하여 만들어낸 작업은 2017년부터 시작된 Spring 연작에서 더욱 명확해진다 Fig. 17. Spring 연작의 조형적 특징은 '⊔'자 유닛을 반복 배치하여 이랑과 고랑의 공간적 구조를 기하학적으로 형상화했다는 점, 폴리코트를 통해 단단히 고정된 화면의 질감과 입체성을 강조했다는 점, 빛이 스며드는 구조를 통해 밭의 생장성과 생명력을 암시하고 있다는 점에서 주목된다. 이러한 구성은 남춘모가 유년기 기억 속 밭고랑을 조형적으로 완성해낸 하나의 결과물로, 그가 더이상 기억을 회상하거나 재현하지 않고 기억을 구조화하여 작품 내부로 내면화시켰다는 점에서 중요하다.

The image of vinyl sheets spread across furrowed fields is directly evoked in *Beam 17-112* (2017)Fig. 16. The slightly skewed alignment between the upper and lower halves of the canvas recalls how furrows are gently curved by natural movements to avoid large rocks, while the bent forms of the ⊔ -shaped units stand in marked contrast to the precisely straight, rigid, and mechanical lines of Western geometric abstraction or Minimalism. The protruding lines of the units, as viewed head-on from the edge of the canvas, are naturally uneven and crooked, reminiscent of farmland shaped by ox carts, rather than by modern farming machinery.

The image of furrowed fields thus provides a fundamental linear structure, serving as the visual and sensory archetype of the "H-beams" and ⊔ -shaped units that recur in Nam Tchun-Mo's paintings. Rather than emerging from Minimalist experimentation, these structural units are actually condensed from childhood landscapes and bodily experiences. As archetypes drawn directly from the artist's psyche, they mark the pivotal point at which his work expands beyond formal experiment into the realm of art manifested from personal memory and sense of place.

The visualization of memory becomes more explicit in the *Spring* series, which began in 2017 Fig. 17. The works in this series are characterized by the repetitious arrangement of ⊔ -shaped units, which serve as geometric replications of furrowed fields; by an emphasis on texture and three-dimensionality, achieved by affixing the surface with polycoat; and by the suggestion of fertility and vitality through structures that allow the permeation of light. Thus, in this series, Nam Tchun-Mo was not simply recalling or representing memory, but rather structuring and internalizing it within the work itself.

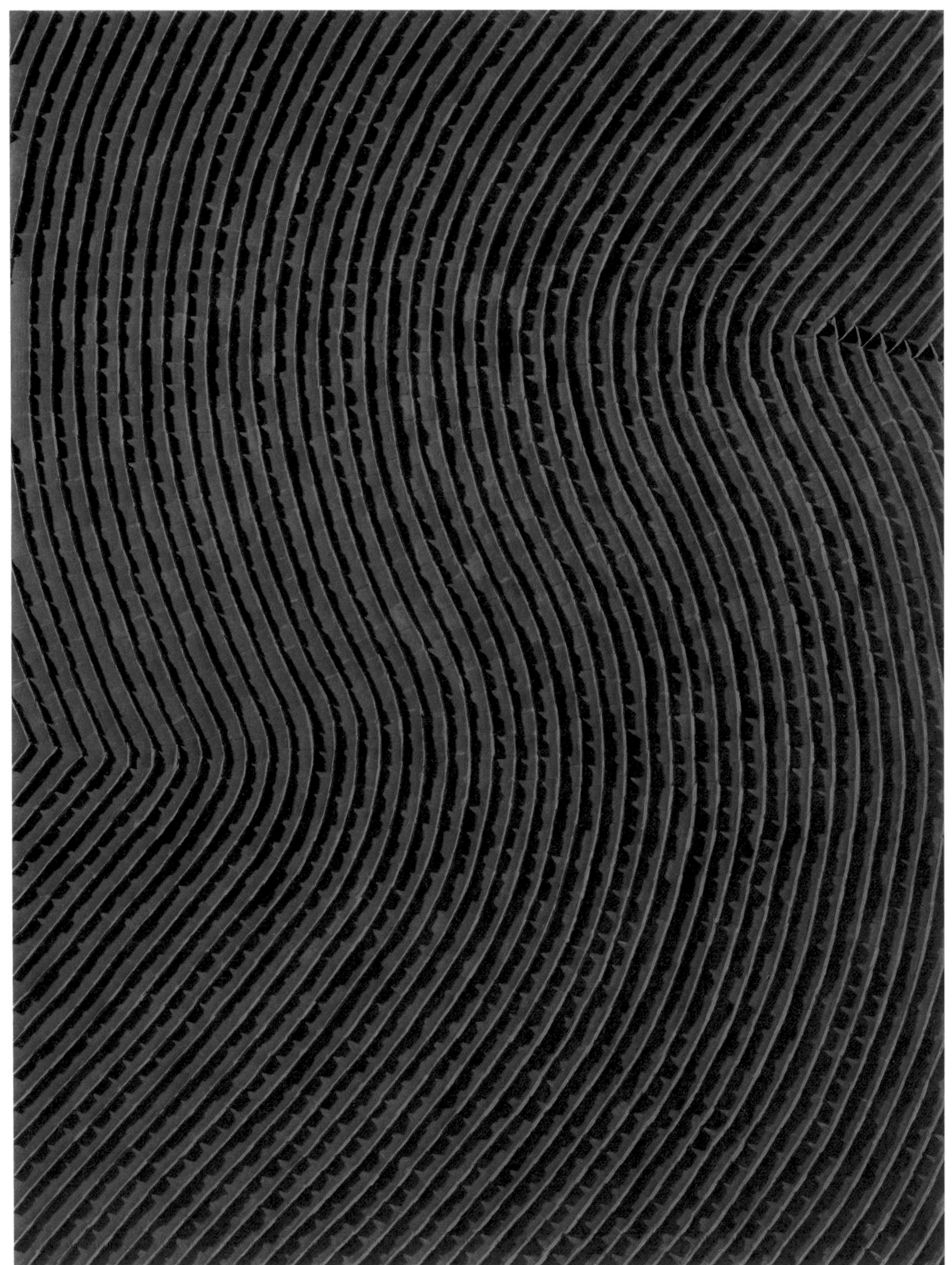

Fig. 17
Spring 18-22
Acrylic on coated fabric, 210 x 160 cm, 2018

'Spring'이라는 작품 제목은 단지 계절적인 은유가 아니라, 밭을 처음 준비하는 몸의 행위, 즉 땅과 처음으로 맞닿는 '경작의 시작'을 상징한다. 실제 농사에서 밭을 경작하는 작업, 즉 땅을 갈고 고르고 두둑을 만들고 멀칭을 깔거나 거름을 뿌리는 등의 준비 작업은 이른 봄(3월~4월) 본격적인 파종 전에 이뤄진다. 따라서 "밭을 만드는 행위"는 대부분 봄에 이뤄지며, 여름은 그 위에서 작물이 자라고 가을에 수확을 하게 된다. 남춘모의 Spring 연작에서 '봄'은 밭고랑의 리듬, 두둑과 이랑의 패턴을 공간화한 것이며, 그 리듬은 밭을 '심기 위해 준비하는 몸의 기억', 즉 봄철 경작의 행위에서 비롯된 것으로 볼 수 있다. 실제로 남춘모가 '⨆'자 유닛을 하나하나 접착제로 붙여나가는 작업만큼은 절대 그 누구에게도 맡기지 않고 직접 작업한다는 점에서도, 이 과정은 단순한 제작이 아니라 실제 밭고랑을 만드는 행위와 동일한 신체적 실천임을 보여준다. 따라서 그의 Spring 연작은 감각의 리듬이 '형태화'된 조형적 성취이며, 밭고랑이라는 감각적 원형의 '표면적 응축'이라고 할 수 있다.

남춘모의 Spring 연작이 유년기의 밭고랑을 구조화하고 반복을 통해 조형적으로 완성한 작업이라면, From the Earth 연작은 그러한 완성의 질서를 다시 해체하고, 흙이라는 물질을 통해 감각의 원형으로 회귀하려는 원초적 실천이다.

2023년 대구 인당미술관에서 열린 《From the Earth》 전시를 통해 선보인 이 연작은, 실제 땅의 형태를 직접 떠내어 조형 언어로 전환시키는 '현물적 번역'의 실험이다 Figs.18, 18-1. 이 작업의 배경에는 작가의 실존적 물음이 자리한다. 해외 전시를 위해 장기간 쾰른과 파리의 작업실에 머물고 팬데믹을 겪으며 축소된 생활 반경 속에서 작가가 스스로에게 던진 "나는 어디서 왔는지"에 대한 물음, 그 답이 "인간과 필연적으로 연결된 대지"임을 깨달은 과정이 이 작업에 고스란히 담겨 있다.

The title *Spring* invokes the physical act of preparing the land—the beginning of cultivation—when one first touches the soil. In farming, early spring is the time when many preparatory tasks must be performed before planting, such as tilling and leveling the ground, building ridges, laying mulch, and spreading fertilizer. Thus, the act of making a field takes place in spring, before the crops can grow in summer and be harvested in autumn. In Nam Tchun-Mo's *Spring* series, "spring" spatializes the rhythms and patterns of ridges and furrows, which originate from his own memories of preparing fields for cultivation. Notably, Nam never delegates the repetitious task of adhering the ⨆ -shaped units to his works, but insists on doing it himself. Thus, every work is imbued with his bodily actions and labor, the equivalent of creating furrows in a field. In his *Spring* series, the rhythm and memory of physical sensation is given physical form, with each work becoming a surface condensation of the sensory archetype of furrowed fields.

However, after stylizing and idealizing the furrowed fields of his childhood through repetition in the *Spring* series, Nam later introduced his *From the Earth* series, in which he engaged in a more primal practice of dismantling this order of completion, seeking to return to the sensory archetype through the materiality of soil. Presented at his 2023 exhibition *From the Earth* at Indang Museum in Daegu, this series was an experiment in literal/material translation, wherein he directly cast actual earthen forms into a painterly language Figs.18, 18-1. These works were rooted in the artist's existential inquiries. During long stays in Köln and Paris for overseas exhibitions, and while confined by the pandemic, Nam Tchun-Mo confronted the ultimate question: "Where do I come from?" He eventually realized that his origin and existence were inextricably linked to the earth, which then found its way into his work.

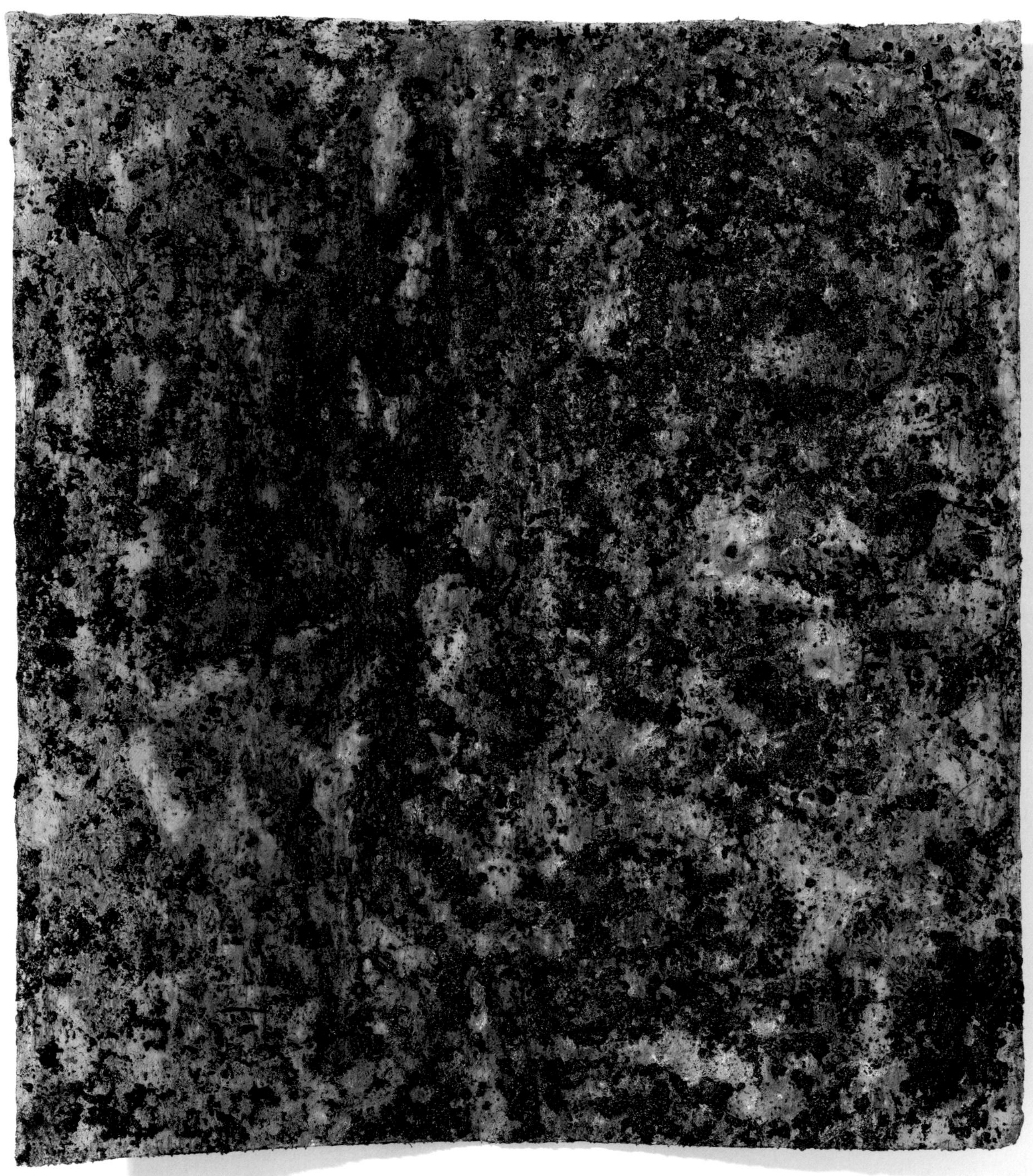

Fig. 18
From the Earth 2602
Mixed media on coated fabric, 210 x 195 cm, 2023

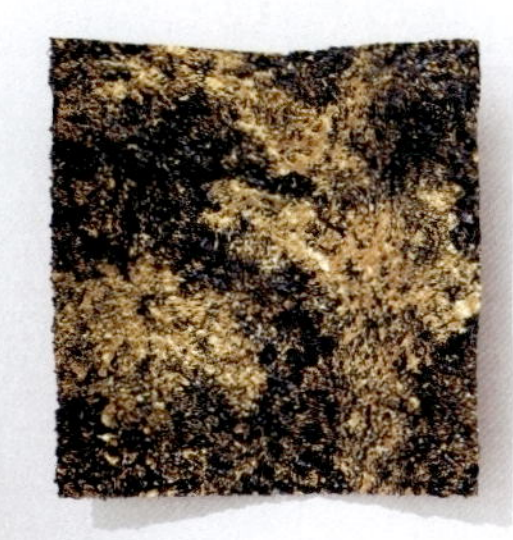
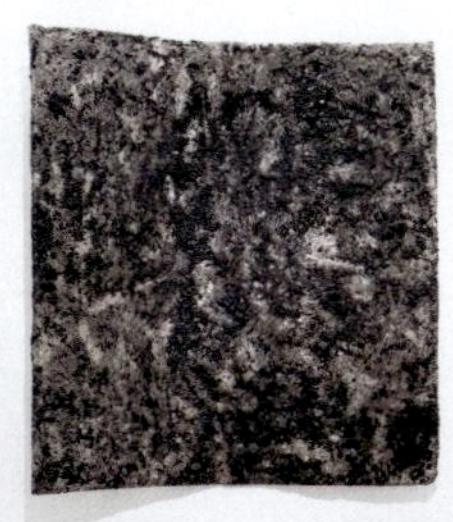
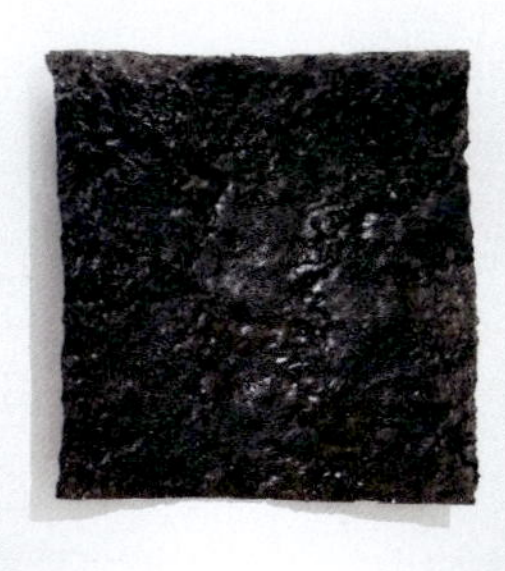

Fig. 18-1 From the Earth Mixed media on coated fabric, 210 x 195 cm, 2023 each

구체적 제작 과정을 보면, 작가는 청도의 폐교에서 농기구로 땅을 고르게 한 후 광목천을 깔고, 그 위에 폴리코트를 입혀 땅의 굴곡을 자연스럽게 표출할 수 있도록 밑작업을 한다. 그 위에 실제 땅의 흙을 입혀 굳혀낸 후, 이렇게 만들어진 흙 표면을 캔버스 삼아 채색하고 선을 그어 작품을 완성한다. 이는 유년기의 시각적 원형인 밭고랑에서 출발해, 그것을 현물적 방식으로 재현하는 독자적인 회화적 실천이라 할 수 있다Plate 3.

과거 한국 근현대 미술의 한 페이지를 장식한 화가들 가운데에도 흙을 재료로 사용한 사례는 많았다. 최영림(1916-1985)이 황토색 흙모래를 사용하여 전통 미감을 구현하거나 고구려 고분벽화를 재해석한 것은 '한국성'을 구현하려는 시대적 요청에 대한 응답이었다고 평가된다. 그러나 남춘모의 경우는 그러한 요청을 선행하는 감각적 충격에서 출발한다는 점이 다르다.

남춘모가 From the Earth 연작에서 보이는 방식은 특정한 전통에 호소하거나 재현하기보다는, 자신의 유년기 감각에 기반한 토포필리아(topophilia), 즉 장소에 대한 애정과 감응에서 비롯된 감각적 전이라고 볼 수 있다. 여기서 밭고랑은 단순한 '농촌적 풍경'이 아니라, 몸으로 기억한 땅의 요철, 그리고 반복된 노동 속에서 형성된 감각적 지형이다. 이 땅을 매끄럽게 다듬는 행위는 단순한 표면처리가 아니라, 남춘모가 일종의 회화적 리추얼(ritual)로 수행하는 '땅과의 접속'이자, 회화의 기원을 다시 호출하는 행위인 것이다.

To create these works, Nam used farming tools to level the ground at a closed school in Cheongdo. He covered the ground with cotton cloth, which he then coated with polycoat, preserving the natural ridges and grooves of the soil. Next, he poured dirt onto the polycoat surface and allowed it to harden. Finally, he painted and inscribed lines on this hardened surface, which served as his canvas. Through this unique process, he was able to literally materialize the visual archetype of furrowed fields from his childhoodPlate 3.

Nam Tchun-Mo is not the first Korean artist to use soil as a medium. In the postwar era, for example, when many artists were searching for ways to express "Koreanness" through art, Choi Youngrim (1916–1985) used ocher-colored earth and sand to recreate traditional aesthetics and reinterpret Goguryeo tomb murals. Even so, Nam's approach is distinguished in that it begins from the shock of sensory experience, which precedes such historical imperatives.

Thus, Nam's *From the Earth* series is not so much a reflection or reproduction of a certain tradition as it is a personal transference rooted in topophilia, an indelible response to and affection for place, grounded in childhood perceptions. The furrowed fields are not simply rural scenery, but a sensory topography imprinted within the body, the ridges and depressions of land shaped by repetitive labor. The act of smoothing the earth is a way of reconnecting with the land, performed as a type of pictorial ritual, a gesture that re-invokes the origins of painting.

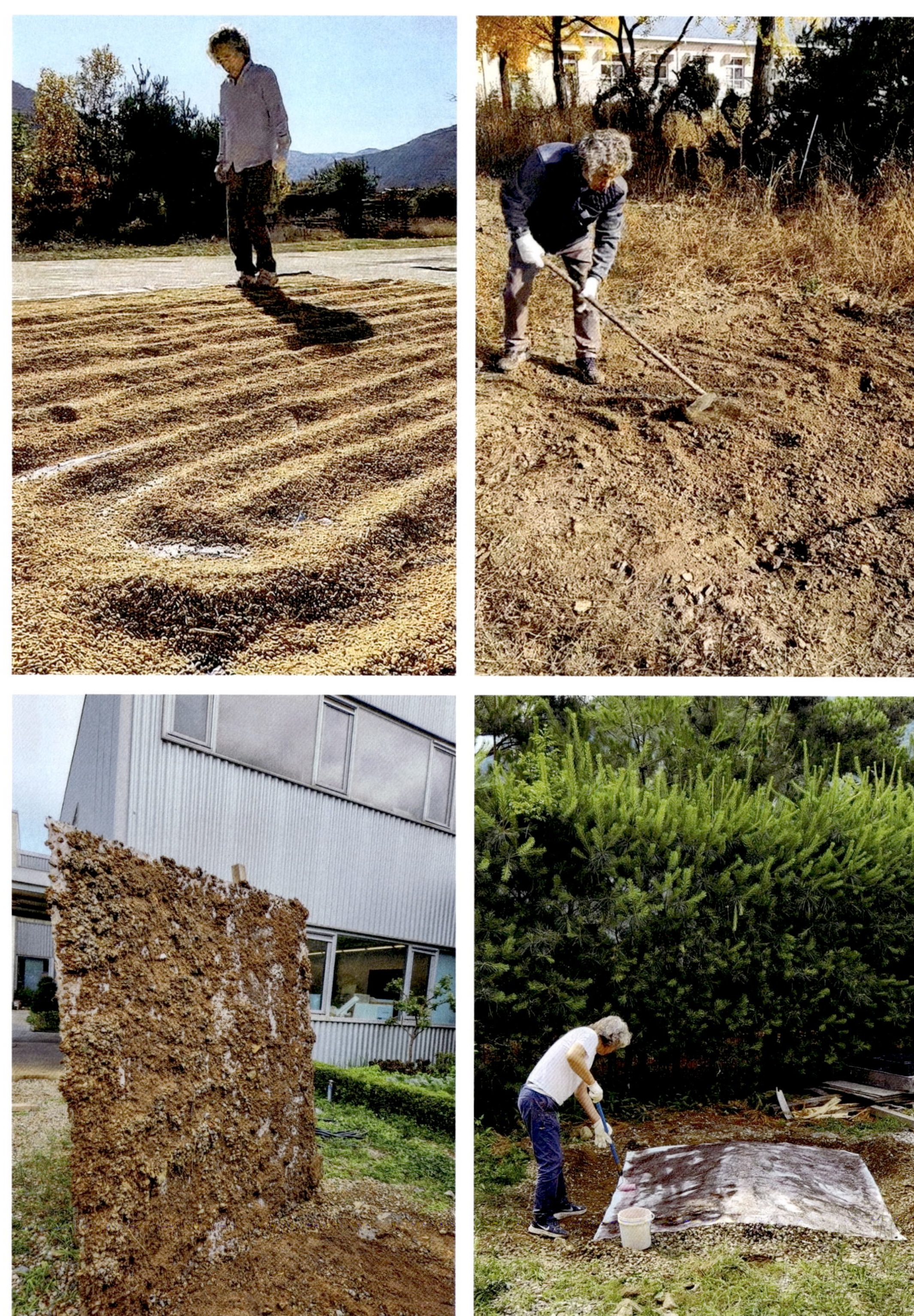

Plate 3
Artist in creation of From the Earth series, artist's studio, Korea 2023

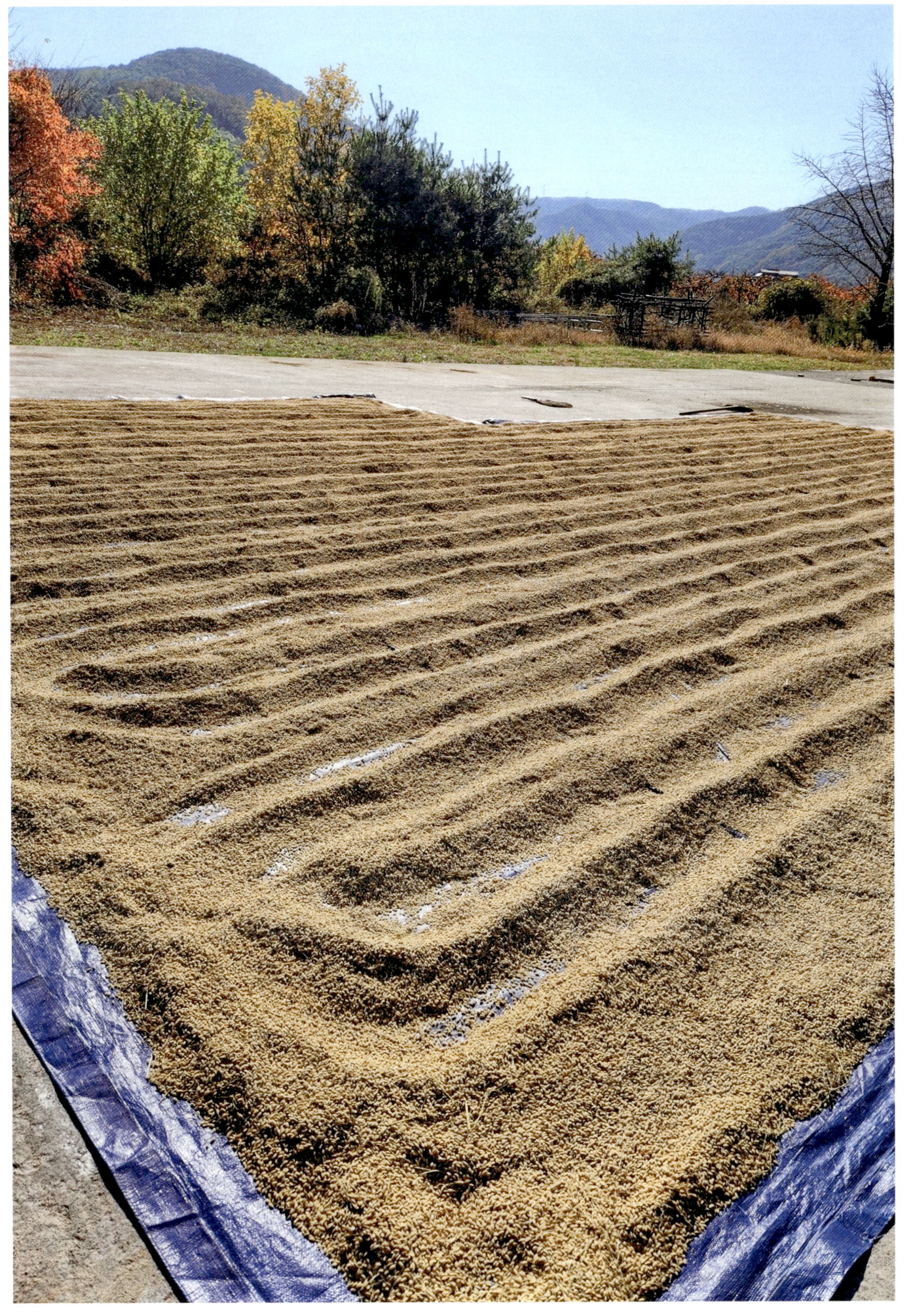

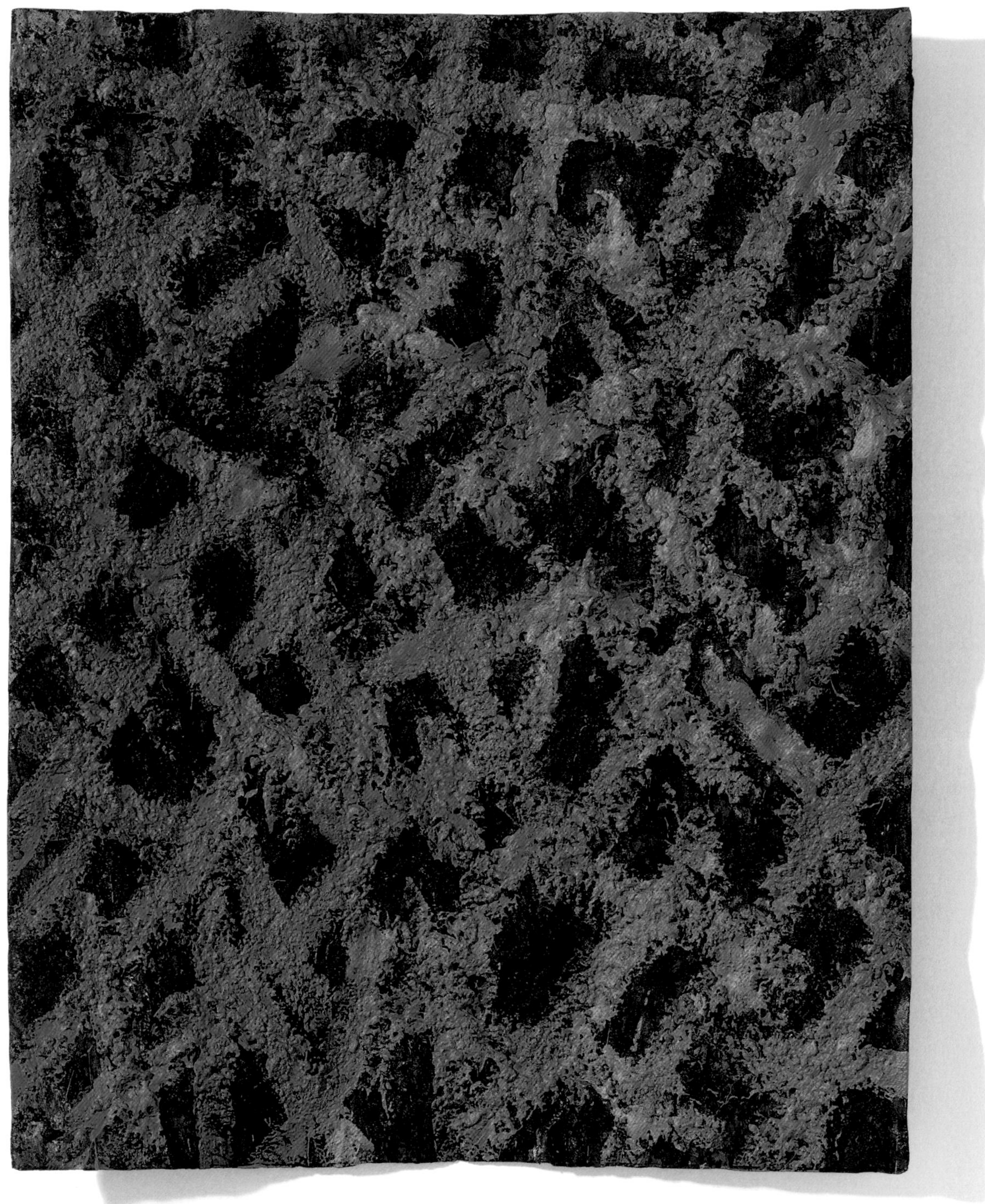

Fig. 19
From the Earth 0212
Mixed media on coated fabric, 160 x 130 cm, 2023

이런 관점에서 보면, From the Earth는 그저 '흙을 사용한 회화'가 아니라, '회화의 바탕을 회화 안으로 끌어들인 사건'이다. 전통적으로 '캔버스'는 회화의 기반이지만 동시에 '비회화적인 것'으로 간주되어 왔다. 그런데 남춘모는 그 경계를 허물고, 실제 땅 자체를 회화의 기반으로 삼음으로써 회화의 출발점을 '재물질화'한다. 다시 말해, From the Earth는 흙이 아닌 '대지 그 자체'의 현현(顯現)이며, 그 위에 Stroke 회화를 올리는 행위는 마치 그 땅 위에 자신의 기원을 덧입히는 회화적 자전(自傳)처럼 작동한다[Fig. 19].

특히 Spring 연작과 From the Earth 연작, 이 두 작업은 단절되지 않고, 오히려 하나의 감각적 기억을 축으로 하여 회화를 구축하고 다시 해체하는 변증법적 순환 구조 속에 놓여 있다. 밭고랑은 그에게 단지 유년의 상징이 아니라, 회화를 움직이게 하는 감각적 원형이자, 구축과 해체 사이를 왕복하는 조형적 리듬의 원천인 것이다.

남춘모의 회화에서 밭고랑은 이처럼 작가의 '몸의 기억'을 환기시키는 원형적 지형이며, 그의 회화적 실천은 단순한 이미지의 반복이 아니라, 기억과 감각, 구조와 감정이 중첩된 감각이 축적된 지층의 구축이라 할 수 있다. 이는 헤르더가 말한 인류가 지구상의 모든 장소에서 자신을 풍토화하는 과정의 예술적 구현이며, 남춘모가 폴리코트와 광목천이라는 일관된 재료를 통해 보여주는 극히 개인적 진정성의 물질적 증거이다.

결국, '밭고랑'이라는 원형적 감각은 이처럼 양극단의 작업을 잇는 공통의 감각적 뿌리로 작동하며, 남춘모의 회화는 "몸-기억-물질-구축-해체"라는 다섯 층위 사이를 왕복하는 회화적 존재론을 구성한다. 계절이나 기후에 따라 변하는 풍경은 단지 변하여 없어지는 현상의 모습에 불과하지만, 이 풍경의 변하지 않는 구조와 구성이야말로 남춘모가 목적으로 하는 예술의 결과다. 그의 밭고랑은 '보는 대상'이 아니라 '지나온 삶을 반복적으로 구축하는 행위'로 존재하며, 이는 그 자체로 진정한 한국성의 자연스러운 발현인 것이다.

Rather than paintings made with soil, the works of *From the Earth* are events in which the very ground of painting is drawn into painting itself. Traditionally, the foundation of painting has been the canvas, but the canvas itself is distinct from a painting. By instead making the earth the ground of his painting, Nam Tchun-Mo collapses that discrepancy, rematerializing painting's point of departure. In other words, *From the Earth* is not made from soil; it is a manifestation of the earth itself. As such, the act of combining his *Stroke* paintings with *From the Earth* functions like a painterly autobiography, layering his own origins upon that earth[Fig. 19].

The *Spring* series and *From the Earth* series exist within a dialectical cycle in which painting is constructed and then deconstructed around the axis of a single memory. The furrowed fields of his childhood serve as sensory archetypes that animate and engender painting, a source of this rhythmic structure that oscillates between construction and dissolution.

In Nam Tchun-Mo's work, furrowed fields evoke the memory of the body. His artistic practice is not a repetition of images, but the accrual of stratified layers of memory, sensation, and emotion, an artistic realization of what Herder described as humanity's process of acclimatizing itself to every place on earth. The deeply personal authenticity of these works is evidenced by his persistent use of the materials of polycoat and cotton cloth.

The furrowed fields of Nam's childhood serve as the common root uniting his seemingly disparate works, which constitute an artistic ontology traversing the five strata of body, memory, matter, construction, and deconstruction. Although landscapes change with the seasons or climate, sometimes even disappearing altogether, their underlying structures and compositions remain unchanged. The furrows in Nam Tchun-Mo's work are not objects to be looked upon, but physical acts of repeatedly constructing a life, and thus a natural manifestation of true "Koreanness."

2. 몸의 언어: 신체를 통한 조형 행위

"나는 그림 그리는 일이
농사짓는 일과 같다고 생각해요."

남춘모의 이 말은 단순한 비유가 아니다. 그에게 회화는 표현의 수단이 아닌 생존의 행위이며, 붓을 잡는 손은 곧 호미를 잡던 손의 기억을 담고 있다. 앞 장에서 살펴본 밭고랑의 시각적 원형이 '본 것'의 기억이라면, 이 장에서는 '한 것'의 기억, 즉 농사와 회화 사이에서 반복되는 신체의 리듬과 그것이 어떻게 조형 행위로 전이되는지를 탐구하고자 한다.

남춘모의 회화에서 '반복'은 단지 동일한 형식을 재현하는 행위가 아니다. 그것은 매번 다른 감각과 리듬, 힘의 강약을 수반하는 신체적 실천이며, 물질을 다루는 '노동'의 궤적이자, 존재를 견디는 윤리적 행위다. 그는 회화 행위를 '표현'이 아닌 '짓는 행위'로 받아들이며, 그 안에서 자신의 시간과 신체를 깊이 각인시킨다.

농사의 과정을 살펴보면 땅을 갈고 고르며 이랑과 고랑을 만드는 '경작', 비닐로 밭을 덮는 '멀칭', 씨를 뿌리고 작물을 기르는 '재배' 단계로 구분된다. 남춘모의 회화 작업 역시 광목천을 준비하고 표면을 다듬는 '기반 구축', 폴리코트를 발라 'ㄩ'자 유닛을 만드는 '재료적 처리', 유닛들을 화면에 부착하거나 선을 그어 작품을 완성하는 '조형 작업' 단계로 이어진다.

2. The Language of the Body, Form Through the Body

"Painting is like farming."

For Nam Tchun-Mo, painting is not so much a means of expression as it is an act of survival; the hand that now holds the brush carries the memory of the hand that once held a hoe. If the visual archetype of furrowed fields reflects the memory of what was seen, this chapter explores the memory of what was done—the bodily rhythms shared between farming and painting, which are transferred into acts of art creation.

In Nam Tchun-Mo's painting, repetition is not the act of reproducing the same form. It is a corporeal practice that continually yields different sensations, rhythms, and intensities. It is the trajectory of labor, of working with material, and an ethical act of enduring existence. He embraces painting not as "expression," but as "construction," deeply inscribing his own time and body into each work.

The processes of farming can be divided into stages: preparation—plowing and leveling the soil, creating furrows and ridges; mulching—covering the fields with vinyl sheets; and cultivation—sowing seeds and nurturing crops. Likewise, Nam Tchun-Mo's painting process involves various stages: groundwork—preparing the cotton fabric and smoothing the surface;

Plate 4
Artist's studio, Daegu, Korea 2025

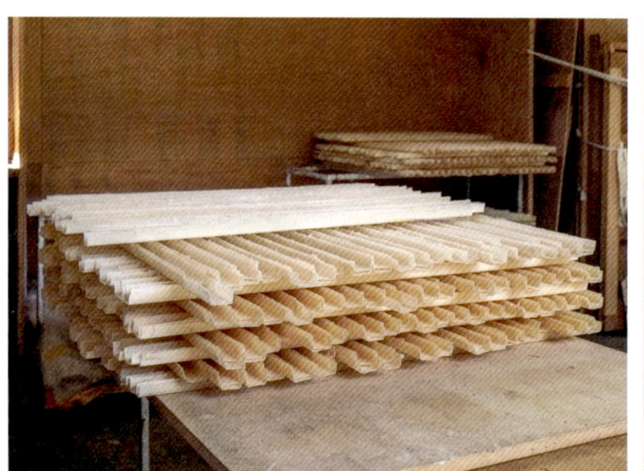

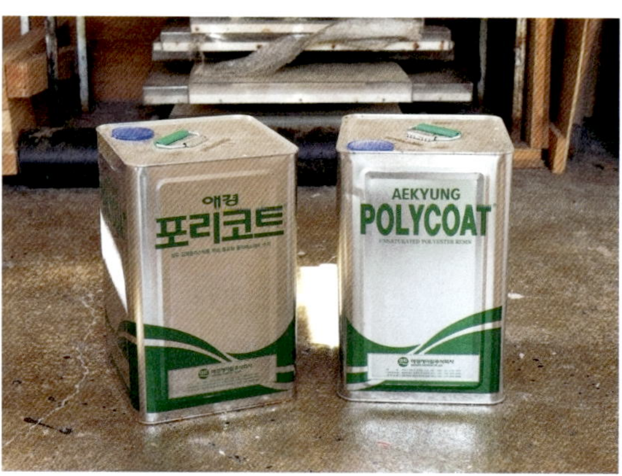

Plate 5

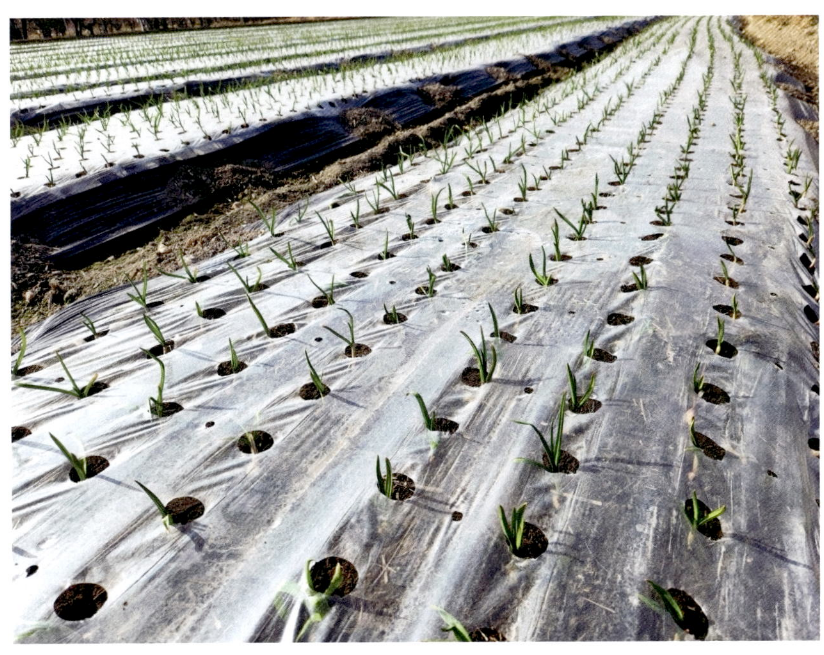

특히 주목할 점은 폴리코트의 역할이다. 이는 작품을 보호하는 마지막 단계가 아니라, 'ㅂ'자 유닛이라는 조형 요소를 생성하는 핵심 과정이다. 'ㅂ'자 유닛이라는 '조형의 씨앗'을 만들기 위해 폴리코트라는 '재료적 멀칭'을 하는 것이다Plate 4. 비닐멀칭이 농작물을 보호하면서 동시에 생장의 기반을 마련하듯, 폴리코트는 유닛을 견고하게 형성하면서 화면에서의 안정적 정착을 돕는다. 이는 작가의 무의식에 각인된 농사의 리듬이 창작 과정에 자연스럽게 스며든 결과다.

이러한 신체적 기억의 전이는 목탄 드로잉 연작 〈Spring Beam〉(2012)에서 직관적으로 드러난다Figs.20, 20-1. 화면에 일정한 간격으로 배치된 검은 원들은 마치 무를 심기 위해 비닐멀칭에 뚫어놓은 구멍들을 연상시킨다Plate 5. 실제 농사에서 비닐구멍을 뚫고 한 구멍에 무씨 2립을 넣어 심는 과정처럼, 작가는 화면에 '그림이 숨 쉴 수 있는 구멍'을 만들어낸다.

material treatment—applying polycoat to create the ㅂ -shaped units; and making forms—attaching the units to the surface or drawing lines to complete the work.

Here, the role of polycoat is particularly important. Instead of being applied as the final step for protecting the work, polycoat becomes the core material that actually forms the ㅂ -shaped units. To create these units—the "seeds of form"—the artist applies polycoat as a type of mulching with a new materialPlate 4. Just as vinyl mulching protects crops while providing the basis for growth, polycoat solidifies the units and secures them to the surface. This process demonstrates how the rhythm of farming, imprinted in the artist's unconscious, permeates his creative practice.

This transference of memory intuitively appears in the charcoal drawings of Nam's series *Spring Beam* (2012)Figs.20, 20-1, in which black circles are arranged at regular intervals across the surface, evoking the holes punctured in vinyl mulching for planting radishesPlate 5. Just as in actual farming, where two radish seeds are placed into each hole, the artist creates breathing holes for the painting.

Fig. 20
Spring-Beam
Charcoal on paper, 57 x 77 cm, 2012

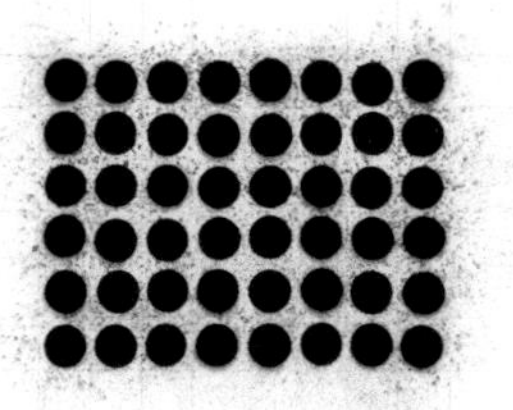

Fig. 20-1
Spring-Beam
Charcoal on paper, 57 x 77 cm, 2013

Stroke 연작에서는 이러한 '숨구멍'의 개념이 더욱 구체적으로 발전한다Figs.21, 21-1. 남춘모는 필획만으로 이루어진 평면 작업을 하면서도, 캔버스나 광목천을 콜라주하여 화면에 요철을 만들어낸다. 이는 시각적 질감을 위한 장식적 기법이 아니다. 그에게 '평평한 표면'은 애초에 존재하지 않았다. 어린 시절 경험한 땅은 돌멩이를 피해 만든 고랑, 자연스러운 흙의 요철, 비닐멀칭 아래 울퉁불퉁한 땅의 기복으로 이루어져 있었기 때문이다. 광목천 콜라주로 만든 울퉁불퉁한 표면은 획이 미세한 틈새와 돌출부를 타고 자연스럽게 흘러가도록 하는 촉각적 통로들을 형성한다. 요철로 만든 바탕은 선과 화면 사이에 물리적 긴장을 조성하며, 그가 그은 선이 천의 주름을 타고 흐르고, 중첩된 콜라주 위에서 방향을 달리하며, 캔버스의 물리적 저항을 만날 때, 그는 단순히 선을 그리는 것이 아니라 획의 감각을 체현하고 있다. 이는 전통적인 용필(用筆)의 차원과 맞닿아 있으면서도, 그 자신만의 독특한 필획 감각을 보여준다.

This concept of "breathing holes" is further developed in the *Stroke* seriesFigs.21, 21-1. Even in these supposedly two-dimensional works comprised of brushstrokes, Nam Tchun-Mo uses canvas or cotton fabric to form collages with irregular surfaces. Rather than a decorative technique for augmenting the texture, this process is simply a reflection of his reality. For him, there is no such thing as a flat surface, for his childhood was spent on rough fields of earth filled with ridges, hollows, and crooked furrows. In his works, the textured ground of the cotton fabric generates physical tension between line and surface. Moreover, the uneven surfaces create tactile channels through which the strokes flow naturally, tracing the subtle creases and protrusions. The lines he draws flow along the folds of the fabric, shifting direction and encountering the physical resistance of the canvas. As a result, he is not merely drawing a line, but embodying the sensation of the stroke itself. This sensation hearkens back to the traditional principle of "*yongpil*" (用筆, "use of the brush"), while simultaneously revealing his own distinct sensibility of the brushstroke.

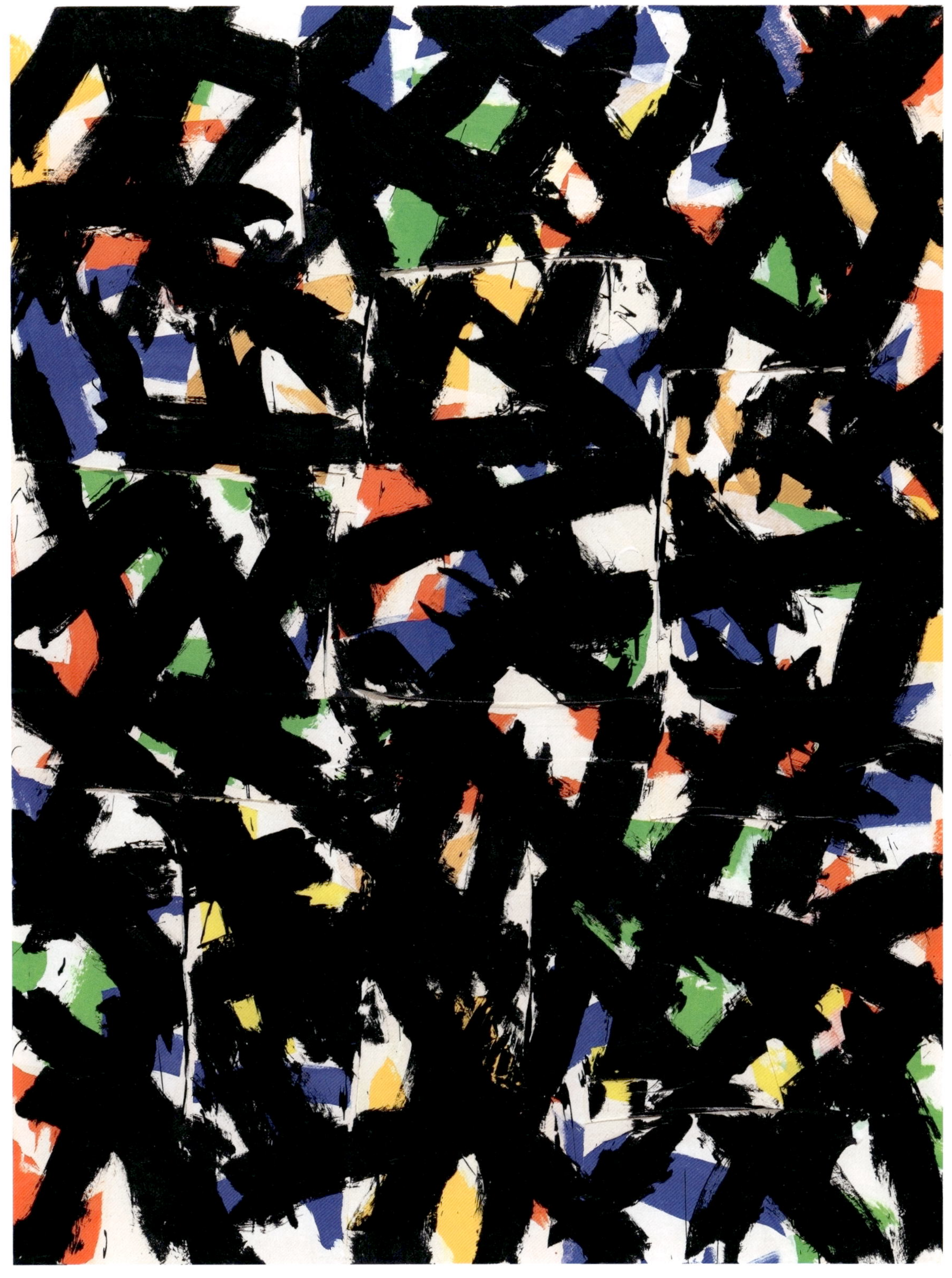

Fig. 21
Stroke-Lines 0506
Acrylic on canvas, 210 x 160 cm, 2025

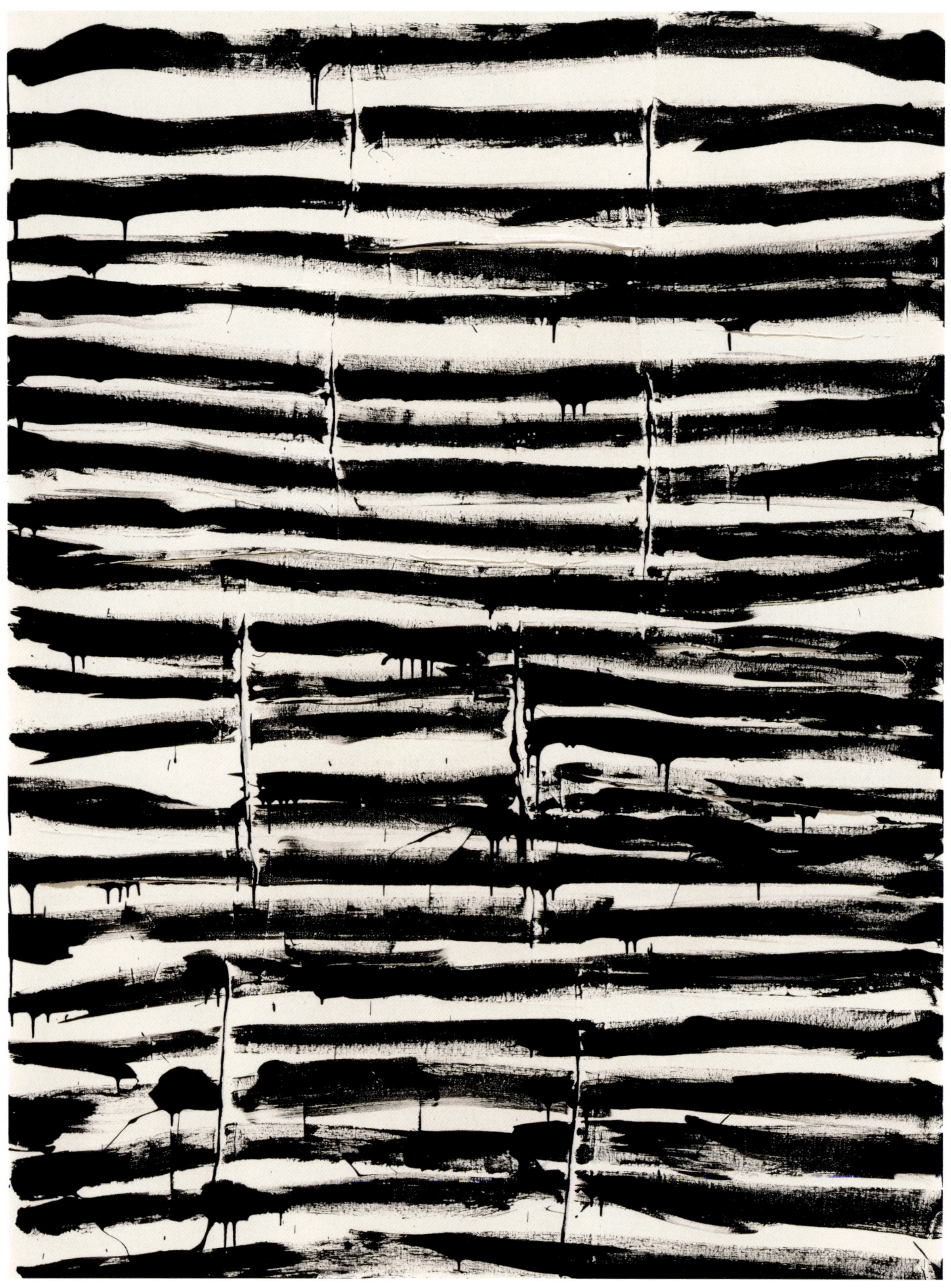

Fig. 21-1
Lines 22-129
Acrylic on canvas, 210 x 160 cm, 2022

이는 2025년에 선보인 From the earth 연작에서 극대화되는데, 그가 회화에 찍어 내려간 둥근 획들이 화면 전체에 리듬감 있게 분포하면서 마치 씨앗을 심은 밭의 전경을 보는 듯한 시각적 경험을 제공한다. 여기서 각각의 둥근 획은 단순한 형태가 아니라, 생명이 움틀 수 있는 잠재적 공간으로 작동한다Figs.22, 22-1.

나아가 이러한 '숨구멍'의 개념은 Beam 시리즈에서도 각기 다른 방식으로 구현된다. 'ㅂ'자 유닛들 사이의 간격은 서구 미니멀리즘의 기계적 격자 구조와는 확연히 다르다Figs.23, 23-1. 작가가 의도적으로 만들어낸 "약간은 엉성하게 삐뚤빼뚤한 구조적 틈새"들은 돌덩이를 피해 자연스럽게 형성된 밭고랑의 불규칙한 간격을 연상시킨다. 이 틈새들은 단순한 조형적 여백이 아니라, 작품이 호흡할 수 있도록 하는 생명적 공간이다. 빛이 스며들고 시선이 쉬어갈 수 있는 이 구조적 여백들은, 비닐멀칭 아래에서도 작물이 숨 쉴 수 있도록 뚫어놓은 구멍처럼, 회화가 경직되지 않고 살아 움직일 수 있는 여유를 제공한다.

이러한 표면 처리는 비닐멀칭-폴리코트의 반복적 준비 행위와 구조적으로 유사하며, 결국 남춘모 회화 전체를 관통하는 "몸의 리듬과 기억에 각인된 회화적 습속"의 결과로 해석해야 한다.

메를로 퐁티의 현상학적 관점에서 본다면, 이는 체험된 공간의 기억이 신체적 창작 행위를 통해 드러나는 과정이라 할 수 있다. 남춘모의 반복은 겉으로 보기에는 동일한 유닛을 쌓아가는 시각적으로 쌓아가는 행위지만, 그 과정은 감각의 리듬과 신체의 미세한 떨림을 통해 구현되는 살아 있는 지각의 표출이다.[6]

이는 농사를 통해 체험한 공간의 기억이 회화의 표면으로 옮겨지는 과정이며, 신체와 작품 사이의 통일성을 보여준다.

6 메를로 퐁티, 류의근 역, 『지각의 현상학』(서울:문학과지성사, 2002) 참조.

This approach reaches its pinnacle in the new works of his *From the Earth* series, unveiled in 2025, wherein impressions of round strokes spread rhythmically across the entire plane, recreating the experience of looking out over a field sown with seedsFigs.22, 22-1. More than mere shapes, each circular stroke is a potential space where life can sprout.

The "breathing holes" appear in another guise in Nam's *Beam* series. As opposed to the mechanical precision and symmetry that generally characterizes grids from Western Minimalism, the spacing between the ㅂ-shaped units in these works is irregular, recalling the subtle shifts of furrows formed around stones Figs. 23, 23-1. Much more than empty gaps, these spaces are vital components that allow the work to breathe, while also enabling light to filter in and providing a place for the viewers' gaze to rest. Just like the holes in vinyl mulching, which let the underlying crops breathe, these uneven spaces keep the painting from becoming rigid, allowing it to remain alive and moving.

This surface treatment is akin to the repetitive preparatory acts of vinyl mulching and polycoat application, demonstrating the painterly habitus imprinted with bodily rhythm and memory that runs through Nam Tchun-Mo's entire works.

From a phenomenological perspective, following Merleau-Ponty, these works embody how the memory of experienced space is revealed through bodily acts of creation. Nam Tchun-Mo's repetitive acts, such as the stacking of identical units, are expressions of living perception, realized through the rhythm of sensation and minute tremors of the body.[6]

They are the process by which the memory of space experienced through farming is transposed onto the painterly surface, creating unity between body and work.

6 Maurice Merleau-Ponty, *Phenomenology of Perception*, trans. Ryu Uigeun (Seoul: Moonji Publishing, 2002).

결국 남춘모의 회화에서 반복은 단순한 조형 어휘가 아니다. 그것은 삶의 지속, 신체의 증언, 감각의 윤리로 이어지는 긴 여정이며, 한국적 추상회화가 가질 수 있는 윤리적 지평의 가능성을 제시한다. 그의 회화는 '그림'이 아니라 '살아낸 구조'이며, 반복의 매 순간이 예술가의 존재를 증명하는 실천으로 작동한다.

Ultimately, in Nam Tchun-Mo's painting, repetition is not merely a formal vocabulary. It is a long journey that encompasses the persistence of life, the testimony of the body, and the ethics of sensation, presenting a new horizon of ethical possibility within Korean abstract painting. His paintings are not a picture, but a lived structure, in which each moment of repetition testifies to the artist's existence.

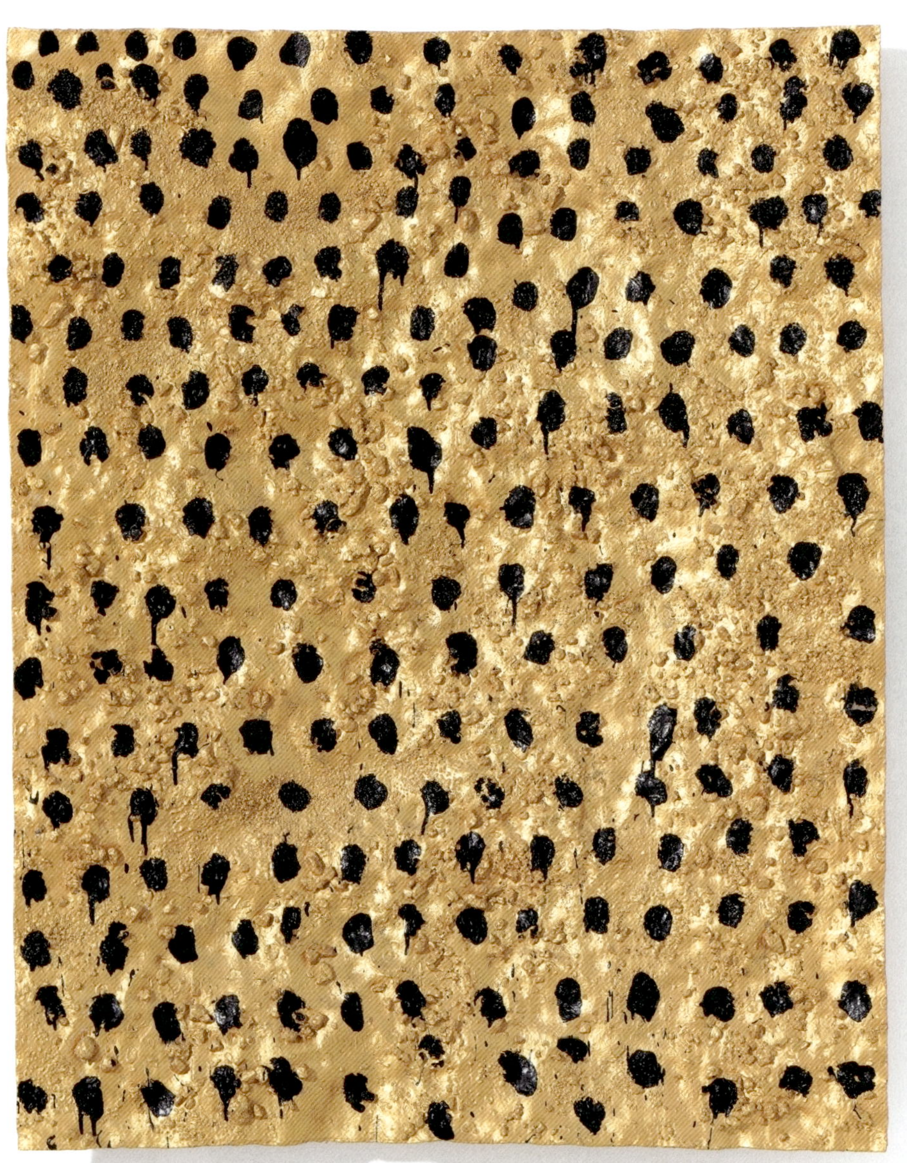

Fig. 22
From the Earth 2606
Mixed media on coated fabric, 160 x 130 cm, 2024

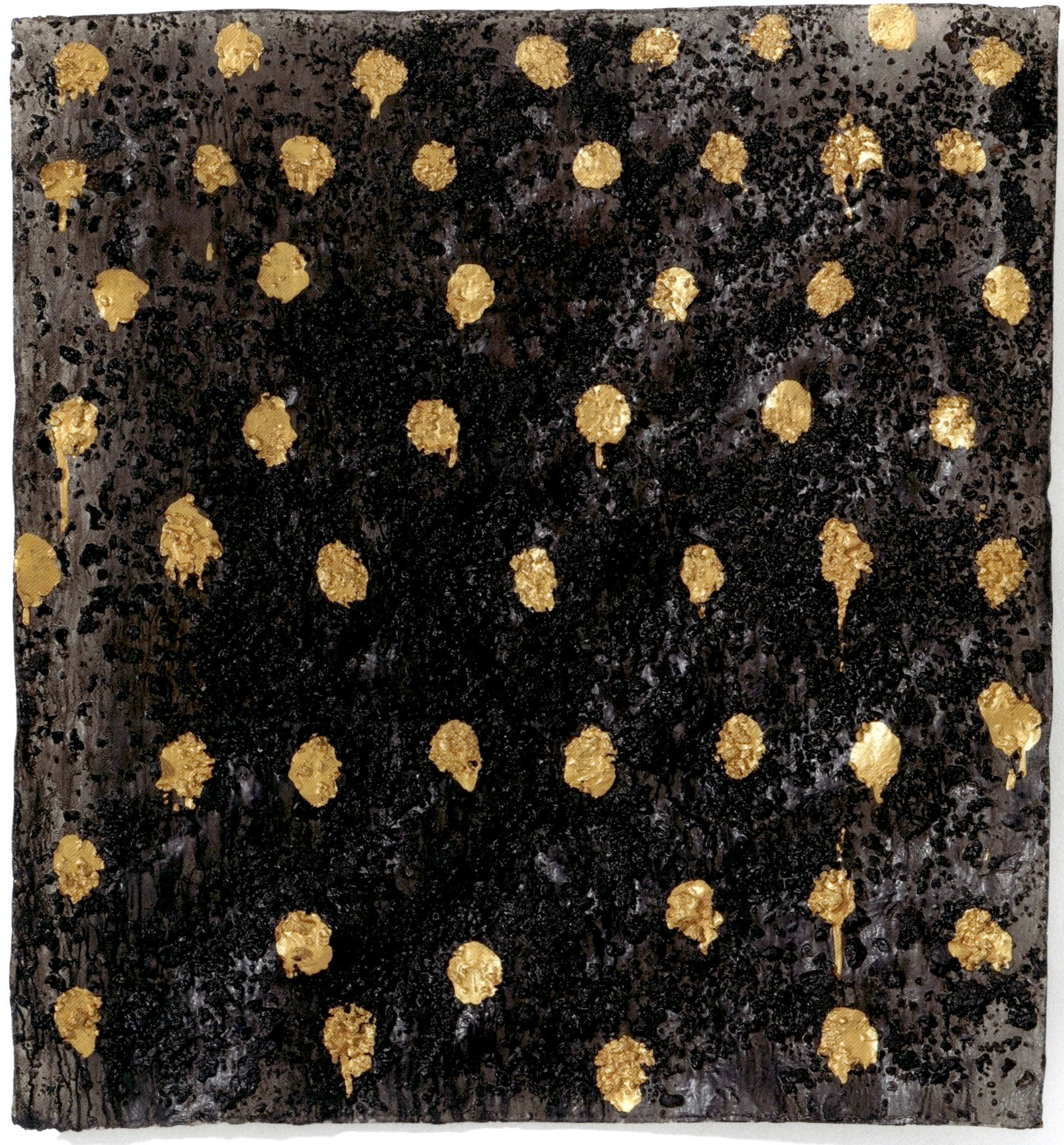

Fig. 22-1
From the Earth 2706
Mixed media on coated fabric, 105 x 100 cm, 2024

Fig. 23
Beam 24-4
Acrylic on coated fabric, 160 x 120 cm, 2024

Fig. 23-1
Beam 2013
Acrylic on coated fabric, 210 x 160 cm, 2013

Ⅳ. 井의 구조와 감각

1. H빔의 창조적 변환: '凵'유닛의 탄생과 구조적 본질

남춘모의 회화는 '선'을 통해 구축된 평면 회화를 넘어서, 모듈화된 구조체와 전통 건축의 상징성을 융합해 감각적 공간성을 창출한다. 그 중심에는 '凵'자 유닛이라 불리는 조형 단위가 존재한다. 이 구조는 작가가 폴리코트를 덧입힌 유닛(약 3×3×1 cm)을 반복적으로 부착함으로써 형성한 것으로, 단순한 표면의 텍스처를 넘어서 화면의 골격이자 감각의 단위로 기능한다Plate 6.

이러한 '凵'자 유닛의 탄생 배경을 이해하려면 남춘모의 학문적 여정을 살펴볼 필요가 있다. 그는 대학원에서 「현대미술에 나타난 기계기술의 영향에 관한 연구」라는 제목의 석사논문을 통해 서구 기계미학에 대한 이론적 탐구를 수행했다. 이후 독일 유학 시절, 그는 바우하우스의 본고장에서 "모든 조형 행위의 궁극적 목표는 건축이다"라는 모더니즘 철학과 예술과 기술의 통합을 직접 체험할 수 있었다. 하지만 이러한 서구적 기계미학의 탐구를 통해 그가 깨달은 것은, 단순한 수용이 아닌 자신만의 독창적 조형 언어를 찾아야 한다는 필연적 과제였다.

남춘모가 주목한 것은 H빔의 구조적 순수성이었다. H빔은 최소한의 재료로 최대한의 강도를 내는 산업 형태로, 현대 건축의 가장 기본적이면서도 구조적으로 완결된 부재다Plate 7. 더 이상 단순화할 수 없는 최소한의 구조적 형태이자, 기능과 형태가 완벽하게 일치하는 순수한 구조체인 것이다. 바우하우스가 주구한 기능주의 미학의 완벽한 구현체로서, H빔은 서구 산업문명이 만들어낸 가장 합리적이고 효율적인 구조적 해답이었다.

Ⅳ. The Structure and Sensation of "井" ("Well")

1. Creative Transformation of the H-Beam: Structural Essence of 凵-shaped Units

Transcending two-dimensional works, Nam Tchun-Mo's paintings are constructions formed by lines, with a vital spatiality that combines modular structures with the symbolism of traditional Korean architecture. At the heart of this structure are the 凵-shaped units (approx. 3 × 3 × 1 cm) that he repetitively assembles and attaches, before applying layers of the polycoat that serves as the framework and sensory unit of the canvasPlate 6.

The origins of the 凵-shaped units can be traced back to Nam Tchun-Mo's student days. For his master's thesis, *A Study on the Influence of Mechanical Technology in Contemporary Art*, Nam conducted theoretical explorations of Western mechanical aesthetics. He then went to study in Germany, where he directly encountered the integration of art and technology in the birthplace of Bauhaus, which famously espoused that "The ultimate goal of all creative activity is architecture." Through these studies of Western mechanical aesthetics, he came to realize the imperative task of discovering his own original artistic language.

In this period, Nam became fascinated by the structural purity of the H-beam. An industrial element that achieves maximum strength with minimal material, the H-beam is the most basic and purest structural form in modern architecturePlate 7. As such, it represents the ideal symbiosis of form and function, irreducible to anything simpler. As the consummate embodiment of the functionalist aesthetics promoted by the Bauhaus, the H-beam was the most rational and efficient structural solution produced by Western industrial civilization.

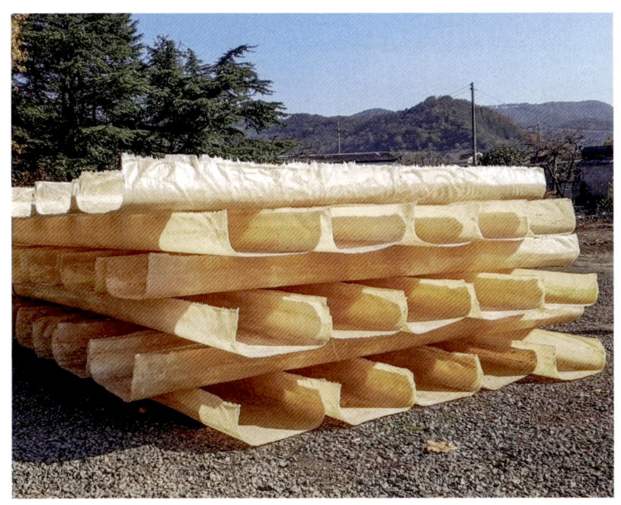

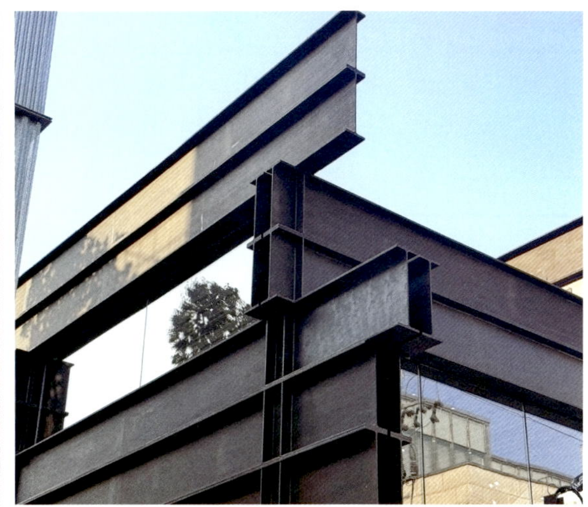

Plate 6
Artist's studio, Korea 2017

Plate 7

하지만 남춘모는 이 서구적 산업 구조체를 한국적 맥락으로 창조적 전환시켰다. '차가운 강철'에서 '따뜻한 광목천+폴리코트'로, '기계적 압연'에서 '수공적 반복'으로, '건축적 구조체'에서 '회화적 단위'로의 변화를 통해 '⊔'자 유닛을 탄생시켰다. 이는 단순한 형태적 차용이 아니라, 구조의 본질을 다른 매체로 이식하는 창조적 변환이다. 구조의 DNA를 그대로 유지하면서도 완전히 다른 감각적 경험을 만들어낸 것이다. 그의 <Beam17-134>는 H빔의 구조적 본질을 회화적 언어로 번역한 대표작이다. 작가는 '⊔'자 유닛의 돌출 부분에만 선택적으로 색을 입힘으로써, 마치 공사현장에 쌓인 H빔 더미를 보는 듯한 강렬한 착시 효과를 창출했다[Figs.24, 24-1]. 이는 전체 표면을 단색으로 처리한 다른 Beam 연작들이 일반적인 미니멀리즘 작품의 시각적 특성을 보이는 것과는 확연히 구별되는 접근이다. 단순한 형태적 차용을 넘어서, H빔의 구조적 논리 자체를 회화 공간에 이식한 결과다.

However, Nam Tchun-Mo reconfigured this Western industrial structure within a Korean context by transforming cold steel into warm cotton and polycoat; mechanical rolling into handcrafted repetition; and the architectural component into a painterly unit, ultimately giving rise to his ⊔ -shaped units. While preserving the inherent essence of the original structure, he enacted a creative transformation, changing an industrial material into a new medium to generate an entirely different sensory experience. This transposition is perhaps best exemplified by *Beam 17-135*[Figs.24, 24-1]. By applying color only to the protruding parts of the units, he conjured an optical illusion, reminiscent of H-beams stacked at a construction site. Notably, this work stands out within the Beam series, which typically features monochrome surfaces that evoke the visual characteristics of conventional minimalist works.

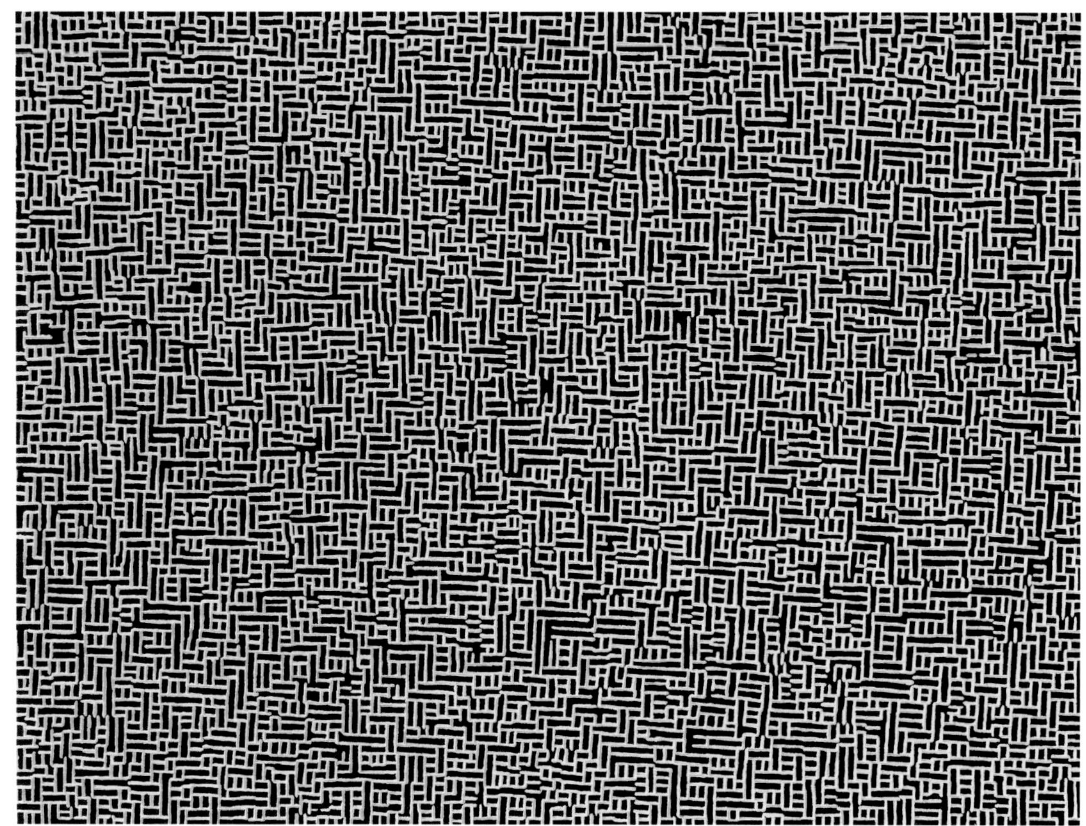

Fig. 24
Beam 2007
Acrylic on coated fabric, 260 x 194 cm, 2007-2023

결국 남춘모의 'ㅂ'자 유닛은 서구 모더니즘의 구조적 순수성과 한국적 풍토와 정서가 만나 탄생한 독특한 조형 언어다. H빔이라는 산업문명의 상징을 동양적 맥락으로 전환시킨 이 과정은, 단순한 문화적 절충을 넘어서 작가의 오랜 고민과 체험이 만들어낸 창조적 결과를 보여주는 사례라 할 수 있다. 더이상 단순화할 수 없는 구조적 본질을 추구하면서도, 그것을 따뜻한 감성의 재료와 손의 경험으로 감싸 안은 남춘모의 'ㅂ'자 유닛은 이후 그의 모든 작업의 핵심적 토대가 되었다.

In the end, Nam Tchun-Mo's ㅂ -shaped units represent a unique artistic language born from the encounter between the structural purity of Western modernism and the climate and sensibility of Korea. The repositioning of the H-beam, an icon of Western industrialism, into an Eastern context is the creative outcome of Nam's entire lifetime of reflection and experience. Upon discovering the irreducible essence of structure, he enveloped it in material warmth, personal sensitivity, and the memory of the hand. In accordance, the ㅂ -shaped units became the foundational core of all his subsequent works.

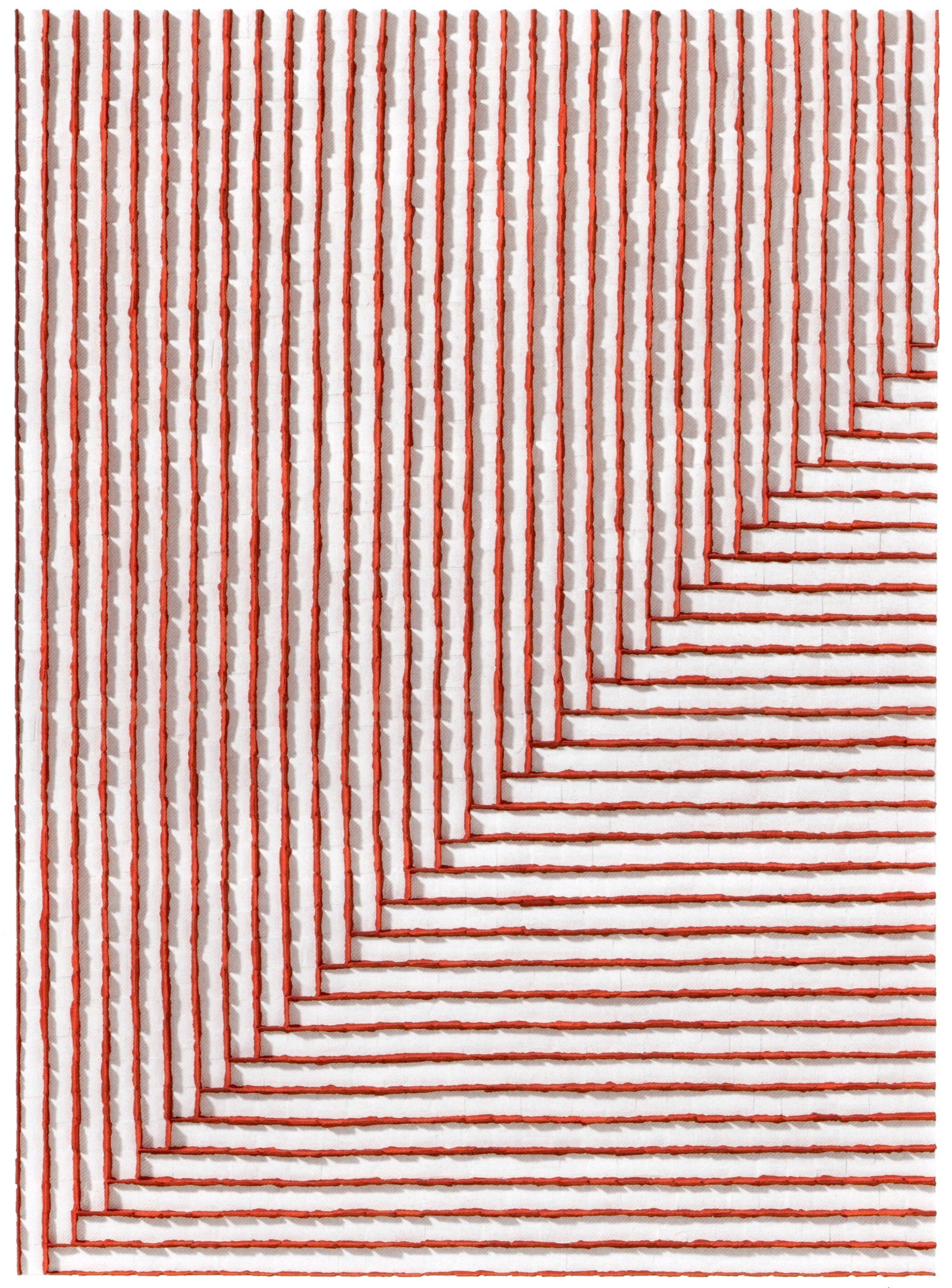

Fig. 24-1
Beam17-03
Acrylic on coated fabric, 160 x 120 cm, 2017

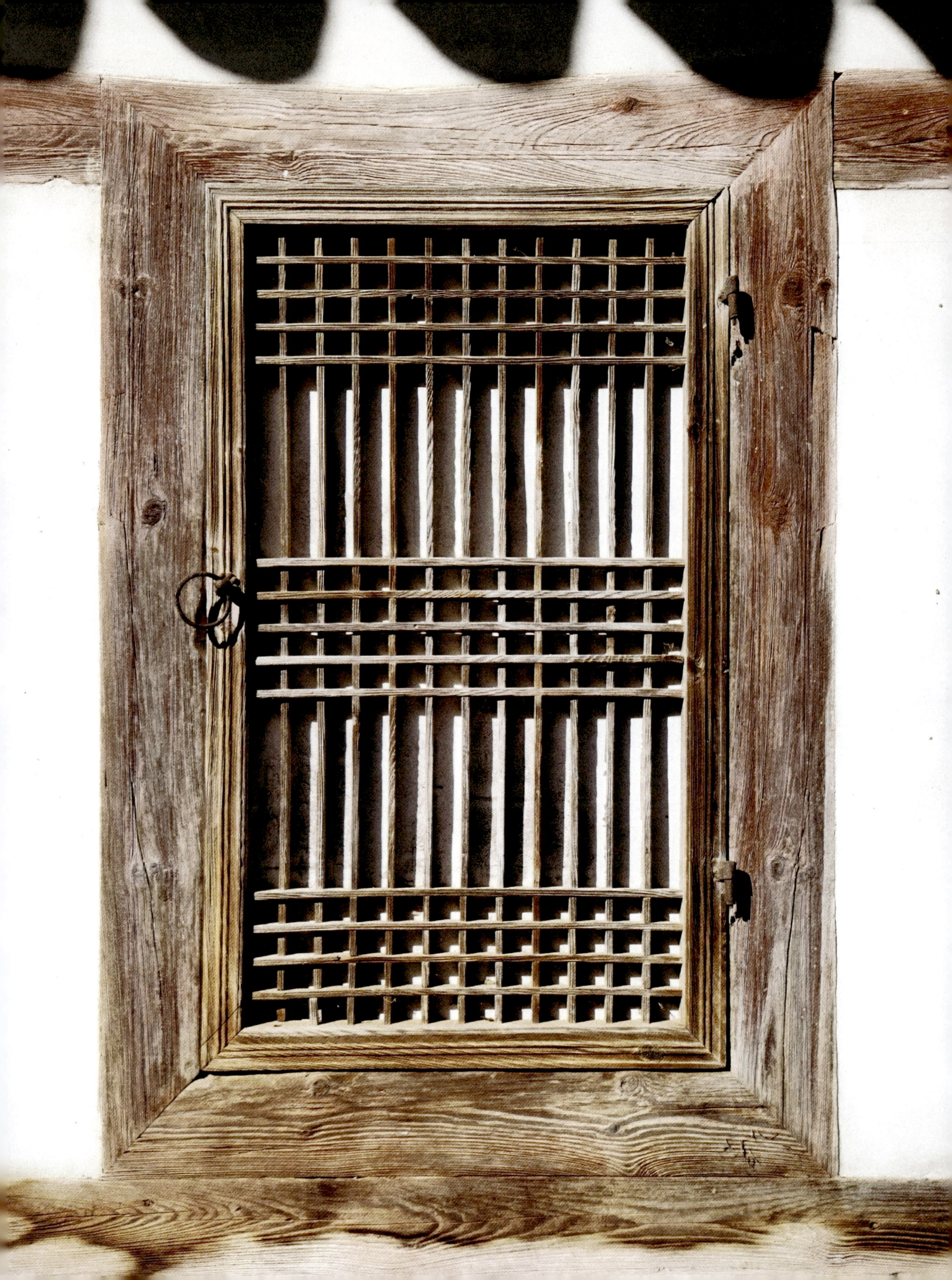

2. 한옥의 공간 미학: 빛과 그림자의 회화적 변환

이렇게 탄생한 '⊔'자 유닛은 평면에서 격자를 이루어 밭고랑의 윤곽선을 연상시키는 동시에, 전통 건축의 창호 구조와도 연결된다. 특히 한옥의 창살이나 격자창에서 보이는 기하학적 질서와 빛의 분할 방식이 남춘모의 작업에서 현대적으로 재해석되고 있다. 각각의 유닛이 만드는 그림자와 빛의 변화는 시간에 따라 화면 위에서 미묘한 변화를 일으키며, 평면 회화임에도 불구하고 공간적 깊이와 시각적 움직임을 만들어낸다.

전통 창호에서 '정자살'은 창호의 외곽 틀인 울거미 안에 한자의 '井'자 형태로 격자를 짜넣은 구조를 가리킨다 Plate 7. 부석사 무량수전이나 수덕사 대웅전의 전면 창호가 대표적인 사례로, 이는 단순한 장식이 아니라 채광과 환기, 그리고 구조적 안정성을 동시에 확보하는 기능적 설계였다. 정자살 창호는 차양(遮陽)으로도 활용되었는데, 창호지를 바르지 않은 채 가로로 길게 설치하여 시원한 바람의 통로를 만들면서도 강한 햇빛은 차단하는 역할을 했다.

한국 창호의 핵심은 독특한 호지법(糊紙法)에 있다. 중국과 일본이 창호지를 바깥면에 바르는 것과 달리, 한국은 안쪽면에 창호지를 발라 마무리한다. 이러한 차이는 단순한 시공법의 문제가 아니라 공간 경험의 본질적 차이를 만들어낸다. 한국 건축은 외적으로는 창살의 선적(線的) 구성을, 내적으로는 창호지의 면적(面的) 구성을 이룬다. 이로써 외부에서는 기하학적 패턴이 강조되고 내부에서는 부드러운 면이 강조되는 이중적 구조를 갖게 된다.

2. Spatial Aesthetics of the Hanok: Painterly Transformation of Light and Shadow

While the grids formed by the ⊔-shaped units elicit the outlines of furrowed fields, they also recall the structures of windows in traditional Korean architecture. In particular, Nam Tchun-Mo's works may be understood as a contemporary re-imagining of the geometric order and division of light produced by the latticed windows of a *hanok* (traditional Korean house). As ever-shifting light and shadow slowly move across the ⊔-shaped units over time, the surface undergoes subtle changes, yielding spatial depth and visual movement even within the confines of a two-dimensional painting.

In traditional Korean architecture, many windows are covered by a "*jeongjasal*" ("井-shaped frame"), a type of lattice with crossing slats that resemble the Chinese character "井" Plate 8. Representative examples include the front windows of Muryangsujeon Hall at Buseoksa Temple and Daeungjeon Hall at Sudeoksa Temple. More than mere decorative features, *jeongjasal* are functional elements that enhance the lighting, ventilation, and structural stability. If *jeongjasal* windows are installed horizontally without *changhoji* (Korean traditional paper used to cover doors and windows), they also function as sunshades, allowing cool breezes to pass through while blocking strong sunlight.

Korean latticed windows are distinguished by the unique way in which they are covered with paper. Unlike in China and Japan, where paper is typically applied on the exterior of a window, in Korea, it is applied on the interior. This seemingly subtle discrepancy produces an entirely different spatial experience, with the linear composition and geometric pattern of the lattice being emphasized on the outside, while the planar composition and soft surface of the *changhoji* paper pervades on the inside.

Plate 8
Dosan Seowon, Andong, Korea

이러한 호지법은 한국 건축만의 독특한 공간 정서를 창조해왔다. 창살과 창호지 면 사이로 은은히 스며드는 햇빛은 공간에 소쇄한 기품과 아기자기한 정취를 불러일으킨다. 달 밝은 밤이면 처마나 뜰의 꽃과 나무 그림자가 창호지면에 투영되어 한 폭의 수묵화를 연출한다. 무엇보다 중요한 것은 창살이 창호지면에 드리우는 그림자의 두께와 각도가 시간의 흐름을 가시화한다는 점이다. 이를 통해 거주자는 정갈한 공간 속에서 시간의 변화를 몸으로 체감하며, 공간과 시간이 통합된 사차원적 경험 속에 머물게 된다. 이러한 공간 경험은 어린 시절 전통 한옥에 살았던 남춘모에게 자연스럽게 각인된 정서였을 것이다.[7]

남춘모는 이러한 건축적 요소를 단순한 차용이나 형식적 인용으로 처리하지 않는다. 대신 'ㅁ'자 형태가 화면 위에 수직·수평의 격자형으로 중첩되며 정자살창과 같은 구조적 리듬을 형성하고, 그 안에 빛과 그림자, 또 물성과 공간의 층위가 서로 교차되도록 유도한다. 특히 주목할 점은 남춘모의 이러한 조형 단위가 단순히 평면적 격자를 닮은 것이 아니라, 정자살창이 가진 감각적 기능을 회화적으로 전환했다는 데에 있다. 정자살창은 빛의 흐름을 제어하고, 내부와 외부를 동시에 열고 닫는 '감각의 필터'로 기능한다. 남춘모의 작품에서 이 격자 구조는 회화의 표면을 단순히 '보여지는 곳'이 아닌, 감각이 통과하는 '막(膜)'으로 바꾸어 놓았다.

이러한 감각적 전환의 핵심에는 그가 주재료로 삼는 광목천과 폴리코트의 독특한 특성이 있다. 광목천은 목화로 짠 표백이나 염색을 하지 않은 생지(生地)로, 약간 거칠고 자연스러운 질감을 가진 아이보리빛의 천연 원단이다. 여기에 폴리코트를 바르면 부드러운 천 섬유가 단단하게 굳어지면서 매끄러운 질감과 함께 불투명했던 광목천이 반투명하거나 투명한 상태로 변한다. 또한 시간이 지남에 따라 자연색 광목천이 약간의 황색을 띠거나 더 진한 톤으로 변하는 것은, 창호지를 오래 방치하면 누런 빛으로 세월의 흔적이 보이는 것과 같은 효과를 낳는다Figs.25, plate 9. 이로써 캔버스는 창호지로 된 겹창을 덧붙여 놓은 것처럼 동양적 공간의 구성 요소로 인식된다.

7 주남철, 『한국의 문과 창호』(서울: 대원사, 2001) 참조.

This papering method gives Korean architecture a unique duality and spatial sensibility. Sunlight filtering gently through the lattice and *changhoji* paper imbues the interior with a special elegance and pleasant charm. On moonlit nights, the shadows of eaves, flowers, and trees from the courtyard are cast upon the *changhoji* paper, unfolding like an ink wash painting. Most importantly, the passage of time is directly visualized by the changing thickness and angle of the shadows cast by the lattice onto the paper. The residents physically sense temporal change within a tranquil space, inhabiting a four-dimensional realm in which space and time are integrated.[7] Such spatial experiences would have been naturally imprinted in Nam Tchun-Mo, who grew up in a traditional *hanok*.

By assembling his ㅁ-shaped units into vertical and horizontal grids on the canvas, Nam generates a structural rhythm akin to *jeongjasal* windows, inducing a layered interplay of light, shadow, material, and space. As such, he translates the sensory function of *jeongjasal* into the form of a painting. Regulating the flow of light, his version of *jeongjasal* serves as a filter of sensation that continuously opens and closes the interior and exterior. Hence, the surface of the painting is transformed from a site of visual presentation into a membrane through which sensation passes.

At the heart of this sensory transformation are the artist's chosen materials: untreated cotton fabric and polycoat. He prefers to work with plain cotton fabric with an ivory tone, unbleached and undyed, with a slightly rough natural texture. When polycoat is applied, the soft fibers harden into a smooth, firm surface, and the previously opaque cotton fabric becomes translucent or even transparent. Over time, the natural tone of the fabric becomes darker and more yellowish Figs.25, plate 9, just as *changhoji* paper turns yellow with age, marking the traces of time. Thus, the canvas comes to be perceived as an element of East Asian spatial aesthetics, like a window covered with *changhoji* paper.

7 Ju Namcheol, *Korea's Doors and Windows* (Seoul: Daewonsa, 2001).

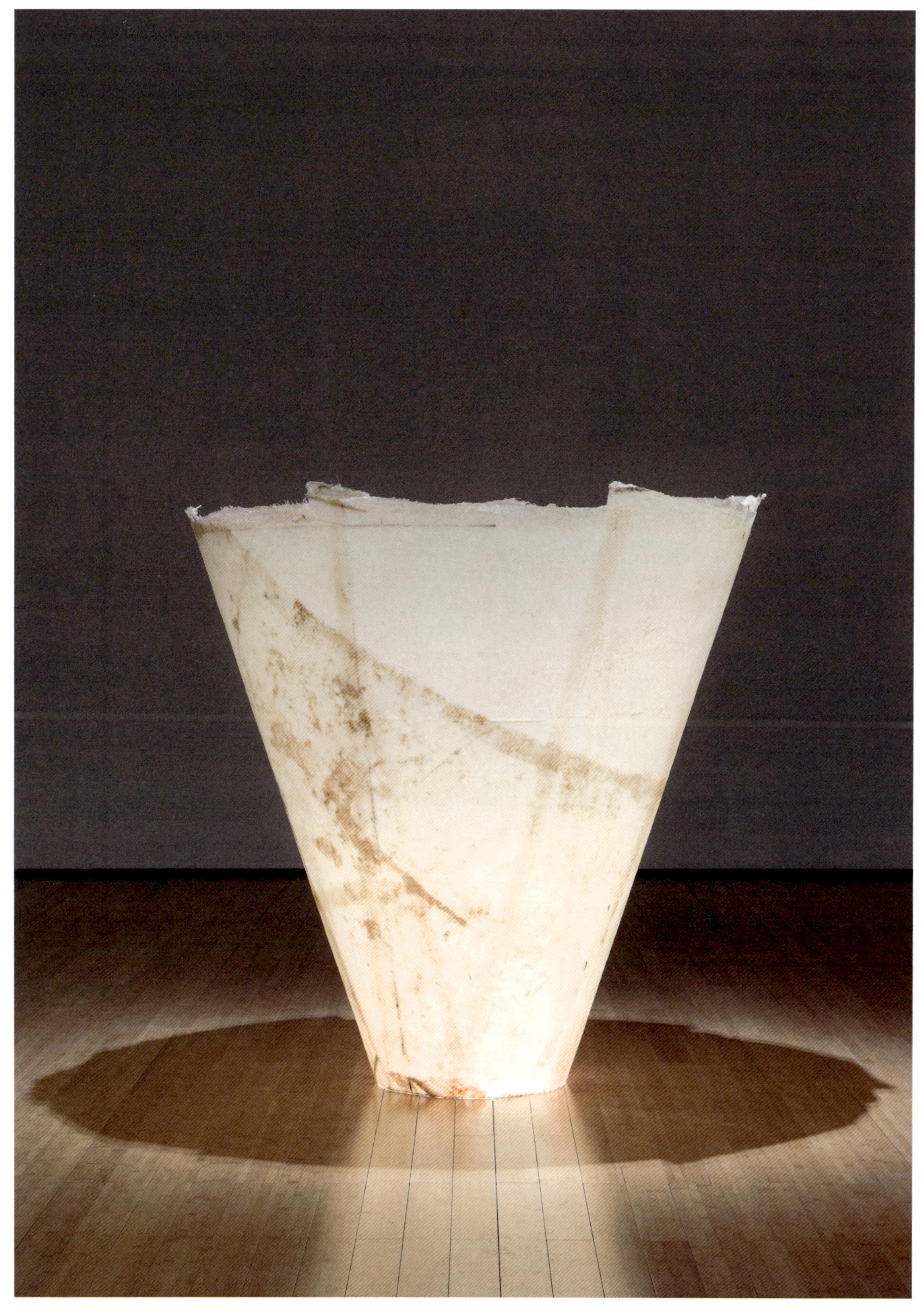

Fig. 25
Coated fabric, 160 x 155 cm, 2017
Installation, Daegu Art Museum, 2018

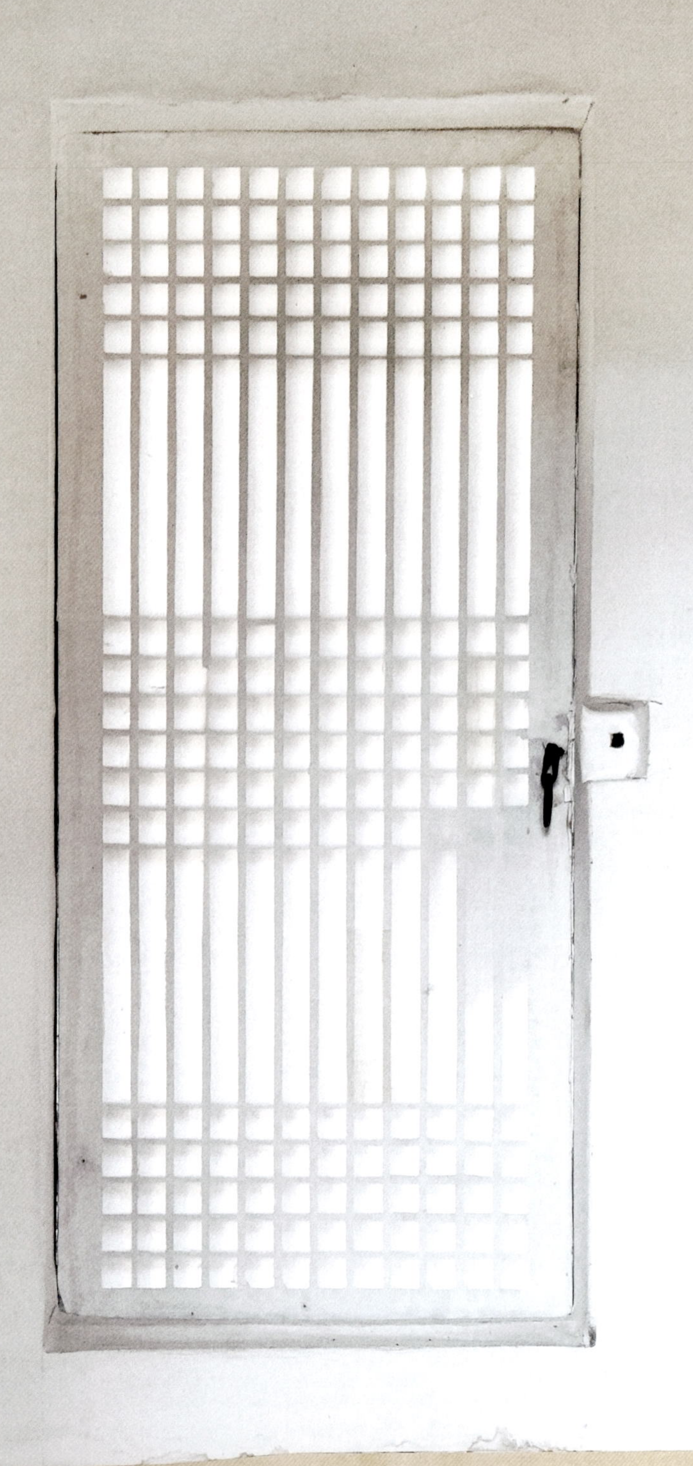

더 나아가 그는 '⊔'자 유닛의 끝을 경사지게 오려 빛이 모듈 사이로 통과하도록 설계함으로써, 화면에 실질적인 '투광성'을 부여한다. 불규칙하게 처리된 격자 모듈은 그림자의 리듬감도 증폭시킨다. 이로써 회화는 더이상 빛을 반사하는 평면이 아니라, 빛을 거르고 유도하며, 그 흐름을 담아내는 공간으로 전환된다. 흥미로운 것은 그의 창작 근원인 밭고랑과 플라스틱의 밀접한 연관성이다. 현대 농업에서 고랑과 이랑을 만든 후 플라스틱 비닐로 멀칭 작업을 하는 과정에서, 남춘모는 바람에 펄럭이는 비닐이 빛에 반짝이는 모습을 보고 "빛을 작품에 가두고 싶다"는 발상을 얻었다. 이는 그의 현재 작업 방식을 완성해나가는 결정적 계기가 되었다.

이러한 전통적 격자의 현대적 전환은 2025년부터 시도한 From the Lines 연작에서 새로운 차원으로 발전한다[Figs.26, 26-1]. 이 작품들에서 남춘모는 한지를 콜라주 기법으로 사용하여 정자살창의 격자 문양과 놀랍도록 유사한 효과를 창출한다. 각각의 한지 조각들이 만드는 미묘한 단차와 겹침은 마치 전통 창호의 살들이 만드는 그림자 효과를 연상시키며, 동시에 한지라는 전통 재료의 고유한 질감이 더해져 현대적 해석과 전통적 정서가 절묘하게 결합된다. 이는 "H빔 → '⊔'자 유닛(광목천+폴리코트) → 한지 콜라주"로 이어지는 재료 진화의 과정에서, 작가가 구조의 본질을 유지하면서도 끊임없이 새로운 '감각적 가능성'을 탐구하고 있음을 보여준다.

By cutting the ends of the ⊔ -shaped units at an angle, thus allowing light to pass between them, Nam Tchun-Mo infuses his works with a unique translucence. The irregularly arranged units amplify the rhythm of shadow until the painting is no longer a flat surface that merely reflects light, but a dimensional space that filters, guides, and contains the flow of light. This effect also recalls the vinyl sheets on furrowed fields, the primary archetype of Nam's art. Inspired by his memories of the sheets fluttering in the wind and glittering in the sunlight, he became determined to capture light within his works, marking a decisive turning point in his artistic development.

Nam's transformation of traditional Korean architecture reached a new dimension in his *From the Lines* series, initiated in 2025[Figs.26, 26-1]. Employing a collage technique, he used *hanji* (traditional Korean paper) to create effects strikingly similar to the lattice patterns of *jeongjasal* windows. The subtle unevenness and overlapping of the collaged pieces creates shadow effects reminiscent of traditional lattice windows, while the distinctive texture of *hanji* imbues the work with a delicate mix of traditional sentiment and contemporary interpretation. These works mark a new phase in the ongoing evolution of Nam's materials—from H-beams to ⊔ -shaped units (cotton fabric + polycoat) to collages of *hanji*—preserving the essence of structure while probing new sensory possibilities.

Plate 9
Dosan Seowon, Andong, Korea

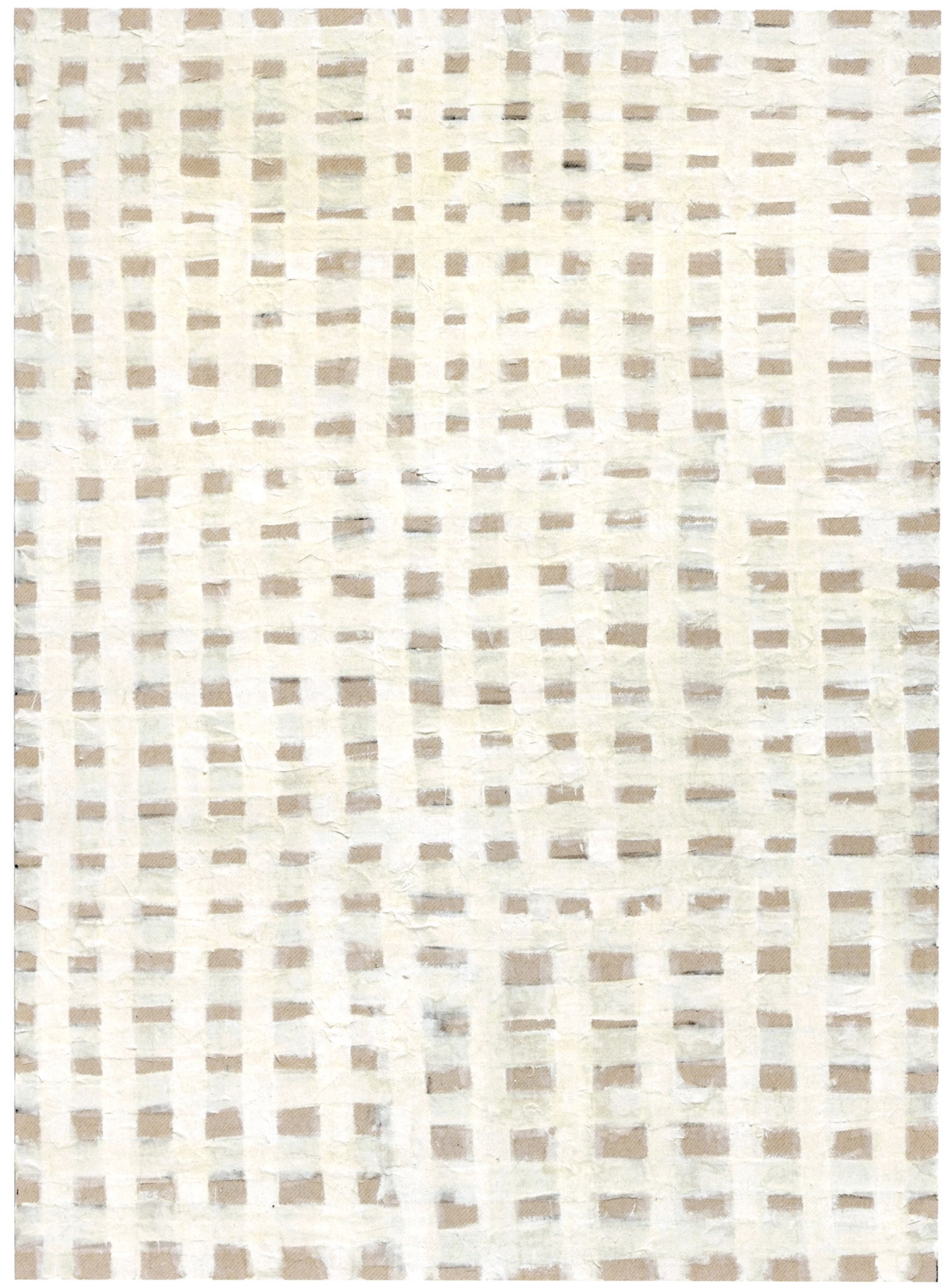

Fig. 26
From the Lines 0905
Acrylic on paper and collage on canvas, 160 x 120 cm, 2025

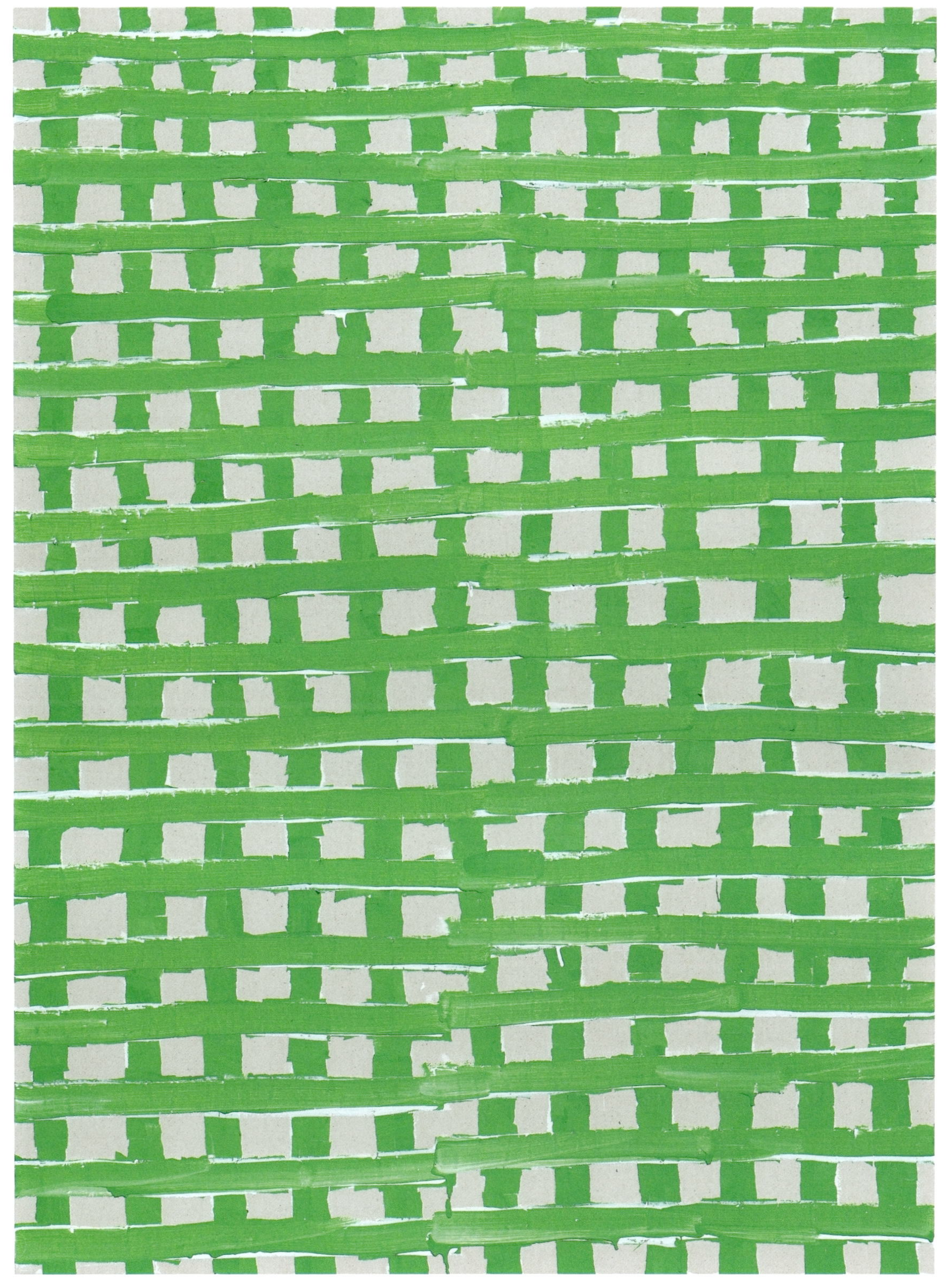

Fig. 26-1
From the Lines 1107
Acrylic on paper and collage on canvas, 160 x 120 cm, 2025

더 나아가 그의 공간 설치작업에서는 평면적 탐구가 삼차원으로 확장된다. 수직으로 배열된 선형 구조들은 마치 한옥의 서까래나 대들보를 연상시키며, 평면에서 시작된 격자의 원리가 삼차원 공간 속에서 어떻게 구현되는지를 보여준다Figs.27, 27-1. 특히 벽면에서 바닥으로 흘러내리는 듯한 경사 설치에서는 중력과 시간의 흐름이 시각화되며, 관람자는 작품 주위를 돌아다니며 서까래 사이로 스며드는 빛처럼 변화하는 그림자와 공간감을 체험하게 된다Figs.28, 28-1. 이때 선형 구조들 사이의 간격은 한옥 처마 아래에서 경험하는 빛과 그림자의 리듬감을 현대적으로 재해석한 것이며, 전통 건축의 공간적 호흡이 현대 미술의 언어로 번역된 결과라 할 수 있다.

In these spatial installations, vertical arrangements of linear structures evoke the rafters or beams of a *hanok*, expanding Nam's two-dimensional investigations into three dimensionsFigs.27, 27-1. In particular, forms that slope diagonally downward from the wall to the floor accentuate the power of gravity and the passage of timeFigs.28, 28-1. Moving through and around this installation, viewers experience shifting shadows and spatial depth, like light filtering between rafters. The intervals between the linear structures reinterpret the rhythm of light and shadow felt beneath the eaves of a *hanok*, translating the spatial respiration of traditional architecture into the language of contemporary art.

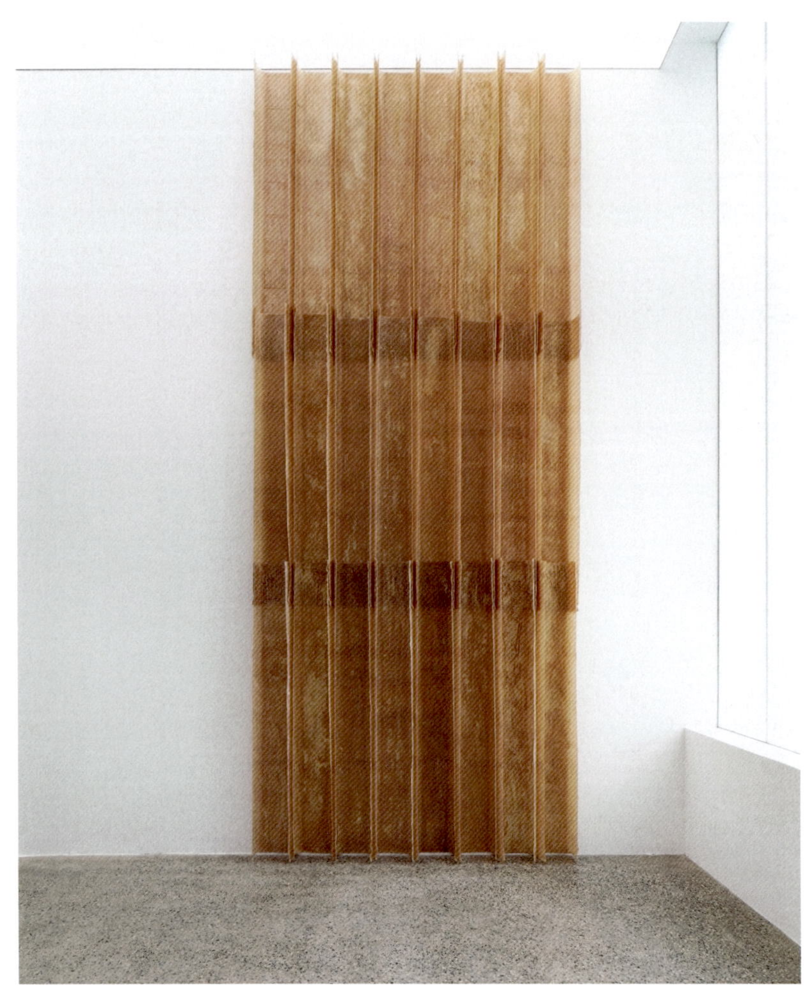

Fig. 27
Spring-Beam
Coated fabric, 960 x 450 x 22 cm, 2024

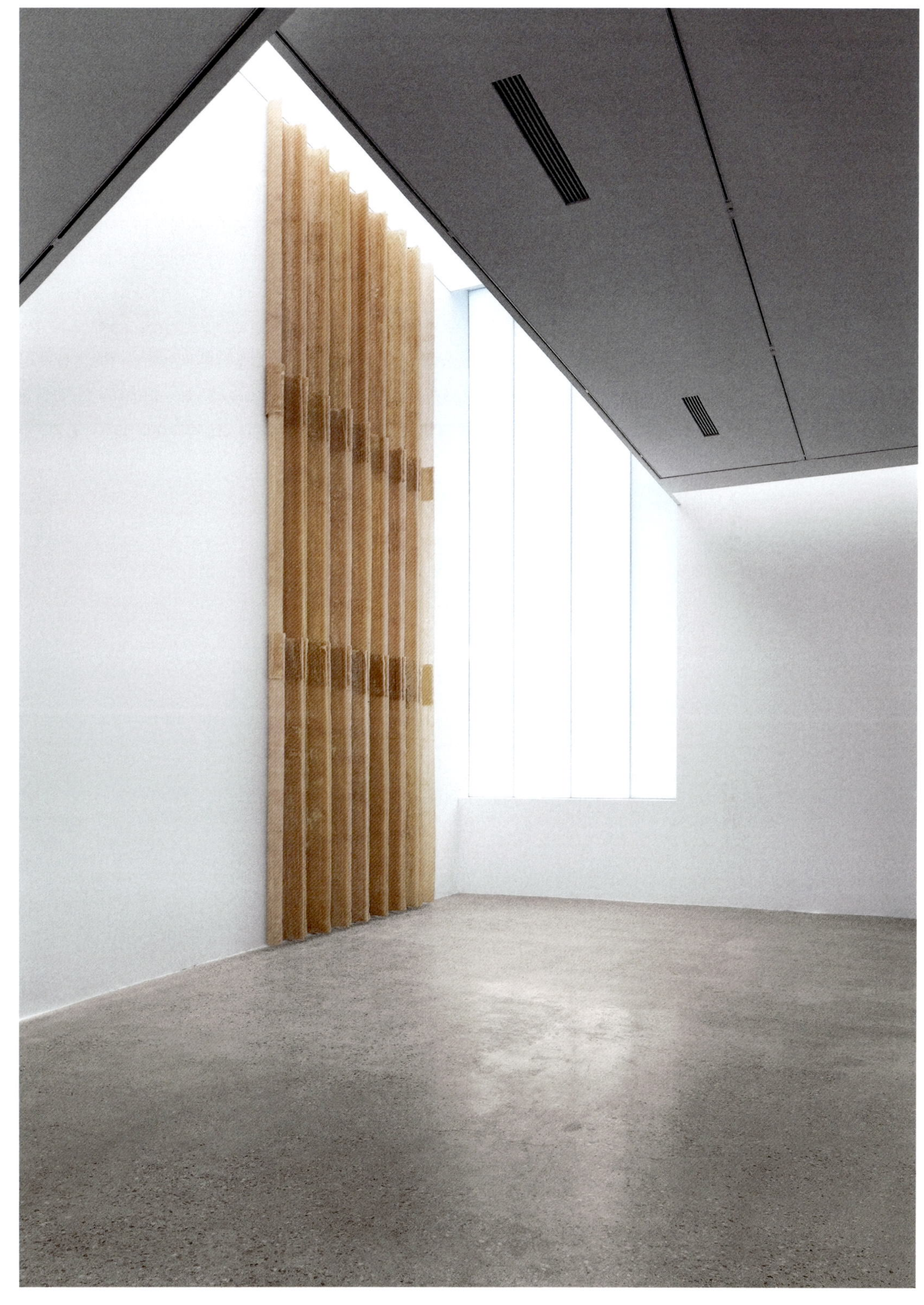

Fig. 27-1
Spring-Beam
Coated fabric, 960 x 450 x 22 cm, 2024, Installation Leeahn gallery

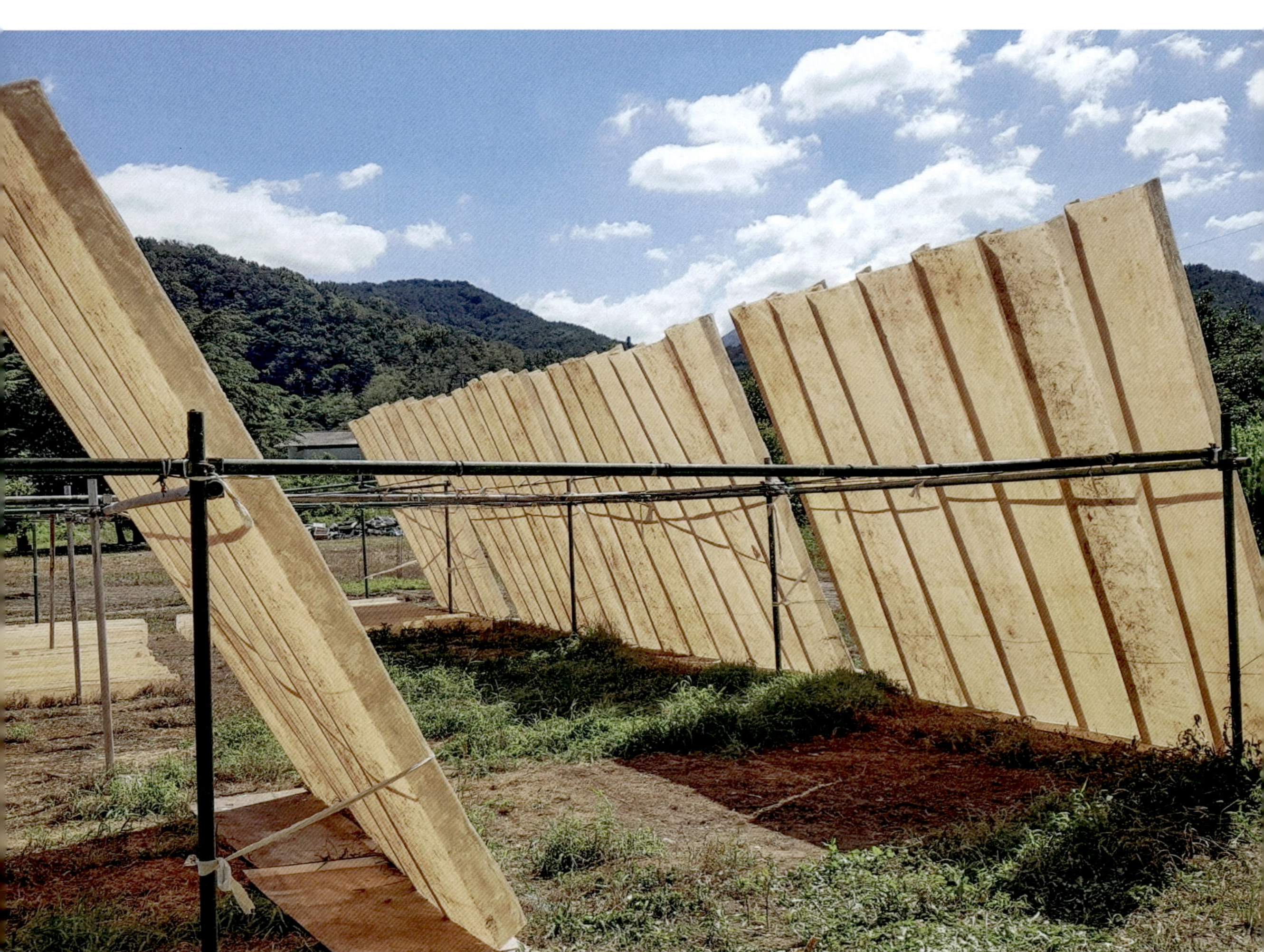

Fig. 28
Spring-Beam
Installation, artist's studio, Korea, 2016

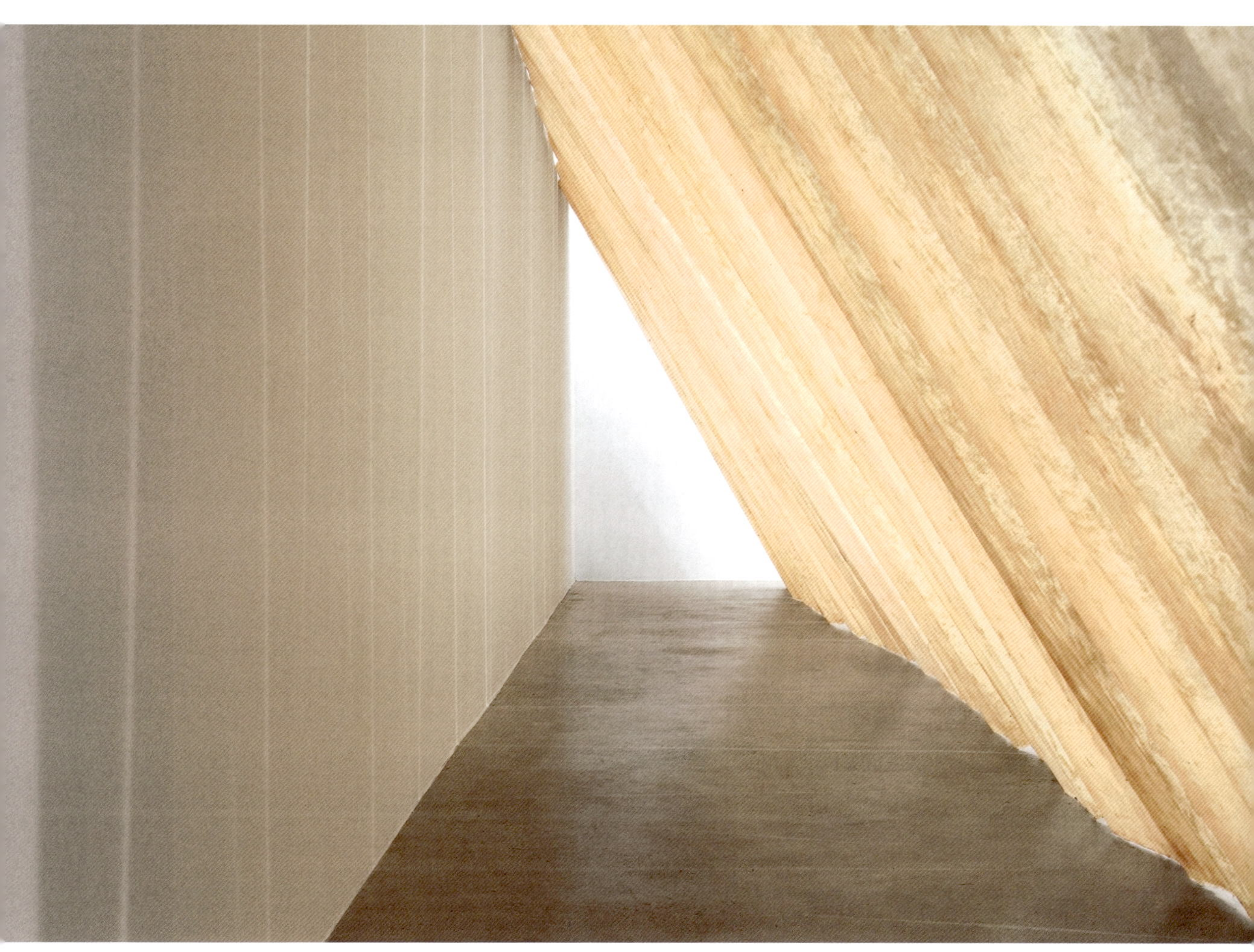

Fig. 28-1
Spring-Beam
Coated fabric, 320 x 45 x 22 cm, 2016, each

이러한 전통 공간성과 현대 미술의 만남은 2024년 9월 창덕궁 낙선재에서 선보인 그의 Void 연작에서 가장 극명하게 드러났다Fig. 29. 전통 한옥의 마루와 대청 공간에 설치된 작가의 '井' 구조 작품은 주변의 정자살창호와 자연스러운 대화를 나누며, 수백 년 된 전통 공간 속에서도 마치 원래 그곳에 있었던 것처럼 조화를 이뤘다. 광목천 콜라주로 만들어진 요철 위에 그어진 붉은, 혹은 푸른 선들이 '井'자 형태를 이루며 전통 한옥의 정자살창과 자연스럽게 호응하면서, H빔에서 시작된 구조적 탐구가 이제 완전히 한국적 공간 감각과 일체화되었음을 보여준다Fig. 30. 이는 작가의 조형 언어가 단순한 현대적 실험이 아니라, 한국 전통 공간의 감각적 질서와 깊이 맞닿아 있음을 보여주는 중요한 사례이다.

This encounter between traditional architecture and contemporary art was most clearly manifested in Nam Tchun-Mo's *Void* series, presented in September 2024 at Nakseonjae, Changdeokgung PalaceFig. 29. Installed in the *maru* (open area with a wooden floor) and main floor room of a traditional *hanok*, the works featured red or blue lines forming the rough shape of the character "井," painted on a relief collage of cotton fabric. Conversing naturally with the surrounding frames, rafters, and lattice windows, the contemporary works seemed as if they truly belonged within the context of the centuries-old *hanok*Fig. 30. With these works, the structural investigations that began with the H-beam fully merged with a distinctly Korean sense of space. In the process, they confirmed that Nam's visual language is not simply a series of contemporary experiments, but is deeply connected with Korean tradition.

Fig. 29
Void 0304
Acrylic on canvas, 115 x 100 cm, 2024

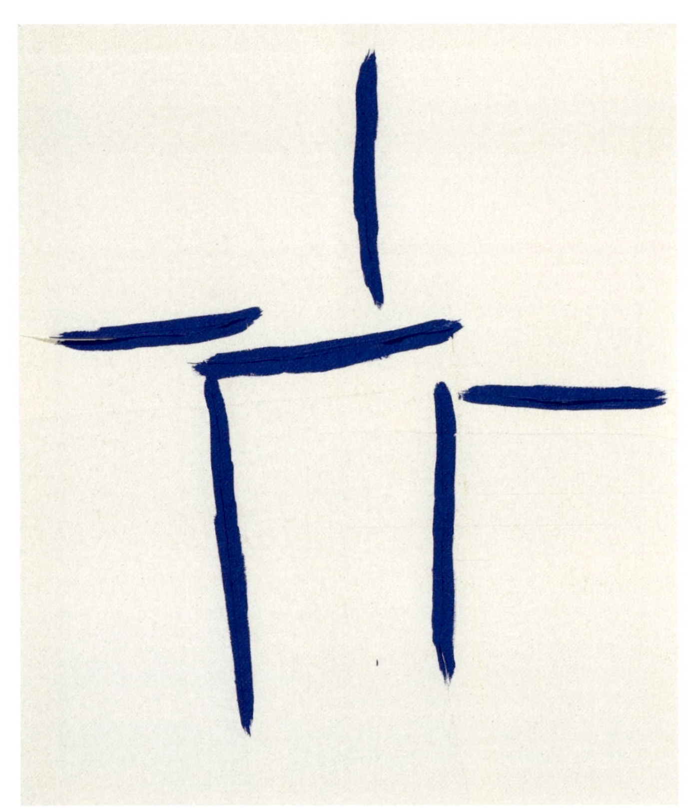

Fig. 30
Installation
Nakseonjae, Changdeokgung Palace, Seoul 2024

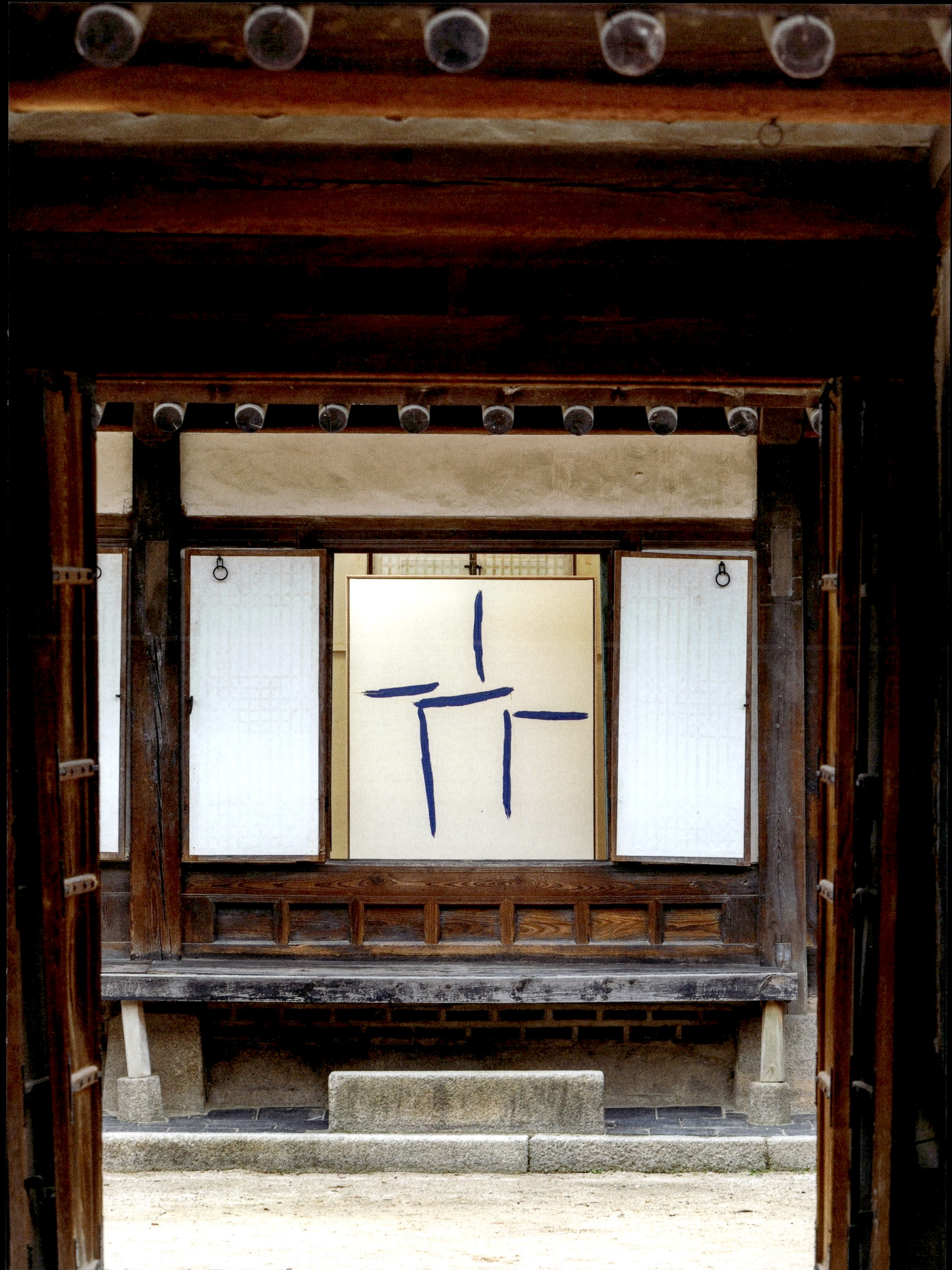

폴리코트로 구성된 격자 구조는 캔버스 표면에서 돌출된 형태로 존재하며, 작품 위에 자연광이나 조명이 닿는 순간, 그 자체로 섬세한 명암의 변화를 발생시킨다. 태양의 각도가 바뀜에 따라 생성되는 장단(長短)의 그림자는 때로는 생동감 있게 변하면서 정적이면서도 동적인 다양한 분위기를 선사한다. 더욱이 매끄러운 폴리코트 표면에서의 빛 반사는 새로운 시각적 효과를 창출하며 빛과 그림자 효과에 직접적인 영향을 준다. 이때 투사되는 그림자는 더이상 부수적 효과가 아니라, 회화의 구성 요소로 적극적으로 기능하며 화면의 입체성과 시간성을 부여한다. 빛은 유닛의 가장자리, 경사면, 혹은 조형적 틈새를 따라 굴절되고 반사되며, 이 과정에서 감상자는 한 점의 고정된 시점이 아닌, 이동 속에서 변화하는 시각적 체험을 하게 된다.

남춘모 작품에서 빛과 그림자의 관계는 전통 회화의 명암 처리와 본질적으로 다르다. 전통적으로 회화가 캔버스 위에 명암을 그려 넣어 입체감을 표현해왔다면, 그의 작품은 실제 갤러리의 조명과 관람자의 움직임에 따라 빛과 그림자가 살아 움직인다. 화면 내부의 표현이 아닌, 화면 바깥의 실제 공간 조건과 반응하는 현상적(phenomenological) 회화인 것이다. 그의 캔버스는 평평하지 않다. 조형 단위가 부조 형태로 솟아오르고, 이 위로 빛이 미끄러지듯 흐를 때 시시각각 다른 그림자를 만들어 낸다. 이때 회화는 더이상 정지된 평면이 아니라 '촉각적인 감광(感光)의 구조'로 재정의되며, 빛에 반응하며 변화하는 살아있는 감각 구조가 된다Figs.31, 31-1. 이러한 부조 효과는 남춘모 회화의 감각적 구축성을 가시화하는 중요한 요소이자, 회화 장르의 확장 가능성을 실험하는 조형 전략으로 작용한다. 중요한 것은 이러한 효과가 회화를 조각처럼 만들려는 의도적 장르 혼성의 결과가 아니라, '선'과 '구조'를 출발점으로 한 회화적 사유가 필연적으로 도달한 감각적 귀결이라는 점이다.

결국 그의 작품 앞에 서면, 우리는 그림을 '본다'는 수동적 행위를 넘어서서 공간과 시간, 빛과 함께 '체험한다'는 능동적 만남을 하게 된다. 이로써 그의 화면은 더이상 감상하는 평면이 아니라, 감응하고 체험하는 구조적 풍경이 된다.

Projecting outward from the canvas, the polycoat grid structures in Nam's paintings produce delicate variations of light and shadow. As the sun moves, the resulting shadows are continuously lengthened or shortened, creating diverse atmospheres that are simultaneously dynamic and serene. This interplay of light and shadow is enhanced by the reflections on the smooth surface of the polycoat. More than incidental visual effects, the shadows function as active compositional elements, endowing the work with three-dimensionality and temporality. Light reflects along the edges, angles, and interstices of the ㅂ-shaped units, giving viewers a perpetually shifting visual encounter that changes with every movement.

The use of light and shadow in Nam Tchun-Mo's works is fundamentally different from conventional shading techniques used in painting. In most paintings, shading is applied in order to add depth and dimension to images on a flat surface. But Nam's works actively animate light and shadow in real time according to the lighting conditions and the movement of the viewer. Rather than an internal representation within the canvas, he produces a phenomenological effect that responds to external conditions. No longer confined as a flat, static surface, his paintings are living structures with a tactile surface that responds to and transforms with lightFigs.31, 31-1. While this relief effect, achieved through Nam's sensory craftsmanship, may be seen as a strategy to experiment with the expandability of painting, it is not a conscious effort at hybridity or to make paintings that resemble sculpture. Instead, it is the inevitable conclusion of the artist's painterly contemplations on the nature of line and structure.

Standing before Nam's works, one is immediately drawn beyond the passive act of seeing a picture into an active encounter of experiencing space, time, and light. More than a plane for viewing, his pictorial surfaces are structural landscapes to be fully sensed and inhabited.

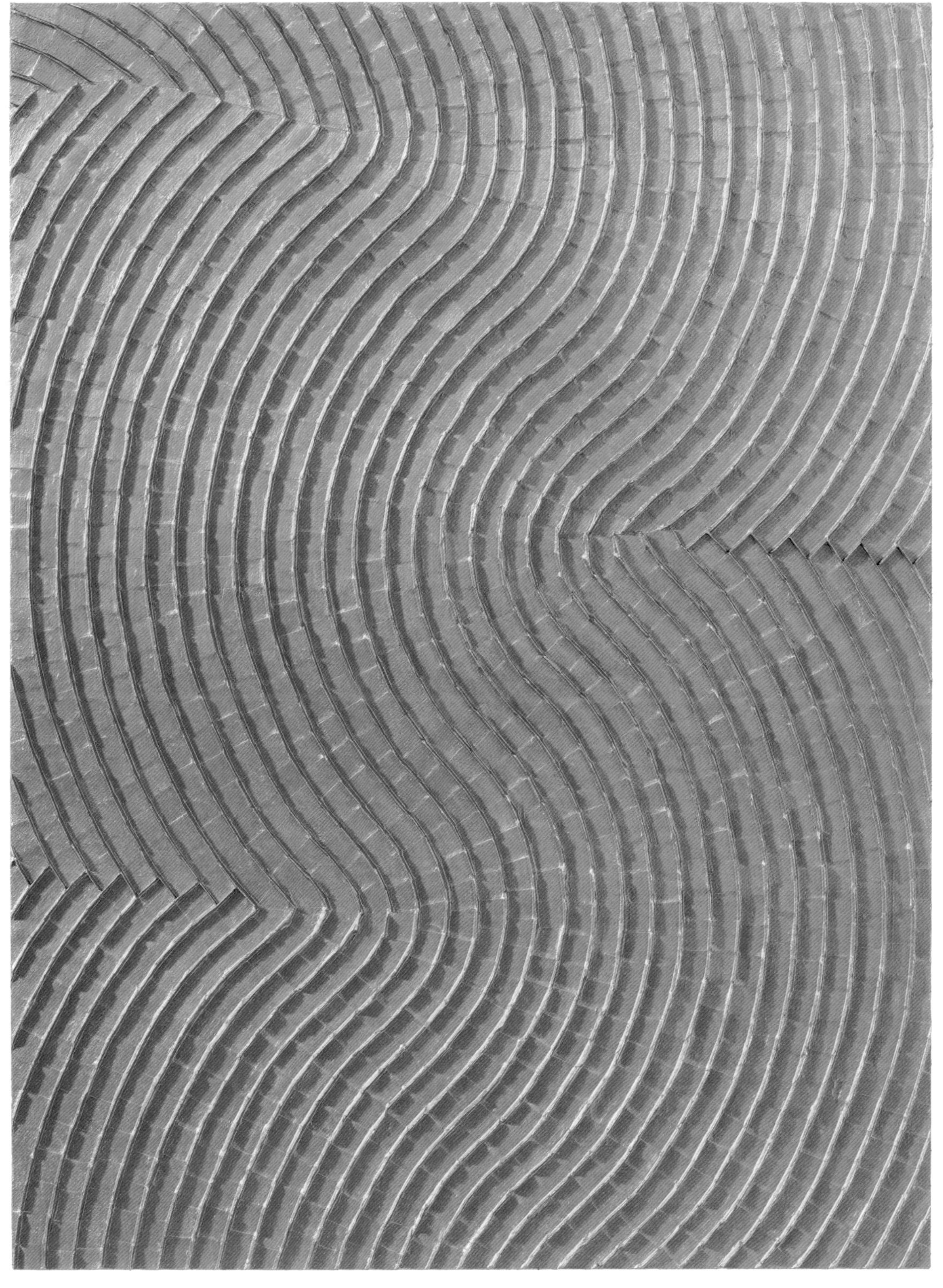

Fig. 31
Spring 20-22
Acrylic on coated fabric, 210 x 160 cm, 2020

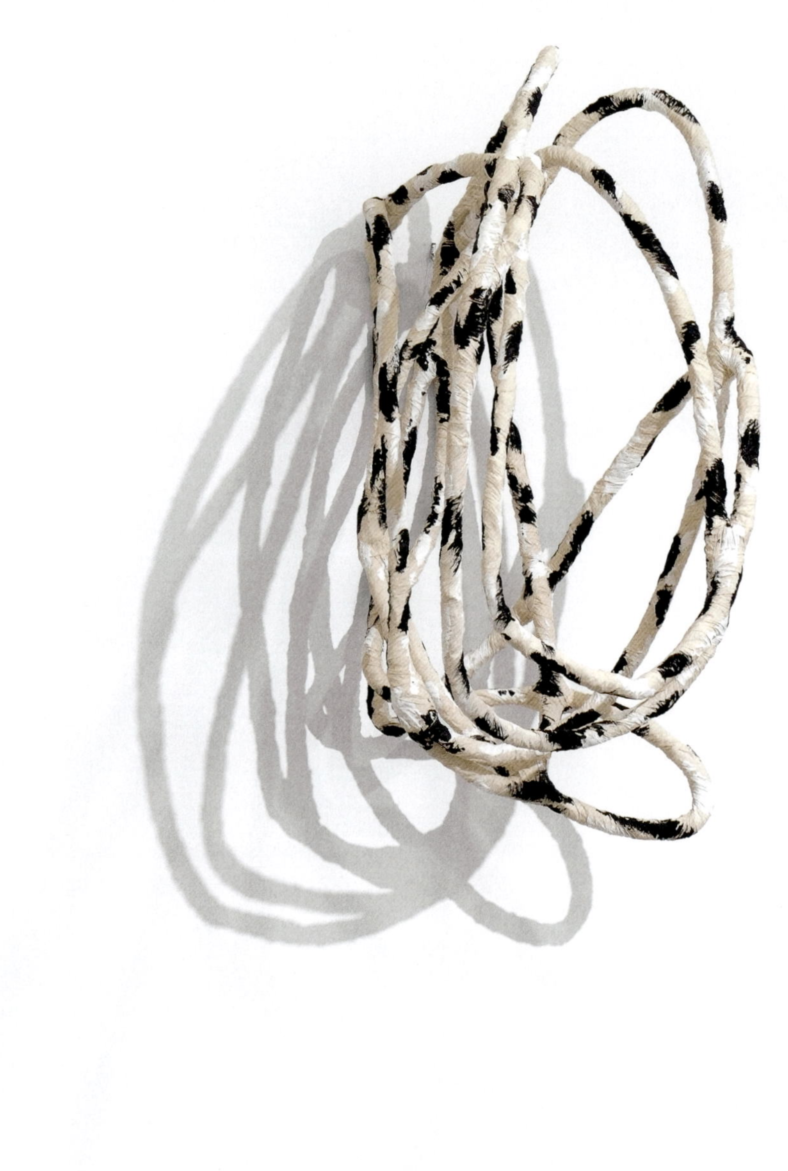

Fig. 31-1
Lines 2023
Fabric on stainless steel, 105 x 60 x 66 cm, 2023

3. 정자(井)에서 해시태그(#)까지: 격자의 상징과 확장

남춘모 회화의 격자 구조는 단순한 형식적 장치에 머무르지 않는다. 그것은 전통과 현대, 개인과 사회, 감각과 개념을 연결하는 이중의 상징 구조이자, 조형 언어의 전이 지점을 드러내는 기호적 기반이 된다. 무엇보다 그의 작업에서 빈번히 등장하는 이러한 격자 형상이 '井(우물 정)' 자와 '#(해시태그)'의 이중적 이미지로 해석될 수 있다는 점에서 매우 흥미롭다.

'井'은 고대 동아시아 문화에서 물의 근원지이자 공동체 생활의 중심 공간이었다. 우물은 생명의 기원을 상징하며, 동시에 깊이와 내면을 향한 시선을 유도하는 심층적 공간의 은유로 작동한다. 한국의 전통 건축에서 우물은 단순한 물의 공급처를 넘어, 공동체를 하나로 묶어주는 정신적 중심 공간으로 여겨졌다[Plate 10]. 반면, 이와 겹쳐 보이는 현대의 상징 '#(해시태그)'는 디지털 환경에서의 정보 연결망, 분류 체계, 소통 방식의 구조를 나타낸다. 이는 개인의 발화가 공동체적 네트워크로 확산되는 구조를 함축하며, 탈중심적이고 유동적인 현대 사회의 관계성을 시각화하는 기호이기도 하다. 남춘모는 이 두 기호, 즉 전통의 중심성과 현대의 유동성을 격자의 형상 안에 병치함으로써, 고정된 상징이 아닌 감각적 전이(轉移)의 장으로서의 회화를 실현한다.

3. From 井 to #: Symbolism and Expansion of the Grid

One of the recurring motifs in Nam Tchun-Mo's painting is the grid. Beyond mere formal devices, these grids function as dualistic symbols linking the traditional and contemporary, the personal and social, and sensation and concept, while also providing a figurative foundation that reveals transition points within his visual language. Perhaps most intriguingly, Nam's grids have a double semiotic meaning, as they can be read as both the Chinese character "井" (*jeong*, meaning "water well") and the modern hashtag, "#."

In East Asian culture, a village well ("井") was not merely the source of water and the center of communal life. The well symbolized the origin of life, while also functioning as a metaphor for a contemplative space where one could gaze into the depths of the inner self. Thus, in Korean traditional architecture, wells were not just practical structures for collecting water, but spiritual centers that bound communities together[Plate 10]. In contrast, the hashtag (#) now signifies the dispersed structure of information networks, taxonomies, and modes of communication in the digital environment. Encapsulating the diffusion of individual utterances among communal networks, the hashtag visualizes the decentered, fluid relationality of contemporary society. By juxtaposing these two signs—the centrality of tradition and the fluidity of the contemporary—via the grid, Nam Tchun-Mo transforms paintings from fixed symbols into fields of sensory transference.

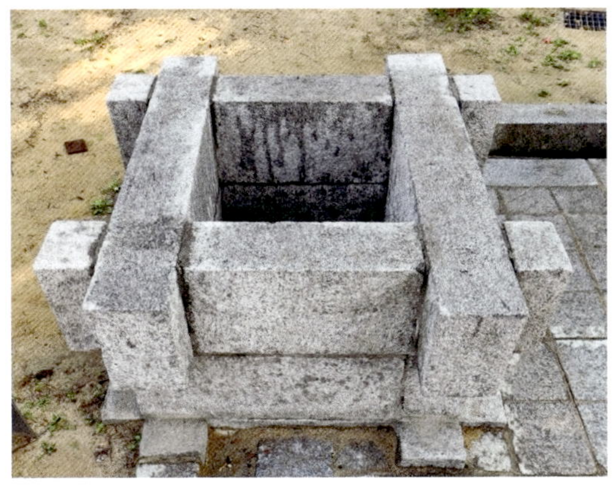

Plate 10
Dosan Seowon, Andong, Korea

남춘모가 Beam, From the line, Void 연작 등에서 보여주는 격자 구조는 바로 이러한 전통적 ‘井’의 공간 개념을 추상화한 것이다. 격자의 규칙성과 중심축을 따라 구성된 화면은 단순한 평면 분할을 넘어, 전통 공간의 질서와 기억을 회화 속에 구현하는 정신지리학적 조형이 된다. 특히 주목할 점은 작가가 이를 단순한 도안이나 기호로 그리지 않고, 물질의 밀도와 중첩을 통해 형상화한다는 점이다. 폴리코트나 광목과 같은 재료 위에 반복적으로 구축된 격자는 화면의 표면에서 솟아오르며, 감각적 구조를 물질화한다.

이러한 맥락에서 2024년부터 시작된 Void 연작은 특별한 의미를 갖는다. ‘Void’라는 제목이 함축하는 공허, 빈 공간에 대한 관심은 기존의 ‘⊔’자 유닛들 사이의 빈 공간에서 이제 그 빈 공간 자체를 직접적으로 다루는 단계로 발전했다. <Void 0307>에서 붉은 색의 강렬한 선들은 기존의 정형화된 격자 구조에서 벗어나 훨씬 자유롭고 역동적인 형태를 취한다[Fig. 32]. 각 선마다 붓질의 흔적과 물감의 농담 변화가 그대로 살아있으며, 선의 시작과 끝에서 붓의 압력과 속도감이 생생하게 전달된다. 주목할 점은 자유로워 보이는 선들이 여전히 전체적인 격자의 질서를 완전히 해체하지 않은 채 유지하고 있다는 것이다. 이는 수십 년 간의 구조적 탐구를 통해 체화된 조형 감각이 이제 완전히 내재화되어, 의식적 통제 없이도 자연스럽게 발현되고 있음을 보여준다.

이러한 평면 작업에서 탐구된 ‘井’의 개념은 조각을 거쳐 공간 설치로 확장되면서 더욱 풍부한 의미를 획득한다. 벽면에 부착된 조각 작업에서 ‘⊔’자 유닛들은 평면에서 벗어나 실제 공간을 차지하는 3차원 형태로 발전하며, 이는 회화적 격자 구조가 물질적 볼륨과 실제적 그림자를 갖는 조형물로 전환되는 중간 단계를 보여준다. 벽면에서 돌출된 ‘井’ 구조는 더이상 그려진 이미지가 아니라 만질 수 있는 물질이 되며, 관람자와의 관계에서 새로운 차원의 감각적 체험을 제공한다[Figs.33, 33-1]. 이러한 조각적 탐구를 거쳐 ‘井’ 구조는 비로소 공간 전체를 변화시키는 설치 작업으로 발전할 수 있었다.

In series such as *Beam*, *From the Line*, and *Void*, the grid motif abstracts the traditional spatial concept of the “井.” Compositions ordered by the regularity and axiality of the grid are not merely surface divisions, but psychogeographic forms that embody the order and memory of traditional space within painting. Notably, Nam does not simply draw or paint the grids as flat diagrams or symbols, but physically constructs them from layers of polycoat and cotton, thereby materializing the sensory structure itself.

Within this context, the *Void* series, begun in 2024, holds special significance. As implied by the title, the works of *Void* engage directly with emptiness itself, extending Nam's earlier exploration of the gaps between ⊔ -shaped units. For example, *Void 0307* features a relatively free and dynamic arrangement of intense red strokes within an open white background, departing from the regimented grid structure[Fig. 32]. Each line preserves traces of the brush, variations of the color, and palpable shifts in pressure and speed, particularly at the beginning and end of the stroke. But despite their seemingly loose configuration, these lines still have not completely abandoned the underlying order of the grid, suggesting that the structural sensibility internalized through decades of exploration now manifests naturally without conscious control.

The concept of the “井” explored in these paintings gains further resonance when extended into sculpture and, eventually, spatial installation. In sculptural works mounted on walls, the ⊔ -shaped units are given fully three-dimensional forms that cast real shadows. No longer a drawn image, the “井” structure becomes a tangible object, offering viewers a new sensory experience[Figs.33, 33-1]. These sculptural investigations set the stage for the “井” structure to be expanded into huge installations that transform entire spaces.

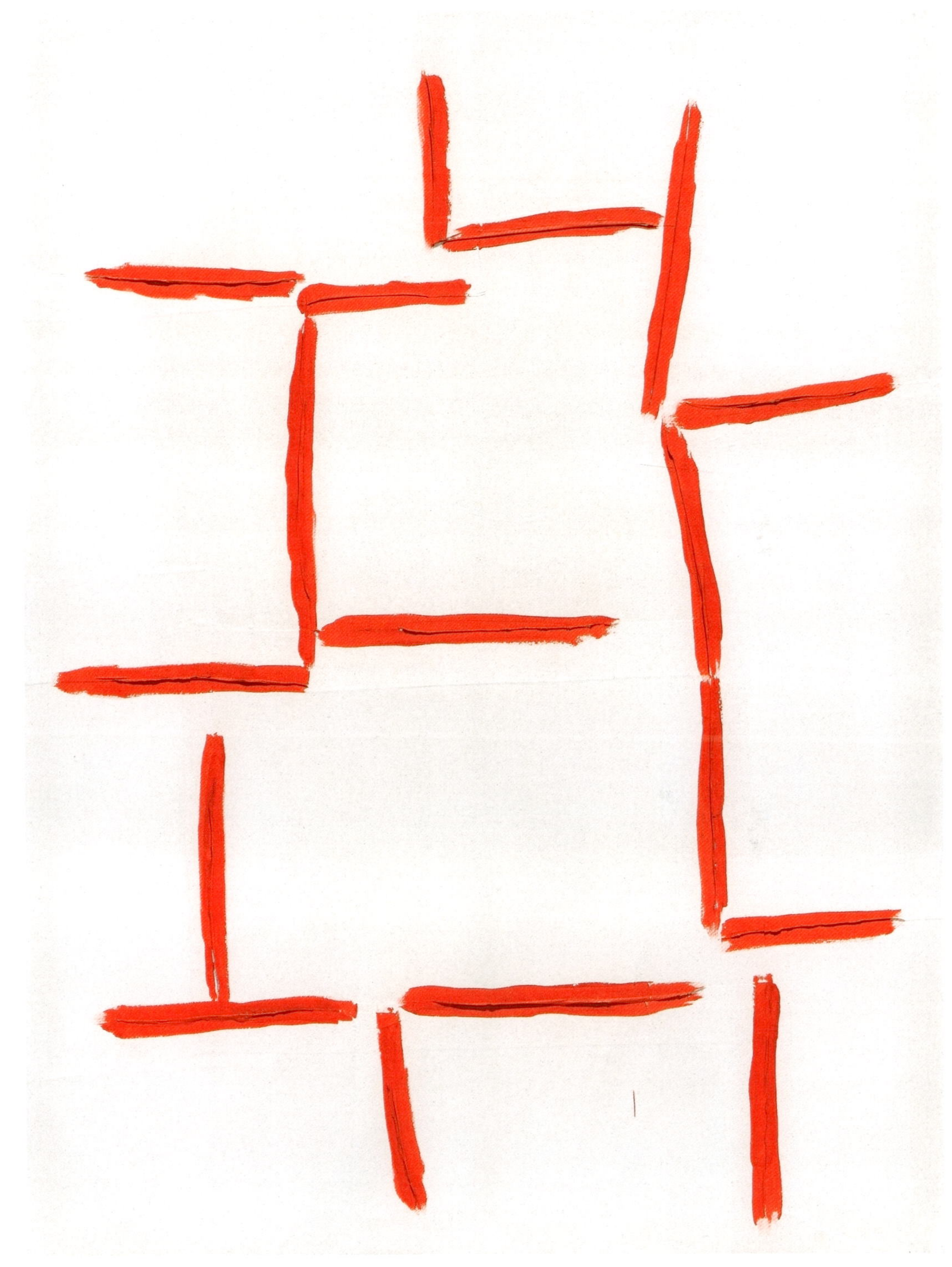

Fig. 32
Void 0307
Acrylic on canvas, 210 x 160 cm, 2024

2025년 초 프랑스 랭스의 샴페인 포므리에서 열린 《익스피리언스 포므리(Experience Pommery) #18- 지하실의 멜로디(Melodies in the Basement)》 전시는 이러한 확장의 첫 번째 차원을 보여준다. 작품이 설치된 브랑켄 포므리 도메인(Domaine Vranken-Pommery) 지하실은 2015년 유네스코 세계문화유산으로 지정된 장소다. 고대 로마시절 만들어진 길이 18km, 깊이 30m에 이르는 지하동굴이라는 독특한 공간에 설치된 '井'자 구조물은 시간의 깊이와 공간의 깊이를 동시에 체험하게 한다Fig. 34. 2000년 전 로마인들이 파낸 지하 공간에서 한국의 전통 우물 구조를 만나는 순간, 관람자는 단순한 미술 감상을 넘어 문명과 문명의 대화를 목격하게 된다. 특히 지하 30m 깊이에서 위를 올려다보는 체험은 실제 우물 밑바닥에서 하늘을 바라보는 원초적 경험을 연상시키며, '井' 구조가 만드는 기하학적 패턴을 통해 무한한 상승감을 체험하게 한다.

This expansion was perhaps most powerfully achieved at Nam Tchun-Mo's 2025 exhibition *Experience Pommery #18 – Melodies in the Basement*, held at Champagne Pommery in Reims, France. To be specific, the installation took place in the Domaine Vranken-Pommery, the underground cellars of the estate, which were designated as a UNESCO World Heritage Site in 2015. Installed within this unique setting—an 18-km manmade cavern dating from the Roman era, which descends 30 meters below ground—Nam's "井"-shaped structures generated an unparalleled collusion of temporal and spatial depthFig. 34. The juxtaposition of a traditional Korean well structure within a 2,000-year-old Roman quarry transcends mere art appreciation, enacting a dialogue between civilizations. The striking experience of looking upward from 30 meters underground recalled the primal sensation of gazing at the sky from the bottom of a well, while the geometric patterns created by the "井" structure imparted an overwhelming sense of soaring toward infinity.

Fig. 33
Spring-Beam
Oil on coated fabric, 263 x 234 x 15 cm, 2022, Detail view

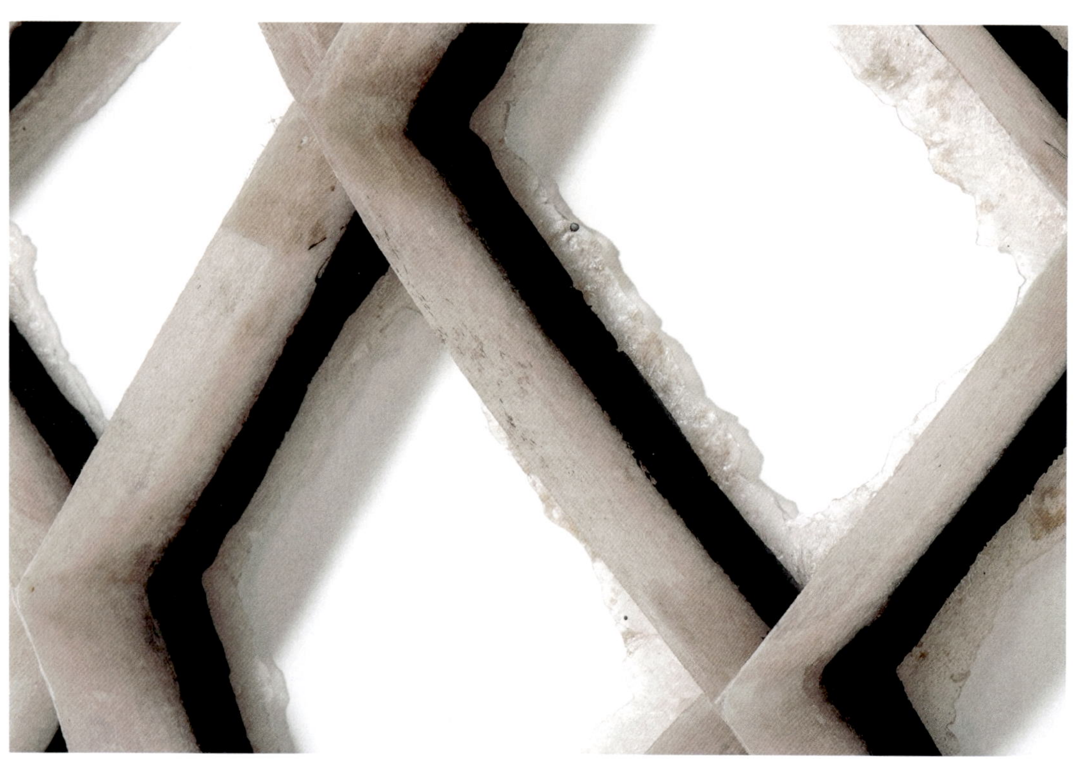

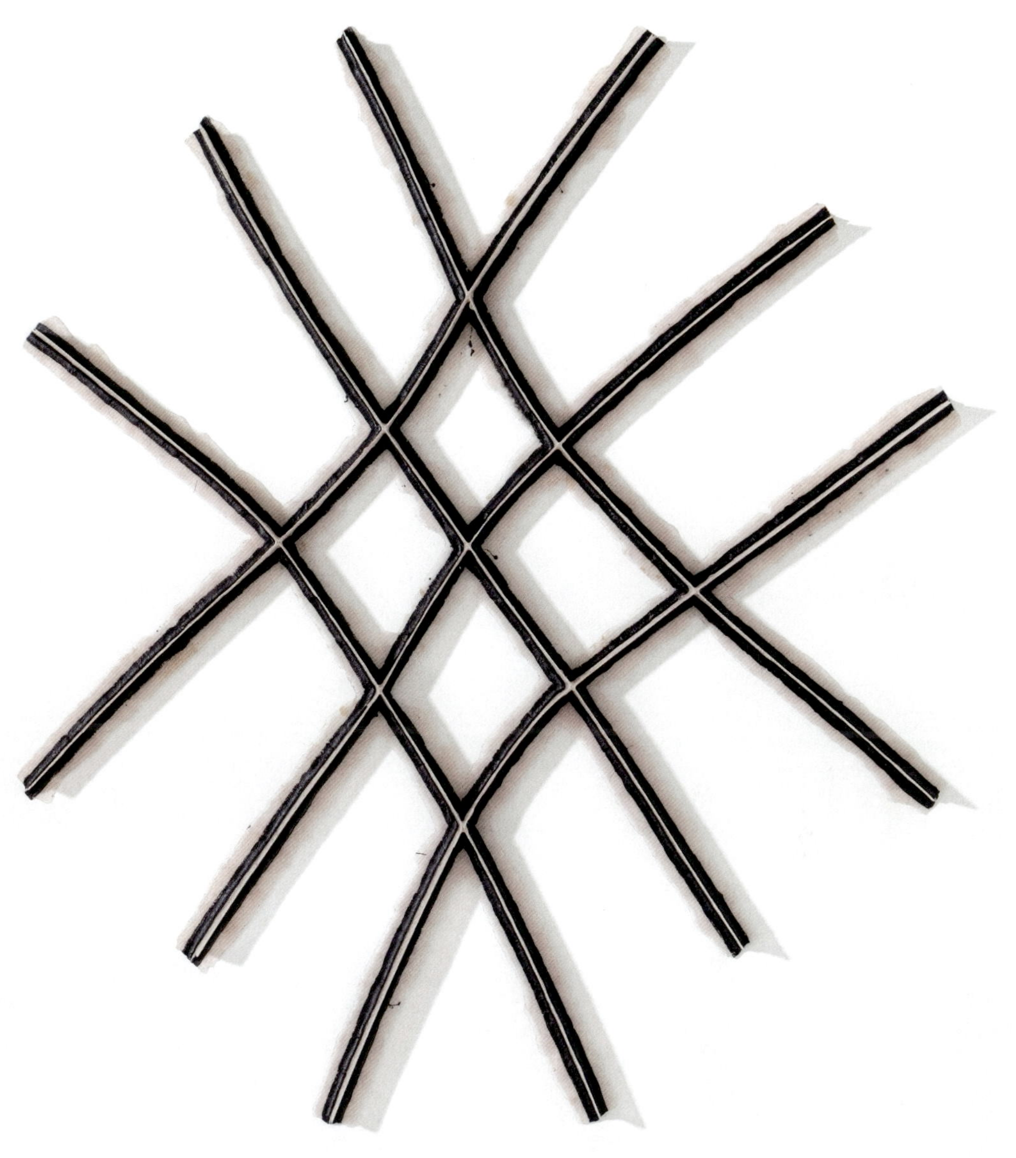

Fig. 33-1
Spring-Beam
Oil on coated fabric, 263 x 234 x 15 cm, 2022

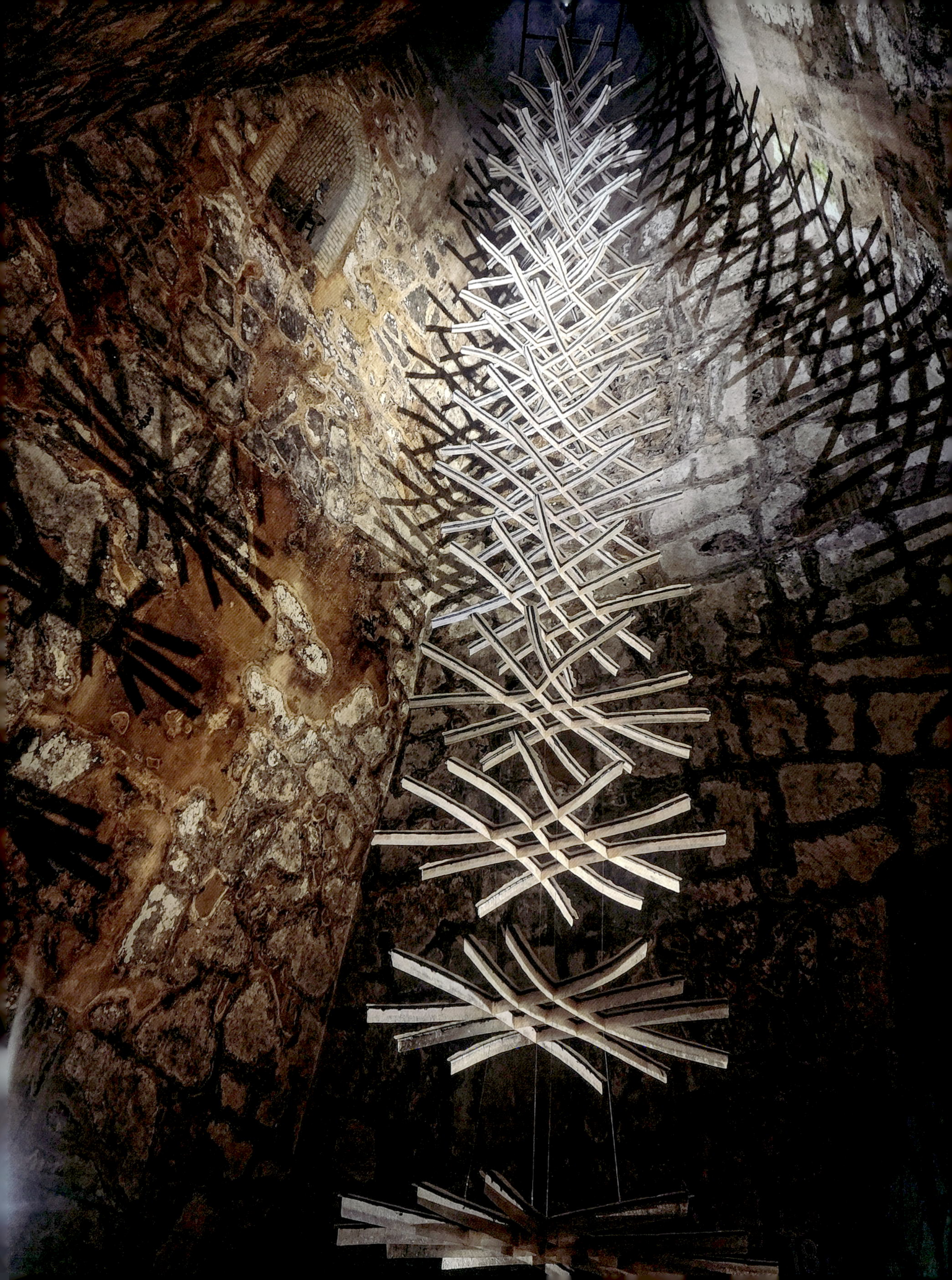

이와 대조적으로 창덕궁 낙선재에서 선보인 '井' 구조 설치 작업은 또 다른 차원을 드러낸다Figs.35, 35-1. 전통 한옥의 마당 공간에 설치된 대형 '井' 구조 작품은 프랑스 지하 동굴의 신비로운 상승과는 완전히 다른 경험을 제공한다. 여기서 '井' 구조는 500년 된 한옥 건축과 만나면서 지상에서의 조화로운 중심성을 보여준다. 전통 기와지붕의 곡선적 흐름과 '井' 구조의 직선적 기하학이 대조를 이루면서도, 마치 마을 중심에 자리한 공동체의 우물처럼 자연스럽게 공간에 뿌리내린다. 관람자는 지하동굴에서처럼 위를 올려다보는 것이 아니라, 열린 마당에서 수평으로 바라보며 '井'구조를 둘러싸고 걸을 수 있다. 이는 실제 마을 우물가에서 사람들이 모여들던 공동체적 경험을 현대적으로 재현하는 것이기도 하다. 한옥의 목재와 작품의 목재가 자연스럽게 호응하고, 전통 창호의 격자 패턴과 '井' 구조의 기하학이 서로 대화를 나누면서, 과거와 현재가 하나의 공간에서 공존하는 순간을 만들어낸다.

In contrast, the "井" structure installed at Nakseonjae in Changdeokgung Palace offered a completely different experience from the mysterious sense of ascent evoked in the underground caverns of France Figs.35, 35-1. Standing in the yard of a 500-year-old *hanok*, the "井" structure created a satisfying harmony with the traditional architecture. The curvaceous flow of the tiled roof and the straight geometry of the "井" stood in contrast, yet together, they ineluctably rooted themselves in the space, like a communal well at the heart of a village. Unlike in the subterranean cellars, where the gaze was directed naturally upwards, viewers at Changdeokgung circled and observed the "井" structure at eye level, resulting in an experience akin to the communal gatherings that once took place around village wells. There was additional resonance between the wooden materials of the *hanok* and the artwork, and between the lattice patterns of the windows and the geometry of the "井" structure, producing a moment in which past and present coexisted in a single space.

Fig. 34
Spring-Beam
Installation, The Domaine Vranken-Pommery, France 2024-2026

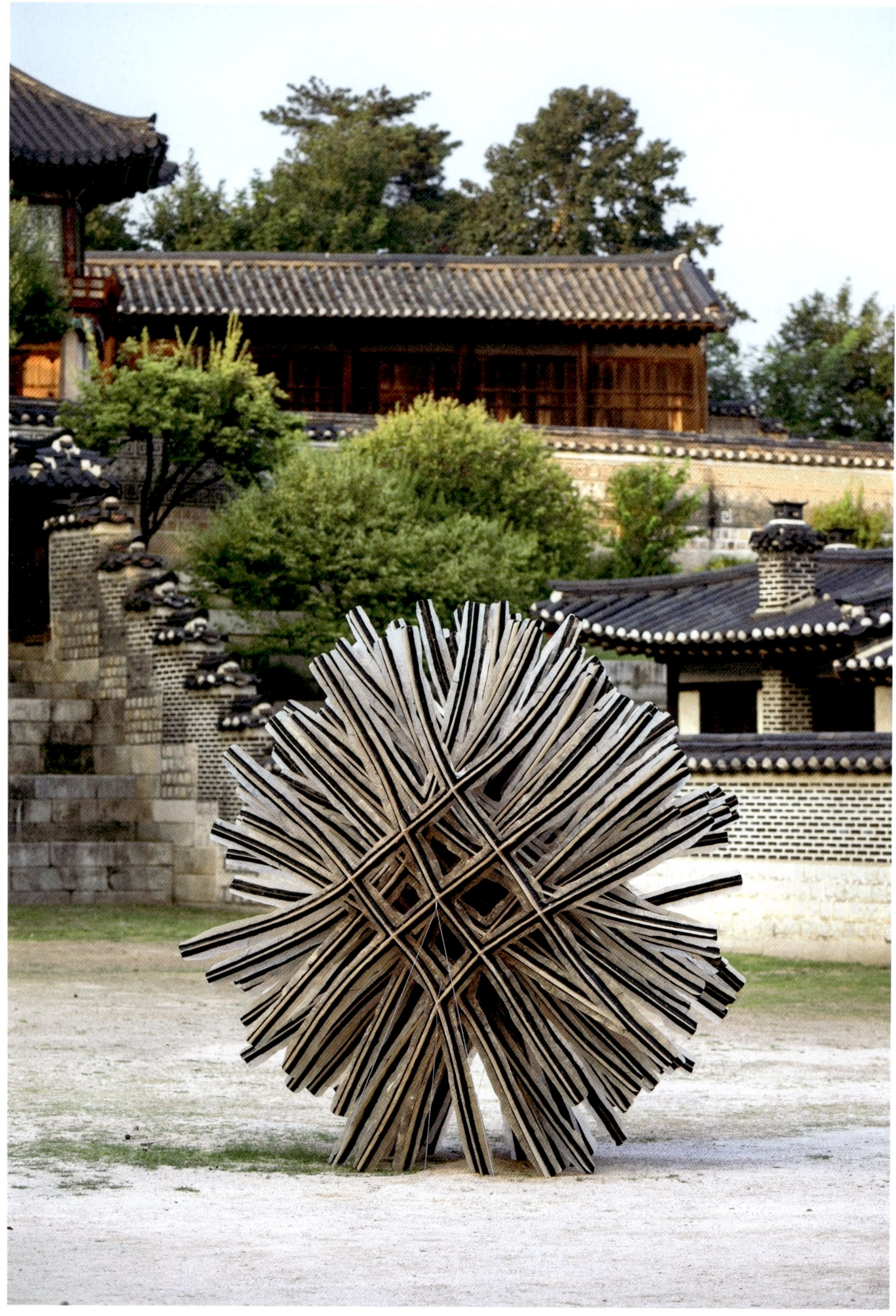

Fig. 35 **Spring-Beam** Nakseonjae, Changdeokgung Palace, Seoul 2024

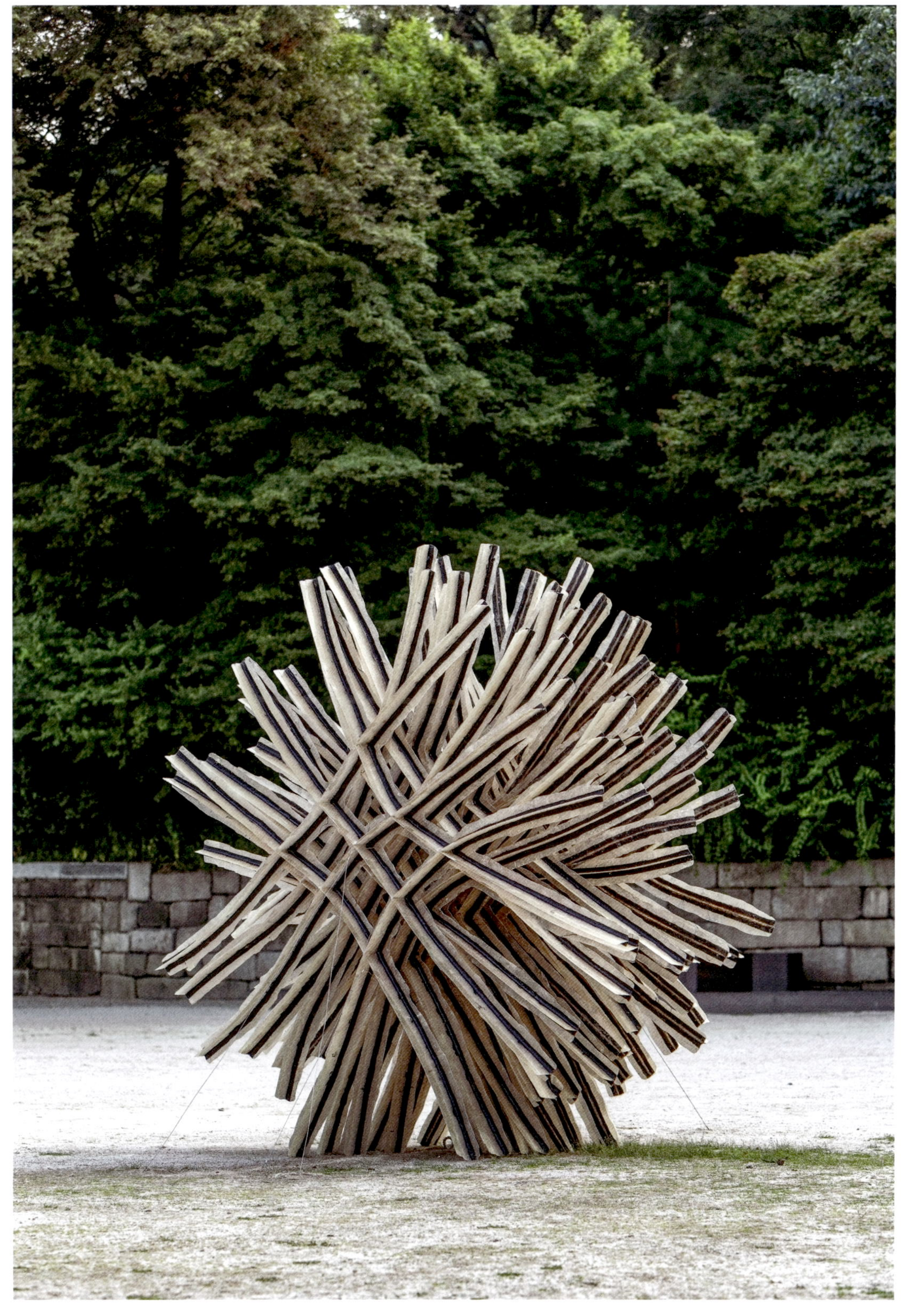

Fig. 35-1 Spring-Beam Installation, Nakseonjae, Changdeokgung Palace 2024

2023년 인당뮤지엄에서의 설치작업은 '井' 구조의 세 번째 차원인 확산과 네트워크의 가능성을 탐구한 전시다 Fig. 36. '井' 구조가 벽면에서 완전히 해방되어 공간 전체를 가로지르며 설치되었는데, 관람자는 작품 사이를 걸어 다니며 다양한 각도에서 井구조를 체험할 수 있다. 이 과정에서 정적인 격자가 동적인 생장의 에너지로 전환되는 것을 목격하게 된다. '봄(Spring)'이라는 제목이 암시하듯, 여기서 '井' 구조는 생명이 움트는 계절적 에너지와 탄력적으로 뻗어나가는 물리적 에너지를 동시에 담고 있다.

이러한 대표적인 세 공간에서의 설치는 각각 '井' 구조의 서로 다른 차원을 드러낸다. 프랑스 지하동굴에서는 '신비로운 상승'(땅에서 하늘로), 창덕궁에서는 '조화로운 중심'(과거와 현재의 만남), 인당뮤지엄에서는 '확산하는 네트워크'(개별에서 전체로)의 경험을 제공한다. 이는 단순한 장소별 적응이 아니라, '井(우물 정)'이라는 원형적 상징이 현대 사회에서 가질 수 있는 다층적 의미를 체계적으로 탐구한 결과다. 특히 이러한 설치들에서 '井'구조는 공간을 단순히 점유하는 것이 아니라 관람자의 동선을 유도하고 감각을 환기시키며 공간의 기운을 드러내는 구조로 기능한다. 그 구조물들은 곧 '선'이자 '뼈대'이며, 골법적으로 공간을 지탱하고 감응하게 하는 장치인 것이다.

In his *Spring* installations at Indang Museum in 2023, Nam Tchun-Mo explored a third dimension of the "井" structure: the possibilities of expansion and network Fig. 36. Completely liberated from the wall, the free-standing "井" structures seemed to traverse the entire space. Visitors could walk between the works, experiencing the structure of "井" from multiple angles, which infused the static grid with a dynamic energy of growth. As the title suggests, the "井" structure of *Spring* embodied the seasonal energy of burgeoning life and the elastic energy of expansion.

The installations in these three respective spaces each revealed a different dimension of the "井" structure. In the French underground cellars, the structure evoked a mystical ascent (from earth to sky); at Changdeokgung, it embodied a harmonious center (the meeting of past and present); and at Indang Museum, it unfolded as an expanding network (from the individual to the collective). Beyond site-specific adaptations, these effects were the result of a systematic exploration of the multilayered meanings that the archetypal symbol of "井" can hold in contemporary society. At each installation, the "井" structures functioned as a framework for guiding the viewer's movement, awakening the senses, and unleashing the energy of the space. In the tradition of *golbeop*, the structures simultaneously served as both lines and frameworks that sustain and evoke space.

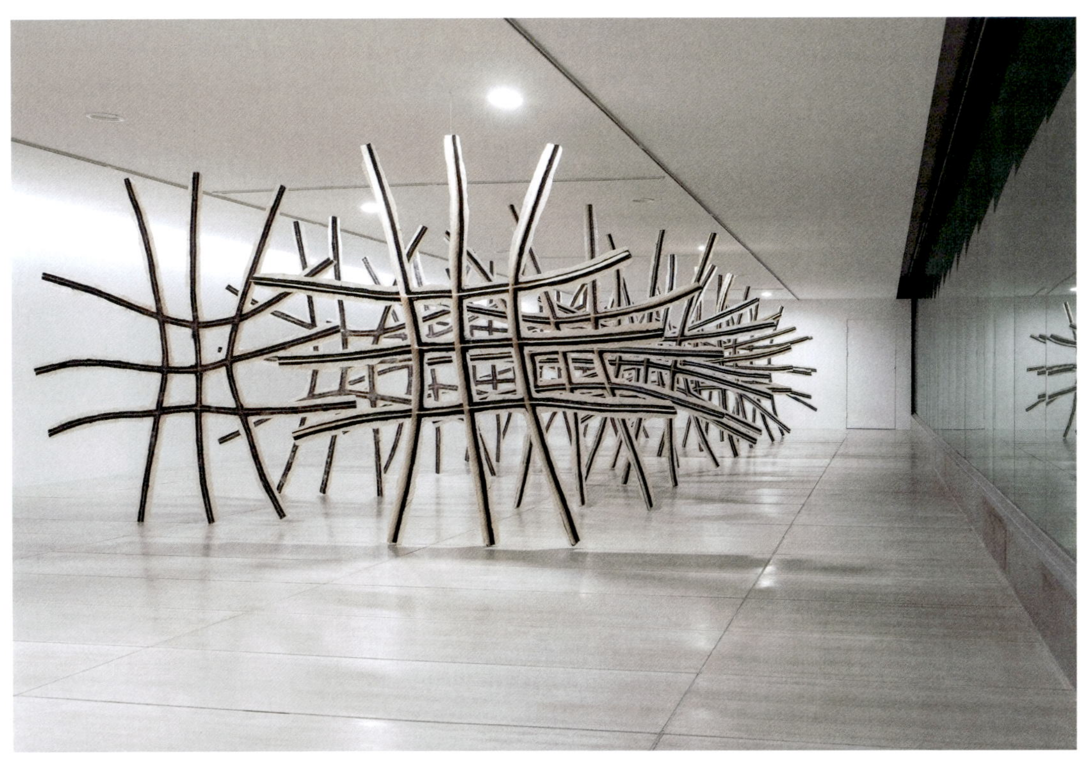

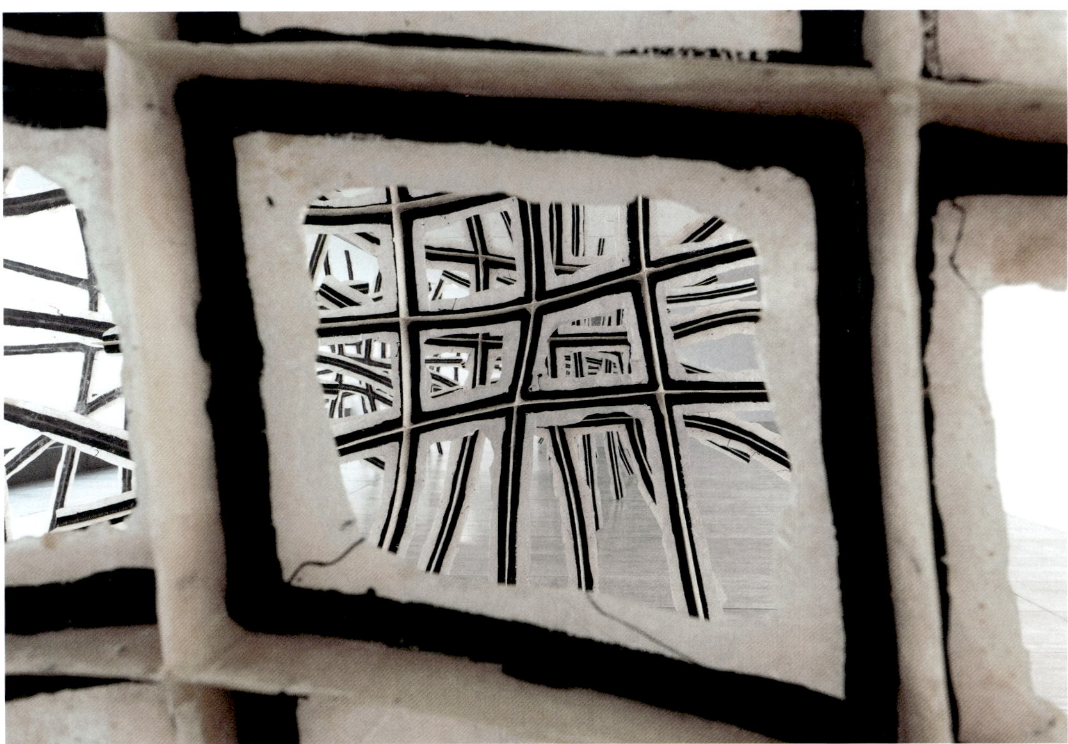

Fig. 36
Spring-Beam
Installation, Indang Museum, 2023

골법이 지향하는 기운생동은 곧 공간에 생기를 불어넣는 것이며, 이는 현대미술의 공간 해체가 추구하는 감각적 활력과 맞닿아 있다. 남춘모의 '井' 구조 설치들은 전통 회화의 기호적 상징 체계를 현대 회화의 물질적 실천으로 전환시킨다는 점에서, 동양적 조형 철학과 포스트모던 공간 감각이 교차하는 지점을 보여주는 중요한 사례가 된다.

요컨대, '井'과 '#'의 중첩 구조는 한국 전통의 내면성과 현대 사회의 연결성을 병치하는 동시에, 남춘모 회화의 상징성과 감각성, 구조성과 시간성을 통합하는 핵심 조형 장치로 기능한다. 그리고 2024-2025년의 최신작들, 이를 테면 Void 연작, From the Lines 연작, 그리고 프랑스, 창덕궁, 인당뮤지엄에서의 설치 작업들은 이러한 탐구가 평면에서 공간으로, 개별에서 공동체로, 전통에서 현대로 확장되고 있음을 보여준다. 이는 남춘모 작업의 사유적 깊이와 미학적 갱신을 동시에 보여주는 중요한 성취라 할 수 있다.

As discussed earlier, the ultimate aim of *golbeop* is to achieve "*giun saengdong*" ("spiritual resonance and life's motion"), the infusion of vitality into space, which resonates with the sensory dynamism pursued through the spatial deconstructions of contemporary art. Thus, Nam Tchun-Mo's "井" installations are crucial examples of how the semiotics of traditional painting can be translated into the material practices of contemporary art, marking a point of intersection between East Asian aesthetics and postmodern spatial sensibilities.

Combining the interiority of Korean tradition with the connectivity of contemporary society, the synchronous structure of "井" and "#" functions as a key compositional device in Nam Tchun-Mo's art, integrating symbolism, sensibility, structure, and temporality. His most recent works from 2024 and 2025—the *Void* series, *From the Lines* series, and his installations in France, Changdeokgung, and Indang Museum—demonstrate how his explorations have expanded from two-dimensional planes into space, from the individual to the communal, and from the traditional to the contemporary, revealing both the philosophical depth and aesthetic renewal of his work.

V. '유위(有爲)의 미학'과 카르마적 실천

1. 플라스틱 시대: 생존의 외피(外皮), 폴리코트

남춘모 회화의 조형적 탐구를 넘어서, 그의 회화는 삶을 살아가는 방식이자 생존의 기술로 작동한 결과물로 이해될 수 있다. 광목천에 그은 반복적인 붓질, 폴리코트를 바르고 굳히는 물리적 공정, 화면 위에 동일한 조형 단위를 수백 개 이상 배치하는 행위는 단순한 조형적 선택이라기보다 일상의 반복과 생의 지속을 내포한 실천으로 이해될 수 있다. 이러한 실천은 그 자체로 행위적(performative)이라고 말할 수 있는데, 예술가의 육체가 고스란히 관여된 감각적 노동의 축적물이다.

우리가 살아가는 시대는 흔히 '플라스틱 시대'라 불린다. 1907년 베이클랜드가 베이클라이트라는 최초의 완전 합성 플라스틱을 만들어낸 후, 석기, 청동기, 철기를 지나 인류 문명은 플라스틱이라는 화학 합성물을 중심으로 생활 양식을 구성하게 되었다. 오늘날 현대 생활에서 우리 문화를 구성하는 가장 보편적인 물질은 바로 플라스틱이다. 플라스틱(plastic)은 '거푸집에 부어 만들다(mold)', '성형하다(form)'라는 뜻을 가진 그리스어 'plastikos'에서 유래했듯이, 그 가변성의 폭이 엄청나게 넓어 지난 100여 년 동안 이전에 사용되던 돌, 청동, 철, 나무, 가죽, 상아 등의 천연재료를 급속하게 대체해 왔다. 이는 급기야 예술가들의 문화적 감수성의 주요 재료로도 부상하였다. 실제 2008년 한양대학교박물관 특별전《제4문화 플라스틱 시대 101》에서는 플라스틱이 단순한 산업소재나 소비재를 넘어, 동시대의 미학과 감각을 담아내는 시각 언어로 작용함을 보여준 바 있다.

남춘모가 회화의 중심 재료로 폴리코트를 선택한 것은 기본적으로 기능적·기술적 이유가 주요했을 것이다. 그러나 이 선택은 보다 넓은 맥락에서 해석될 여지가 있다. 재

V. The Aesthetics of "*Yuwi*" (有爲) and Karmic Practice

1. The Age of Plastic: Polycoat, the Skin of Survival

Beyond formal explorations, Nam Tchun-Mo's works are the tangible outcome of a way of life and a technique for survival. His entire artistic process—from applying brushstrokes on raw cotton to layering polycoat and allowing it to dry to attaching hundreds of identical units to the surface— embodies the repetition of daily life and the persistence of existence. Such practice is, in itself, performative, an accumulation of sensory labor in which the artist's body is fully engaged.

Through the course of history, humanity has moved through the Stone Age, the Bronze Age, and the Iron Age to the current era, which has often been called the "Plastic Age." Since 1907, when Leo Baekeland invented Bakelite, plastic has become a ubiquitous substance shaping human life and culture. Derived from the Greek word *plastikos*, meaning "to mold" or "to form," plastic offers extraordinary variability, allowing it to replace many natural materials, such as stone, bronze, iron, wood, leather, and ivory. Inevitably, plastic also emerged as a primary material for artists. The 2008 special exhibition *The Fourth Culture: The Plastic Age 101* at Hanyang University Museum demonstrated how plastic has transcended its function as an industrial and consumer material to become a visual language ideally suited for expressing contemporary aesthetics and sensibilities.

Nam Tchun-Mo's decision to use polycoat as the central material of his painting was likely driven by functional and technical considerations, but the choice invites broader interpretation. For materials are not

료는 단순한 도구가 아닌 작가의 상상력과 세계관을 형성하는 매개체이기 때문이다. 폴리코트(합성수지)가 갖는 현대적 특성, 즉 가벼운 중량, 뛰어난 빛 투과성, 화학적 안정성 등은 작가가 의도했든 그렇지 않든, 한국 회화의 전통과 현대성 사이의 관계를 재고하게 만드는 결정적 계기가 되어준다.

국립현대미술관 소장 <관계-선>(2001)은 그의 최근작들과 달리 파스텔톤의 폴리에스터를 사용해 마치 맑은 시냇물을 들여다보는 듯한 느낌을 준다[Figs.37, 37-1, 37-2]. 이 작품은 플라스틱 계열의 소재인 플렉시글라스와 폴리에스터를 적극 활용하여 재료의 물성을 충분히 표현하고 있으며, 재료에 대한 그의 다양한 실험적 시도를 보여준다. 플라스틱 특성상 작품 소장의 편의성과 내구성을 동시에 확보했음은 물론이다.

merely tools, but mediators that shape the artist's imagination and worldview. Whether intentionally selected or not, polycoat holds many properties—such as its lightness, chemical stability, and excellent transmission of light—that prompt us to reconsider the relationship between the traditional and the contemporary in Korean painting.

In addition to polycoat, Nam Tchun-Mo has also worked with other plastic-based materials, including Plexiglas and polyester. His adept use of these materials, accentuating their innate characteristics, is demonstrated by *Connection-Lines* (2001)[Figs.37, 37-1, 37-2], from the collection of the National Museum of Modern and Contemporary Art, Korea. Made from pastel-toned polyester, this work replicates the sensation of gazing into the clear water of a mountain stream. Not incidentally, plastic artworks are also very durable and easy to store, qualities intrinsic to the material.

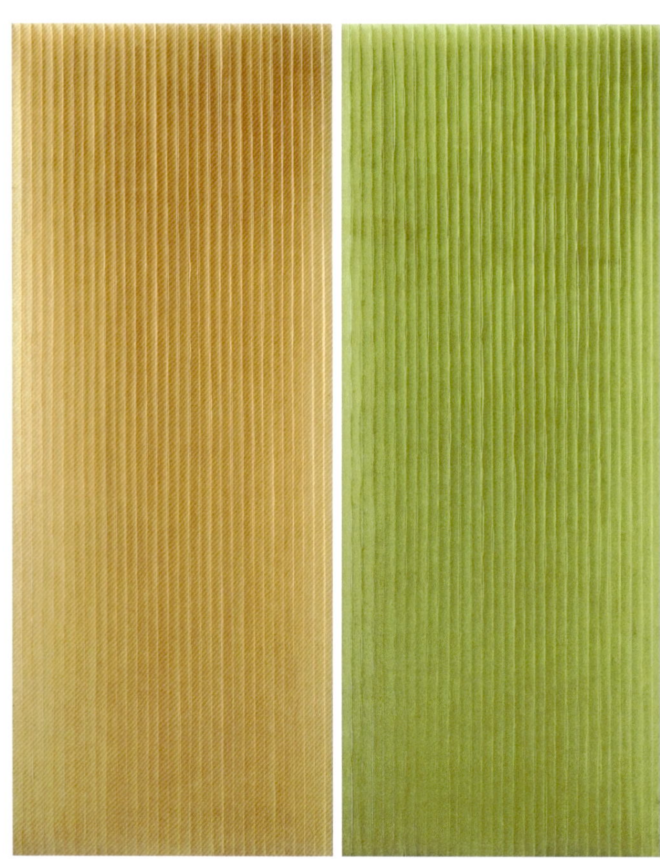

Fig. 37
Connection-Lines
Coated fabric, 175 x 70 x 2 cm each, 2001

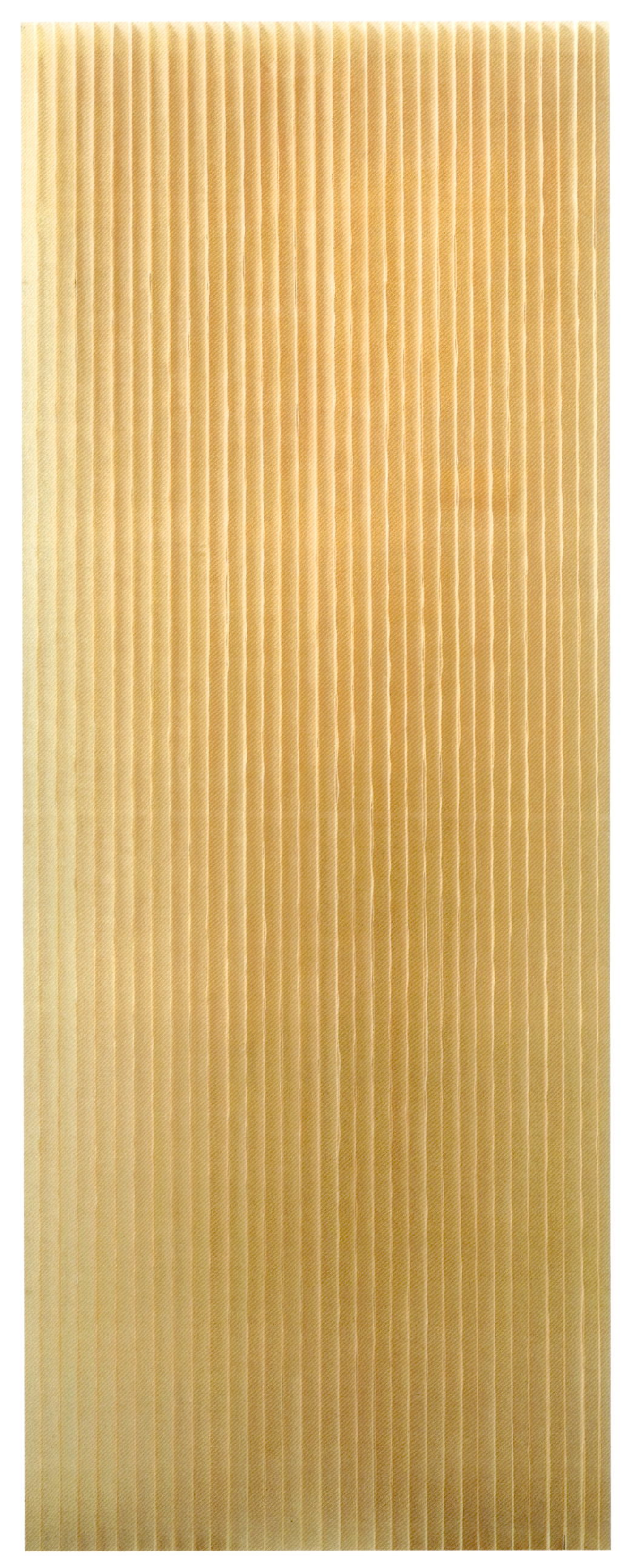

Fig. 37-1
Connection-Lines
Coated fabric, 175 x 70 x 2 cm, 2001

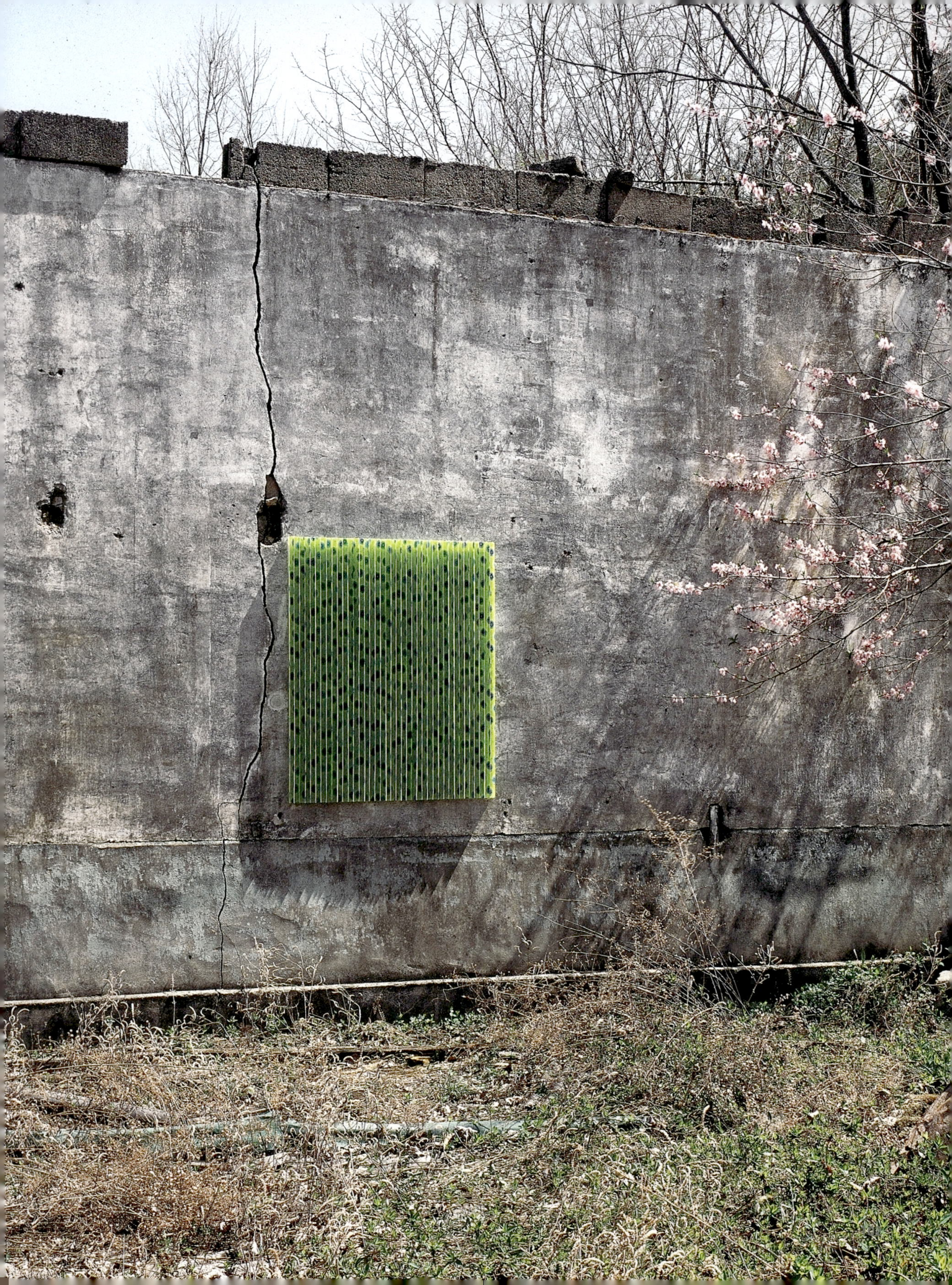

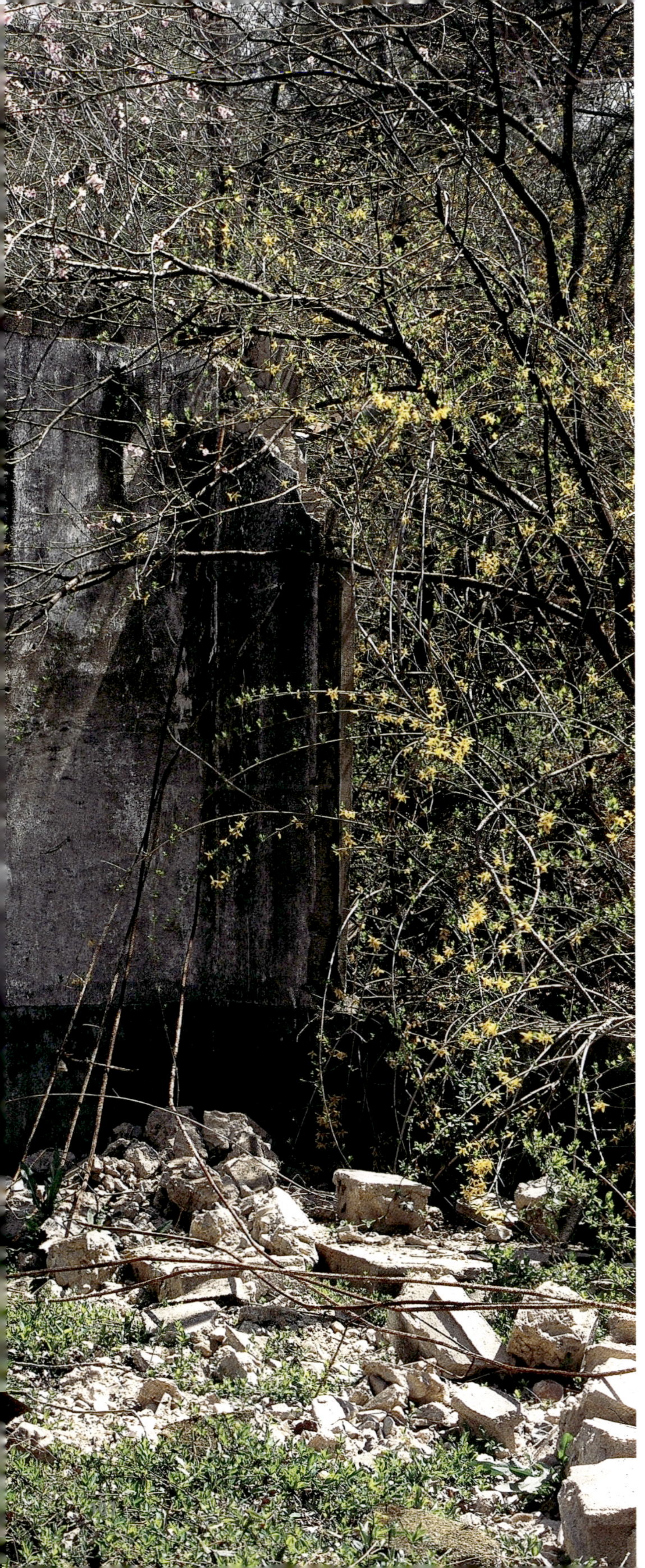

Fig. 37-2
Stroke-Lines
Coated fabric, Sindong, Korea, 2001

익히 알려져 있듯 전통적으로 한국적 정체성을 드러내는 재료로는 한지, 먹, 천연 안료, 목재와 같은 자연 기반 소재가 선호되었다. 남춘모 역시 처음에는 폴리코트 대신 옻칠을 실험한 바 있다. 아마도 단색화 작가들이 그러했듯, '무위(無爲)'에 가까운 미니멀리즘적 반복과 수행성이 강조되며, 전통 매체의 영적(spiritual) 함축이 그에게도 중요하게 여겨졌을 것이다. 그러나 남춘모는 이러한 '한국성의 클리셰(관습적 표현)'에 머무르지 않고, 폴리코트라는 비전통적 재료를 통해 감각적이고 시대적인 '유위(有爲)'의 조형 실천을 실현해냈다.

폴리코트는 본래 산업적이고 비예술적인 용도에서 출발한 물질이다. 그러나 그 표면의 반투명성, 빛을 머금거나 투과시키는 물성, 그리고 반복적으로 코팅되며 생성되는 층위감은 남춘모의 조형 언어 안에서 '감각적 번역'의 매개체가 된다. 그는 이 물질을 통해 전통 회화에서 나타나는 '겹겹이 쌓인 중첩된 준법(皴法)의 밀도', '은은한 여백의 공간과 감성', '작품 전체에 흐르는 리듬과 운율감'을 현대적으로 치환하며, 그 안에 한국적 정서를 담아낸 것이다. 즉 폴리코트는 반복을 견디는 피부이며, 동시에 그 반복을 축적하는 감각의 외피(外皮)로서 드러난다. 남춘모에게 폴리코트는 단순한 재료가 아니라, 생존의 윤리를 각인시키는 '회화적 피부'인 것이다.

한편, 우리는 여기서 '실천(實踐)'이라는 용어 선택에 주목할 필요가 있다. 기존 단색화 담론에서 빈번히 사용되는 '수행(修行)'은 불교적, 도교적 맥락에서 정신적 완성을 추구하는 영적(spiritual) 행위를 함의한다. 반면 남춘모가 강조하는 것은 구체적 노동이며, 일상적 생존 조건과 연결된 물질적 작업이다. 그는 회화 작업을 '수행'이 아닌 '노동'으로, '깨달음'이 아닌 '생존을 위한 실천'으로 이해한다.

As is well known, Korean art has long been centered around materials closely related to nature, such as *hanji* (Korean traditional paper), natural ink and pigments, and wood. In accordance, Nam Tchun-Mo initially experimented with natural lacquer (made from tree sap and wax) before switching to polycoat. Like many Dansaekhwa artists, Nam was likely intrigued by the minimalist repetition and performativity associated with the aesthetics of "*muwi*" (無爲, "nonaction" or "not doing"), as well as by the spiritual connotations of traditional media. Yet rather than devoting himself to such cliché and conventional expressions of "Koreanness," he instead switched to the non-traditional material of polycoat, through which he realized a sensory and contemporary practice of "*yuwi*" (有爲, "action").

Polycoat is an industrial material that was not developed for artistic purposes. But with its layered texture, semi-transparency, and capacity to absorb and transmit light, all of which are accentuated through repeated applications, polycoat has become a medium of sensory translation in the works of Nam Tchun-Mo. Through polycoat, he reinterprets the fundamental qualities of traditional paintings—such as the layered density of texture strokes, the compositional and emotional resonance of blank space, and the overall rhythm and cadence—transposing them to a contemporary context while imbuing them with Korean sentiment. Polycoat thus becomes a skin that endures repetition and, simultaneously, a sensory outer covering that accumulates such repetition. For Nam Tchun-Mo, polycoat is a painterly skin that inscribes his ethics of survival.

이러한 '실천' 중심의 접근은 남춘모가 속한 세대적 조건과도 무관하지 않다. 일제강점기와 전쟁을 겪은 1세대 단색화 작가들에게 '한국적 정체성'과 '수행적 깨달음'은 생존을 위한 절대명제였으리라. 반면 산업화와 경제성장을 경험한 1960년대생들에게는 거창한 담론보다 일상의 구체적 감각이 더 절실한 문제로 다가왔다고 볼 수 있다. 즉, 1세대 단색화 작가들에게 '수행'이 현실적 절실함과 만나는 지점이고, 그것이 한국적 정체성을 규명하는 근거였다면 남춘모의 경우 일상의 감각을 통해 '유위의 실천'을 드러내는 것이 좀 더 진정성 있는 방식이 아니었을까?

중요한 점은, 이러한 작업이 '한국성'을 표방하지 않음에도 불구하고, 오히려 특정한 감각적 리듬과 진정성 있는 태도를 통해 더 깊이 있는 정체성의 층위를 형성한다는 것이다. 남춘모의 작업에서 '한국적'이라는 것은 더이상 재료의 고유성과 민족주의적 기호의 문제로 환원되지 않는다. 대신, 시대를 살아가는 방식, 감각을 조직하는 태도, 진정성을 구현하는 조형적 실천 속에서 그 의미가 새롭게 구축된다.

그의 폴리코트 작업은 외형적 한국성이 아니라, 감각의 진정성을 통해 동시대 미술의 한가운데서 '다르게 존재하는 법'을 제안한다. 이는 단색화 이후 '전통'의 모티프가 어떻게 다시 감각적으로 재구성될 수 있는지를 보여주는 사례이자, 비전통적 재료를 통해 전통을 갱신하는 회화적 실험이라 할 수 있다.

In the discourse on Dansaekhwa, the term "*suhaeng*" (修行), meaning "discipline" or "asceticism," is often invoked to describe the artists' process, usually with reference to Buddhist or Daoist training aimed at mental and spiritual refinement. Notably, however, Nam Tchun-Mo prefers to describe his own process with the term "*silcheon*" (實踐), meaning "practice." For him, painting is not a form of spiritual training, but the concrete labor of daily life. It is not a path to enlightenment, but a practice for survival.

This practice-centered approach is closely related to the social circumstances of Nam's generation. For the first-generation Dansaekhwa painters, who lived through the Japanese colonial period and the Korean War, the search for Korean identity and personal enlightenment through spiritual training was an absolute imperative for survival. By contrast, for those born in the 1960s, who grew up during industrialization and rapid economic growth, the immediacy of everyday sensory experience took precedence over grand discourses. Thus, while the first-generation Dansaekhwa painters felt compelled to pursue muwi (nonaction) and spiritual training as a matter of existential urgency, Nam Tchun-Mo found his own authenticity in practicing *yuwi* (action) through the sensibilities of daily life.

Although Nam's works may not overtly proclaim "Koreanness," their rhythms of sensation and attitude of sincerity nonetheless form a deeper layer of identity. No longer reduced to the essentialism of materials or nationalist symbols, "Koreanness" acquires a deeper meaning expressed through a mode of living in time, an attitude for organizing the senses, and an artistic practice that embodies sincerity.

Eschewing externalized forms of Korean identity, Nam Tchun-Mo's polycoat-based works instead propose a way of being otherwise within contemporary art through the authenticity of sensation. In so doing, they demonstrate how, after Dansaekhwa, the motif of "tradition" can be reconfigured and renewed through painterly experiments with non-traditional materials.

2. 손의 궤적, 업(業)의 회화: 존재를 새기는 조형 실천

남춘모의 작업은 현대미술의 '탈개인적' 경향이나 개념 위주의 작업들과는 다른 길을 걷는다. 그의 회화는 삶의 시간과 감각적 경험을 기록하는 공간이며, 예술가의 몸과 일상의 리듬이 축적된 시간의 층위를 화면 위에 드러낸다. 특히 Beam 시리즈에서 보이는 H빔의 변형된 형태인 'ㅢ' 유닛의 배열은 단순한 반복이 아닌, 시간이 응축된 형상(time-based form)으로 기능하며, 각 유닛은 일정한 노동의 단위를 대변하기도 한다. 이처럼 작가의 행위는 물질의 표면을 변화시키는 동시에, 그 자체로 시간의 흔적을 남기며 화면을 감각적 시간의 구조로 전환시킨다.

주목할 점은 이 반복이 기계적 생산의 효율성과는 무관하게, 오히려 비효율적인 수공의 리듬을 따르고 있다는 점이다. 광목천에 폴리코트를 바르고 덧입히며, 일정한 간격을 유지하면서 구조를 세우는 과정은 마치 장인의 노동처럼 매뉴얼(manual)하고도 느리며, 그 안에는 시간의 압축과 감각의 밀도가 고스란히 배어 있다. 실제로 남춘모는 'ㅢ' 유닛 하나하나를 캔버스에 접착제로 붙이는 작업만큼은 직접 한다. 남춘모는 이러한 감각적 노동을 통해 화면을 '감상하는 대상'이 아닌 '살아가는 과정의 증언'으로 전환시키며, 회화를 통해 생존의 형식을 구축하는 것이다.

그의 회화는 이처럼 반복되는 노동 속에 신체의 시간, 감정의 파동, 삶의 윤리가 차곡차곡 축적되는 '지각의 지층'이자 '삶의 단면'이다. 즉, 카르마(Karma)인 것이다. 그것은 생존의 상황 속에서 이루어지는 '유위(有爲)의 실천'이며, 예술을 통해 삶을 지탱하는 한 인간의 태도, 혹은 시대에 대한 응답이기도 하다

2. Trajectory of the Hand, Painting of Karma: An Artistic Practice that Engraves Existence

Nam Tchun-Mo diverges from the de-personalized and concept-driven approaches that characterize so much contemporary art. Revealing themselves as strata accumulated through time and bodily actions, his paintings are physical records of the artist's daily life and sensory experience. In the *Beam* series, the ㅢ -shaped units, derived from H-beams, are time-based forms, each representing a unit of labor. Thus, the artist's actions not only alter the material surface, but also inscribe traces of time, transforming the pictorial plane into a structure of sensory temporality.

Notably, Nam insists on personally attaching each and every ㅢ -shaped unit to the canvas with adhesive. This repetition does not represent the efficiency of mechanical production, but rather the inefficiency of manual labor and craftsmanship. The process of repeatedly applying polycoat onto raw cotton to "build" structures at regular intervals is slow and arduous, like the work of a craftsperson, carrying within it the compression of time and the density of sensation. Through this sensory labor, he turns the pictorial plane into a testimony of his process of living, and turns the practice of painting into a form of survival.

His painting is a stratigraphy of perception and a cross-section of life, wherein the time of the body, the vibrations of emotion, and the ethics of existence are accumulated through repeated labor. In short, it is karma. It is the practice of *yuwi* (action) carried out for survival, an attitude through which a human being sustains life by means of art, and simultaneously a response to the times.

작가의 손은 단순한 조형의 도구가 아니라, 삶을 꿰뚫는 실천자의 손, 노동의 축적을 인내하는 손, 그리고 성실한 감각적 판단의 원칙을 구현하는 손으로 확장된다. 남춘모가 반복적으로 선을 긋고, 폴리코트를 바르고, 구조를 세우는 과정은 단지 시각적 완성을 위한 조형 행위가 아니라, 삶을 살아가는 방식의 반복적 실천이자, 예술가로서 감내하는 신체적·정신적 시간의 기록이다.

하지만 그의 회화를 기교나 효과를 겨냥한 결과물로 이해해서는 곤란하다. 그는 일정한 구조의 유닛을 인위적으로 배치하지만, 그 배치의 과정에서는 미묘한 흔들림, 리듬, 그리고 예상치 못한 운율이 자연스럽게 생성된다. 남춘모의 '유위'는 서구의 기하학적 추상에서 보이는 정확하고 냉정한 계산으로 산출된 유위와는 다르다. 그의 행위는 철저히 의식적이지만, 그 안에는 감각의 여백, 반복의 리듬, 우연의 윤슬이 녹아있다. 즉, 그의 회화는 '의도된 행위가 우연의 생성을 품어내는 회화적 실천'이라 할 수 있는 것이다.

이러한 반복은 일종의 '회화적 카르마(pictorial karma)'로서, 현재의 행위가 화면 위에 고스란히 각인되며, 과거의 실천과 연결되고 미래의 전개로 나아가는 궤적을 만든다. 붓질 하나, 유닛 하나가 단독으로 존재하는 것이 아니라, 시간의 연쇄 안에서 의미를 획득하며, 반복은 그 자체로 시간의 흔적이자 존재의 증표가 된다Fig. 38.

Nam's hand is not merely a tool for making forms, but the hand of a practitioner who pervades life, the hand that endures prolonged labor, and the hand that embodies sincere principles of sensory judgment. Rather than artistic gestures aimed at visual expression, Nam Tchun-Mo's repetitive acts of drawing lines, applying polycoat, and building structures are practices of living that record the physical and mental time endured as an artist.

Although Nam artificially arranges his structural units with deliberate order, the process naturally entails many subtle tremors and accidental rhythms. Unlike the *yuwi* manifested in Western geometric abstract art, with its cold and calculated precision, Nam Tchun-Mo's *yuwi* is a strategy that contains the sensation of blank space, the rhythm of repetition, and the shimmer of chance. In other words, his work represents a painterly practice in which deliberate action embraces the emergence of chance.

Such repetition functions as a type of pictorial karma. At every moment, the present act is inscribed directly on the surface, linking past practices with future developments. No single brushstroke or unit exists in isolation, instead acquiring meaning within a temporal chain. Repetition itself becomes the trace of time and sign of existenceFig. 38.

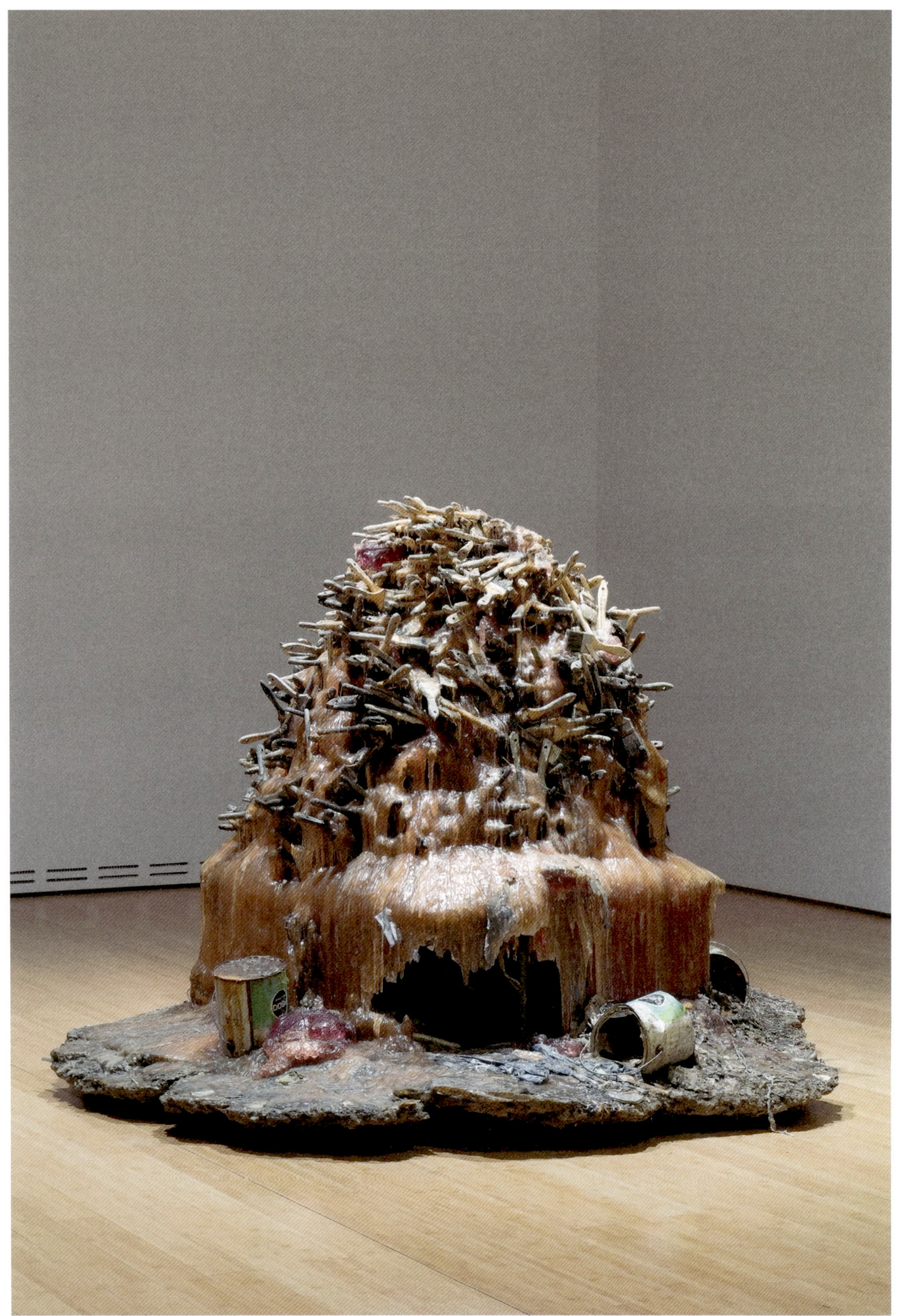

Fig. 38 **Installation** Daegu Art Museum, 2018

이러한 관점에서 '업(業, karma)'은 불교에서 말하는 원인과 결과의 윤회적 고리를 의미하는 개념이지만, 동시에 반복되는 행위가 남기는 궤적이자 존재를 구성하는 흔적의 체계로도 이해할 수 있다. 작가는 결코 즉흥적으로 화면을 휘두르지 않는다. 그는 늘 일정한 리듬, 고된 반복, 세밀한 감각의 조정을 통해 '작업'한다. 이때 작업은 노동(labor)이자 실천(practice)이며, 동시에 자신의 업(業)을 감당하는 행위다. 즉 남춘모의 회화에서 중요한 것은 무엇을 '그리는가'가 아니라, 어떻게 '반복하고 축적하는가'이다.

그의 회화는 단지 결과물로서가 아니라, 과정의 시간성, 행위의 밀도, 손의 흔적이 그대로 남아 있는 물질적 카르마의 실현체라 말할 수 있다. 구조 단위를 수백 번, 수천 번 화면 위에 부착하는 행위는, 감상자에게는 물리적 형태로 보일 뿐이지만, 작가에게는 매일의 반복적인 작업을 견디는 실천의 시간이며, 주체성을 형성하는 과정이다. 이 행위 속에서 축적되는 감각과 기억, 피로와 생존의 원칙은, 그의 작업을 단순한 조형 실험에서 실존적 예술 실천의 현장으로 전환시킨다.

결과적으로 그의 '손의 흔적'은 곧 '시간의 흔적'이며, '행위의 궤적'은 바로 '삶의 리듬'이다. Strokes-Beam 시리즈에서 수많은 선들이 캔버스 위를 가로지르며 형성하는 리듬은 기계적 반복이 아니라, 유일한 행위들의 누적이다. 각 선은 매 순간 달라지며, 선의 굵기와 농도, 방향과 속도, 물성의 밀도는 작가의 호흡과 리듬, 삶의 궤적을 고스란히 담아낸다. 어떤 삶의 태도를 관통하는 반복과 인내, 끈기와 감각의 훈련이 담겨 있다.

Here, karma should be understood not only in the Buddhist sense, as the cyclical link between cause and effect, but also as the system of traces left by repeated action, which constitute existence. Nam Tchun-Mo never impulsively sweeps across the pictorial plane. On the contrary, he always works through steady rhythm, arduous repetition, and meticulous adjustment of sensation. In this sense, his art is his labor and practice, as well as an act of bearing his own karma. What matters in Nam Tchun-Mo's painting is not so much what is "drawn," but how it is "repeated and accumulated."

Each painting is a materialization of karma: temporality as process, density as action, and traces of the hand made visible on the surface. To the viewer, the act of attaching hundreds or thousands of structural units to the canvas may be seen as a physical form, but to the artist, it represents the time of his practice, his endurance of repetitive tasks, and his process of shaping subjectivity. Through this accumulation of sensation, memory, and fatigue—the core elements of survival—his work transcends formal experimentation to become an existential artistic practice.

Capturing the passage of time and trajectory of action, the traces of the hand in his paintings are nothing short of the rhythm of life. In the *Strokes–Beam* series, the countless lines that traverse the canvas generate rhythms not from mechanical repetition, but from the accumulation of singular acts. Each line varies from moment to moment in its thickness, density, direction, and speed, along with the weight of the material, bearing the artist's breath, rhythm, and life trajectory.

반복되는 유닛의 구조화, 폴리코트를 덧입히는 과정, 한 줄 한 줄 선을 긋는 제스처는 모두 무심히 행하는 행위가 아니라 절실한 삶의 태도를 반영한다. 이러한 '유위'의 회화는 일상의 생존과 감각의 지속성을 작품으로 가져오는 구체적인 방식이며, 이는 '예술을 한다'는 것에 머물지 않고, '살아낸다'는 표현을 쓸 수 있을 정도의 작품에 대한 마음가짐과 태도로 읽힌다.

남춘모는 예술을 거창한 이데올로기나 형식의 완성이 아니라, 삶과 노동의 연속선상에 있는 일상의 구축적 행위로 재정의한다. 이는 자본주의 예술시장과 구별되는 작가만의 고유한 실천 방식을 보여주며, 현대 예술이 지닌 존재론적 위기를 회복하는 하나의 대응으로 작용한다. 그의 회화는 감각을 예민하게 정돈하며, 재료와 구조에 끊임없이 개입하고, 반복 속에서 자신만의 감각적 진정성을 형성해간다.

이러한 방식은 동아시아 회화의 이상적 경지인 '예술의 도(道)'를 현대적으로 받아들이는 방식이기도 하다. 그러나 그 방식은 무위의 '자연스러운 발현'이 아니라, 유위의 '의도된 반복과 감각의 축적'이라는 점에서 분명한 차이를 지닌다. 남춘모는 이 유위의 실천을 통해 회화를 삶의 감각적 기록으로 만들고, 예술을 존재의 리듬으로 변화시킨다.

이때의 '업'은 죄업도 아니고, 윤회만을 의미하는 종교적 은유도 아니다. 그것은 오히려 예술가가 자신의 존재를 회화 속에 '물질화'하고, 행위의 궤적을 화면 위에 감각적 구조로 전이시키는 방식, 즉 살아 있는 진정성의 흔적이라 할 수 있다. 남춘모 회화의 반복성과 신체적 특성은 그 자체로 현대적 카르마의 실천이며, 삶과 예술의 일치를 통해 형성된 실존적 진정성을 보여준다.

As such, they embody the repetition, endurance, perseverance, and discipline that form the foundation of a certain attitude toward life. By embedding his paintings of *yuwi* with daily survival and the persistence of sensation, Nam goes beyond "making art," instead demonstrating an ethos and orientation toward painting that can only be described as "living art."

For Nam Tchun-Mo, art does not come from the pursuit of grand ideology or formal completion, but from constructive acts situated on the continuum of life and labor. This attitude and practice clearly separates him from the capitalist art market, serving as a possible response to the ontological crisis of contemporary art. Through patience and repetition, his painting keenly refines sensation, ceaselessly intervenes in material and structure, and builds a sensory authenticity all his own.

This approach can also be seen as a contemporary implementation of the East Asian ideal of the "Tao of art," but through the intentional repetition and accumulation of *yuwi* (action), rather than as a natural manifestation of *muwi* (nonaction). Through the practice of *yuwi*, Nam Tchun-Mo transforms paintings into sensory records of life, and art into the rhythm of existence.

Here, karma is not related to religious notions of sin or reincarnation. It is simply the way the artist materializes his being in painting, transmuting the trajectories of his actions into sensory structures on the surface. The repetitiveness and corporeality of Nam Tchun-Mo's painting constitute a contemporary practice of karma, revealing an existential authenticity formed through the unity of life and art.

VI. 결어

지금까지 살펴본 바와 같이, 남춘모의 회화는 단일한 조형 실험이나 특정 추상 양식의 계보에 국한되지 않는다. 그것은 반복과 구조, 물성, 감각, 정신지리학, 실천적 태도에 이르기까지, 다양한 층위가 복합적으로 쌓인 통합적(integrative) 예술 실천의 모습으로 이해될 수 있다.

그의 작품에서 반복적으로 등장하는 선(線)과 격자(格子), 그리고 폴리코트라는 독특한 재료는 단순한 시각적 장치를 넘어, 감각적 리듬과 존재론적 깊이를 형성하는 핵심 구조로 작용한다. 여기서 '선'은 형태를 긋는 행위를 넘어, 시간을 쌓고 기억을 조직하는 매개로 작용하며, '격자'는 질서와 긴장의 공존, 전통과 현대의 교차를 보여주는 정신의 공간으로 확장된다. 특히 "H빔→'ㅂ'자 유닛→한지 콜라주"로 이어지는 재료의 진화 과정은 구조의 본질을 유지하면서도 끊임없이 새로운 감각적 가능성을 탐구하는 작가의 창조적 여정을 보여준다.

본 논문은 남춘모 회화의 조형적 특성을 '골법'과 '기운생동'이라는 동아시아 회화의 핵심 개념을 통해 해석함으로써, 그의 작업이 단순한 추상의 재현이나 반복의 실험이 아니라, 감각과 태도, 존재와 시간, 내면과 외부가 교차하는 깊이 있는 회화 행위임을 밝혔다. 동시에, '폴리코트'라는 비전통적 물질을 통해 재료와 시대성, 조형성과 한국성을 진정성 있는 감각으로 새롭게 정의하고자 한 작가의 실천은, 동시대 한국 회화의 가능성과 정체성에 대한 중요한 제안을 제공한다.

무엇보다 경북 영양의 밭고랑에서 시작된 개인적 기억이 보편적 조형 언어로 승화되는 과정, 그리고 농사와 회화 사이의 신체적 리듬이 교차하는 지점에서 우리는 남춘모 회화의 독특한 정신지리학적·정신풍토학적 특성을 발견할 수 있었다. 이는 단순한 형식적 탐구를 넘어 '몸의 기억'이 어떻게 조형 실천으로 전환되는지를 보여주는 중요한 사례다.

VI. Conclusion

Nam Tchun-Mo's painting cannot be easily summarized as formal experimentation or confined to the genealogy of any particular abstract style. It is a highly complex and layered artistic practice integrating repetition, structure, materiality, sensation, psychogeography, and attitude.

The recurring elements in his work—lines, grids, and his trademark material of polycoat—function not merely as visual devices, but as key structures that generate sensory rhythm and ontological depth. Here, the "line" exceeds the act of drawing forms to become an autonomous medium that accumulates time and organizes memory, while the "grid" expands into a mental and spatial field infused with tension and order, where the traditional overlaps with the contemporary. Meanwhile, the evolution of his materials—from H-beams to ㅂ-shaped units to *hanji* collage—represents a singular creative journey driven by his devotion to preserve the essence of structure while probing new sensory possibilities.

Interpreting the formal characteristics of Nam Tchun-Mo's painting through core concepts of Eastern ink wash painting theory, particularly "*golbeop*" and "*giun saengdong*," reveals that his practice is not simply an experiment in abstract representation or repetition, but a profound pictorial act involving the intersection of sense and spirit, existence and time, interiority and exteriority. At the same time, through his use of the nontraditional material of polycoat, he reimagines materiality, contemporaneity, and "Koreanness" with an authenticity grounded in sensation. As such, his work poses many compelling propositions for the possibilities and identity of contemporary Korean painting.

Nam's art resonates with a unique psychogeography

또한 '井(우물 정)'에서 '#(해시태그)'에 이르는 격자 구조의 상징적 전이는 전통과 현대, 중심성과 네트워크성이 하나의 조형 언어 안에서 공존할 수 있음을 시사한다. 2024년 창덕궁 낙선재에서의 전시나 프랑스 샴페인 포므리에서의 설치 작업은 이러한 격자 구조가 시공간을 초월한 보편적 조형 원리로 작동함을 입증했다.

남춘모의 회화는 결국 '업(業)'의 반복이자, '생존의 실천'으로서의 예술이다. 이는 기존 단색화의 무위(無爲)적 수행성과 구별되는 유위(有爲)의 미학으로, 매 순간 살아가는 방식이자 예술하는 방식으로 확장된다. 회화를 통해 생존의 형식을 구축하는 그의 실천은 '살아가는 방식의 예술'이자 '회화적 삶(pictorial life)'의 구현이다. 그의 회화는 정지된 이미지가 아닌, 행위의 궤적이며 손의 흔적이고, 존재의 리듬을 기록하는 살아 있는 조형이다.

이러한 관점에서 남춘모의 조형 실천은 현대 예술이 지닌 존재론적 위기에 대한 하나의 응답이기도 하다. 현대 미술계의 제도적 논리와 구별되며 어느 미술사조에도 속하지 않는 작가만의 고유한 실천 방식을 통해, 그는 예술이 단순한 상품이나 관념이 아닌 삶의 구체적 형식임을 증명한다.

그리하여 남춘모의 회화는 단순한 시각 예술이 아닌, '감각의 미학'이며, 시대를 통과하는 하나의 '윤리적 조형 실천'으로서 자리매김할 수 있을 것이다. 그의 작업은 한국 현대 회화가 전통의 형식적 차용에 머물지 않고, 감각의 진정성을 통해 동시대적 의미를 창출할 수 있는 길을 제시한다.

and cultural climatology that derives from his personal memories of working the furrowed fields of Yeongyang, North Gyeongsang Province. By sublimating his childhood experiences into a universal visual language where the bodily rhythms of farming and painting converge, he shows how the memory of the body can be transformed into pictorial practice, beyond mere formal exploration.

With his symbolic transposition of the grid structure—from "井" ("well") to "#" (hashtag)—he suggests how seminal dichotomies such as the traditional and contemporary, and centralized and networked connectivity, can coexist within a single visual language. As confirmed by his recent exhibitions in Changdeokgung Palace and the Pommery in France, this grid structure can operate as a universal compositional principle transcending time and space.

Ultimately, Nam Tchun-Mo's art is the repetition of karma and the practice of survival. As opposed to the performative *muwi* (inaction) of Dansaekhwa, he realizes an aesthetics of *yuwi* (action), using painting to manifest acts of survival. His paintings are not static images, but trajectories of action and traces of the hand, living forms that record the rhythm of existence. Thus, he demonstrates art as a way of living and living as a way of art.

From this perspective, Nam Tchun-Mo's pictorial practice may be read as a response to the ontological crisis of contemporary art. Eschewing the institutional logic of the art world and defying assignment to any art-historical movement, he reminds us that art is not merely a commodity or an abstract idea, but a concrete form of life itself.

Realized through an ethical pictorial practice that transcends its era, Nam Tchun-Mo's works embody an extraordinary aesthetics of feeling and existing. He opens a new path for contemporary Korean painting—one that does not remain bound to the formal appropriation of tradition, but that generates contemporary meaning through the authenticity of sensation.

List of Works

Fig. 1
Stroke-Lines1997-3
Charcoal on paper
57 x 76 cm
1997

Fig. 1-1
Stroke-Lines1997-3
Charcoal on paper
57 x 76 cm
1997

Fig. 2
Stroke-Lines1997-7
Charcoal, oil on paper
57 x 76 cm
1997

Fig. 2-1
Stroke-Lines1997-8
Charcoal, oil on paper
57 x 76 cm
1997

Fig. 3
Lines 0401
Acrylic on paper
105 x 75 cm
2023

Fig. 4
Lines 0603
Charcoal on paper
105 x 75 cm
2023

Fig. 5
Lines_A-203
Charcoal on paper
75 x 105 cm
2020

Fig. 5-1
Lines_A-213
Charcoal on paper
75 x 105 cm
2020

Fig. 6
Stroke-Lines 20-09
Acrylic on canvas
162 x 120 cm
2020

Fig. 6-1
Stroke-Lines
Acrylic on canvas
210 x 160 cm
2020 each

Fig. 7
Beam17-143
Oil on coated fabric
210 x 160 cm
2017

Fig. 8
Stroke-Beam
Oil on coated fabric
143 x 123 x 7 cm
2017

Fig. 8-1
Stroke-Beam
Oil on coated fabric
198 x 134 x 6 cm
2022

Fig. 8-2
Spring-Beam
Coated fabric
ø280 x 10 cm
2017
Installation
Ludwig Museum
Koblenz
Germany
2019

Fig. 8-3
Installation
Gyeongnam Art Museum
2018

Fig. 9
Beam 17-01
Acrylic on coated fabric
160 x 120 cm
2017

Fig. 9-1
Beam
Acrylic on coated fabric
100 x 73 cm
2013

Fig. 9-2
Beam 17-74
Acrylic on coated fabric
2017

Fig. 10
Spring 22-59
Oil on coated fabric
160 x 120 cm
2022

Fig. 10-1
Spring 22-59
Acrylic on coated fabric
160 x 120 cm
2022

Fig. 11
Stroke-lines 20-11
Acrylic on canvas
162 x 120 cm
2020

Fig. 11-1
55 x 320 x 15 cm
2022-23
each
Installation
Indang Museum
2023

Fig. 12
Stroke-Lines 20-83
Acrylic on canvas
210 x 160 cm
2020

Fig. 12-1
Stroke-Lines 20-39
Acrylic on canvas
160 x 120 cm
2020

Fig. 13
Stroke-Lines 20-94
Acrylic on canvas
210 x 160 cm
2020

Fig. 13-1
Stroke-Lines 20-115
Acrylic on canvas
210 x 160 cm
2020

Fig. 13-2
Stroke-Lines 20-107
Acrylic on canvas
210 x 160 cm
2020

Fig. 14
Beam
Oil on coated fabric
210 x 10 x 30 cm
2016 each

Fig. 15
Beam
Acrylic on coated fabric
100 x 73 cm
2014

Fig. 15-1
Beam
Acrylic on coated fabric
210 x 160 cm
2014

Fig. 16
Beam17-112
Oil on coated fabric
210 x 160 cm
2017

Fig. 17
Spring18-22
Acrylic on coated fabric
210 x 160 cm
2018

Fig. 18
From the Earth 2602
Mixed media
on coated fabric
210 x 195 cm
2023

Fig. 18-1
From the Earth
Mixed media
on coated fabric
210 x 195 cm
2023 each

Fig. 19
From the Earth 0212
Mixed media
on coated fabric
160 x 130 cm
2023

Fig. 20
Spring-Beam
Charcoal on paper
57 x 77 cm
2012

Fig. 20-1
Spring-Beam
Charcoal on paper
57 x 77 cm
2013

Fig. 21
Stroke-Lines 0506
Acrylic on canvas
210 x 160 cm
2025

Fig. 21-1
Lines 22-129
Acrylic on canvas
210 x 160 cm
2022

Fig. 22
From the Earth 2606
Mixed media
on coated fabric
160 x 130 cm
2024

Fig. 22-1
From the Earth 2706
Mixed media
on coated fabric
105 x 100 cm
2024

Fig. 23
Beam 24-4
Acrylic on coated fabric
160 x 120 cm
2024

Fig. 23-1
Beam 2013
Acrylic on coated fabric
210 x 160 cm
2013

Fig. 24
Beam 2007
Acrylic on coated fabric
260 x 194 cm
2007-2023

Fig. 24-1
Beam17-03
Acrylic on coated fabric
160 x 120 cm
2017

Fig. 25
Installation
Daegu Art Museum
2018
Coated fabric
160 x 155 cm
2017

Fig. 26
From the Lines 0905
Acrylic on paper and
collage on canvas
160 x 120 cm
2025

Fig. 26-1
From the Lines 1107
Acrylic on paper and
collage on canvas
160 x 120 cm
2025

Fig. 27
Spring-Beam
Coated fabric
960 x 450 x 22 cm
2024

Fig. 27-1
Spring-Beam
Coated fabric
960 x 450 x 22 cm
2024
Installation
Leeahn gallery

Fig. 28
Spring-Beam
Installation
Artist's Studio
2016

Fig. 28-1
Spring-Beam
Coated fabric
320 x 45 x 22 cm
2016 each

Fig. 29
Void 0304
Acrylic on canvas
115 x 100 cm
2024

Fig. 30
Installation
Changdeokgung
Nakseonjae
2024

Fig. 31
Spring 20-22
Acrylic on coated fabric
210 x 160 cm
2020

Fig. 31-1
Lines 2023
Fabric on stainless steel
105 x 60 x 66 cm
2023

Fig. 32
Void 0307
Acrylic on canvas
210 x 160 cm
2024

Fig. 33
Spring-Beam
Oil on coated fabric
263 x 234 x 15 cm
2022
Detail view

Fig. 33-1
Spring-Beam
Oil on coated fabric
263 x 234 x 15 cm
2022

Fig. 34
Spring-Beam
Installation
The Domaine
Vranken-Pommery
2024-2026

Fig. 35
Spring-Beam
Installation
Changdeokgung
Nakseonjae
2024

Fig. 35-1
Spring-Beam
Installation
Changdeokgung
Nakseonjae
2024

Fig. 36
Spring-Beam
Installation
Indang museum
2023

Fig. 37
Connection-Lines
Coated fabric
175 x 70 x 2 cm each
2001

Fig. 37-1
Connection-Lines
Coated fabric
175 x 70 x 2 cm
2001

Fig. 37-2
Stroke-Lines
Coated fabric
Sindong
Korea
2001

Fig. 38
Installation
Daegu Art Museum
2018

Artist's Chronology

남춘모 南春模

1961　　경북 영양 출생
현재　　대구/서울 및 독일 쾰른에서 거주 및 작업

학력

1982-1986　　계명대학교 서양화과 학사
1986-1988　　계명대학교 서양화과 석사

남춘모(1961-)는 선의 반복과 구조를 통해 독창적인 회화 세계를 구축해 온 작가다. 1990년부터 국내외 주요 갤러리 및 미술관에서 개인전과 단체전을 통해 작품을 선보여 왔다. 그의 작업은 한국 단색화 이후 세대를 대표하는 작가로서, 명상적 수행이 아닌 구체적인 손의 노동과 반복을 통해 단색화 너머 새로운 회화의 가능성을 보여준다.

어린 시절 고향 경북 영양에서 본 밭고랑의 기억은 그의 작업 전체를 관통하는 출발점이다. 농사짓는 몸의 리듬, 흙의 감각, 한옥 창살과 서까래의 기하학적 아름다움. 이 모든 기억이 현대적 재료인 플라스틱 수지(폴리코트)를 통해 새롭게 태어난다.

서양 건축의 'H빔'을 '凵'자 유닛으로 변형시키고, 전통 한옥의 '井(우물 정)'자 구조를 현대의 '#(해시태그)'와 연결하는 그의 작업은, 전통과 현대, 동양과 서양의 경계를 자연스럽게 넘나든다. 한지나 먹 같은 전통 재료를 쓰지 않아도, 우리가 살아온 공간과 몸의 기억을 통해 이 시대의 한국성이 무엇인지 보여주는 작가다. 반복되는 손의 궤적 속에서 삶과 예술이 하나가 되는 그의 회화는, 그림이 곧 살아가는 방식임을 보여준다.

개인전

2025	From the Lines, 리안갤러리, 서울, 한국
2024	Strokes and Rhythms, Ceysson & Bénétiére, 룩셈부르크
	From the Earth, 리안갤러리, 대구, 한국
2023	From Lines, 대구보건대학교 인당뮤지엄, 대구, 한국
2022	Spring, Ceysson & Bénétiére, 생테티엔, 프랑스
	Gesture in Lines, Gallery Dorothea van der Koelen, 마인츠, 독일
	Lines from Gesture, 파워롱미술관, 상하이, 중국
	Gesture in Lines, Ceysson & Bénétiére, 뉴욕, 미국
2020	Lines in Space, 리안갤러리, 대구, 한국
	Master of Lines, Ceysson & Bénétiére, 파리, 프랑스
2019	Gesture in Space, 루드비히 미술관, 코블렌츠, 독일
	남춘모, 리안갤러리, 서울, 한국
2018	풍경이 된 선, 대구미술관, 대구, 한국
	선의 충돌과 재확산, 경남도립미술관, 창원, 한국
2017	Blackcolor, 안도파인아트, 베를린, 독일
2016	남춘모, 리안갤러리, 대구, 한국
	Art'Loft, 브뤼셀, 벨기에
2015	남춘모, 리안갤러리, 서울, 한국
	Where Light and Dark Collide, 안도파인아트, 베를린, 독일
	빔 2015, 쿤스트라움21, 본, 독일
2014	갤러리604, 부산, 한국
	갤러리 예동, 부산, 한국
2013	Holly Hunt & Nam Tchun Mo, 홀리 헌트, 뉴욕, 미국
	IBU 갤러리, 파리, 프랑스
	스페이스 홍지, 서울, 한국
2012	갤러리 M, 대구, 한국
	BIBI 스페이스, 대전, 한국
	Galerie Landskron Schneidzik, 뉘른베르크, 독일
2011	IBU 갤러리, 파리, 프랑스
2010	아뜰리에24, 겔터킨덴, 스위스
	데이트 갤러리, 부산, 한국
2009	IBU 갤러리, 파리, 프랑스
	석 갤러리, 대구, 한국
2008	갤러리 우베 삭소프스키, 하이델베르크, 독일
	갤러리 F5, 베이징, 중국
2007	카이스 갤러리, 서울, 한국
2005	아뜰리에24, 겔터킨덴, 스위스
	이현 갤러리, 대구, 한국

2004 조현 화랑, 부산, 한국
2003 카이스 갤러리, 서울, 한국
2002 이현 갤러리, 대구, 한국
2001 박여숙 화랑, 서울, 한국
금호미술관, 서울, 한국
현대예술관, 울산, 한국
갤러리 M, 대구, 한국
2000 시공 갤러리, 대구, 한국
조현 화랑, 부산, 한국
1998 시공 갤러리, 대구, 한국
1996 시공 갤러리, 대구, 한국
1994 갤러리 에피쿠르, 부퍼탈, 독일
1993 갤러리 삭스-물티굴트, 프랑크푸르트, 독일
1992 두빛 갤러리, 대구, 한국
1989 예맥 화랑, 대구, 한국

그룹전

2025 Experience Pommery #18, 뽀메리,랭스.프랑스
Fire, Boghossian Foundation,빌라 엉팡미술관, 브뤼셀, 벨기에
한국추상미술의 하이라이트,대구문화예술회관, 대구
2024 Shapes, Lines & Colors, Lee-Bauwens Gallery. 브뤼셀, 벨기에
이음의 -결.낙선재,창덕궁
단색화의 태도들 : 완료에 정주하지 않는, 서보미술문화공간, 제주
아름다움의 비전, La Gallery, 베니스(In parallel to the Bienniale), 이탈리아
에디터 갑의 집, 오초량, 부산
2023 단색화 넘어 너머로,리안갤러리,대구 한국
Blue-The Colour of the Place, La Galleria Venice. 이탈리아
빛을 찾아서, 수성아트피아, 대구, 한국
2021 클라우디아 훼렌켐퍼/남춘모/헤르베르트 멜러, 빌라프리더미술관, 본, 독일
Lines of Perfection, 헤이그 미술관, 헤이그, 네덜란드
만향, 대구보건대학교 인당뮤지엄, 대구, 한국
2020 텅 빈 충만, 박여숙 화랑, 서울, 한국
2018 한국의 후기 단색화, 리안갤러리, 서울, 한국
Absence, Art'Loft, 브뤼셀, 벨기에
2017 Beautiful Black, 리안갤러리, 대구, 한국
2016 Made in the EAST, MDZ Art 갤러리, 크노케, 벨기에
쿤스트타게 비닝겐, 비닝겐, 독일
변화하는 시간, 쿤스트라움21, 본, 독일
2015 코리아 투모로우 2015, 성곡미술관, 서울, 한국
Leading Artists 2015, 대구문화예술회관, 대구, 한국

	한국현대미술 초대전, 울산문화예술회관, 울산, 한국
2014	AHA, 쿤스트라움21, 본, 독일
	Painting not Painting, 박여숙 화랑, 서울, 한국
2013	갤러리 라우스베르그 10주년 기념전, 뒤셀도르프, 독일
	Trois Accords(이교준, 이배, 남춘모), 동원 화랑, 대구, 한국
	한국 현대미술의 재구성, ICAS, 싱가포르
	색-감성을 속삭이다, 일우스페이스, 서울, 한국
2012	한국의 모노크롬, 반더쿨렌 갤러리, 마인츠, 독일
	한국의 단색화, 국립현대미술관, 과천, 한국
	빛과 색, Space BBK, 쾰른, 독일
2011	Made in Daegu, 대구미술관, 대구, 한국
	기하학적 추상, 갤러리 라우스베르그, 뒤셀도르프, 독일
	절제된 미학, 통인 옥션 갤러리, 서울, 한국
2010	Iwami 국제현대미술제, 이와미, 일본
	In Side Out, 봉산문화센터, 대구, 한국
	오늘의 청년 작가전, 대구문화예술회관, 대구, 한국
2009	리듬, 조형, 교감 : 스펙트럼전, 세종문화회관, 서울, 한국
	8인전, New Painting , 갤러리 yfo, 대구, 한국
	Painted Painting, 아트파크, 서울, 한국
2008	진공의 공간, 갤러리 쌈지, 서울, 한국
	색, 면, 공간, 갤러리목금토, 서울, 한국
2007	Art in Life, 몰테니&C, 서울, 한국
2006	빛과 마음전, 신미술관, 청주, 한국
	2006 부산비엔날레 바다미술제, 부산, 한국
	사각의 색채, 갤러리 M, 대구, 한국
2004	한국평면회화의 어제와 오늘, 서울시립미술관, 서울, 한국
	금호미술관 개관 15주년 특별전, 금호미술관, 서울, 한국
	남춘모-비치가이오전, 라인란트팔츠주 국회의사당, 마인츠, 독일
	SUM of the Contemporary, 대구문화예술회관, 대구, 한국
	나가사키 현대미술전, 나가사키, 일본
2003	아름다움전, 성곡미술관, 서울, 한국
	유쾌한 공작소, 서울시립미술관, 서울, 한국
	Happiness, Art Space M-POST, 서울, 한국
	20주년 기념전, 박여숙 화랑, 서울, 한국
2002	미적인 또 다른 만남전, 나인갤러리, 광주, 한국
	2002 대구현대미술제, 대구문화예술회관, 대구, 한국
	현대미술 초대전, 대구문화예술회관, 대구, 한국
	9월 9인전, BIBI 스페이스, 대전, 한국
	동거동락전, 박여숙 화랑, 서울, 한국
2001	한국미술 2001 : 회화의 복권, 국립현대미술관, 과천, 한국
	休(휴)전, 성곡미술관, 서울, 한국

주요작품소장

갈릴라 홀란더 컬렉션, 브뤼셀, 벨기에

경남도립미술관, 창원, 한국

경북대학교, 대구, 한국

국립현대미술관, 과천, 한국

금호미술관, 서울, 한국

대구문화예술회관, 대구, 한국

대구미술관, 대구, 한국

대구보건대학교 인당뮤지엄, 대구, 한국

대구월드컵경기장, 대구, 한국

루드비히 미술관, 코블렌츠, 독일

리움-삼성미술관, 서울, 한국

미술은행, 과천, 한국

부산시립미술관, 부산, 한국

서울시립미술관, 서울, 한국

스웨덴 한국대사관, 스톡홀름, 스웨덴

코오롱, 서울, 한국

파워롱미술관, 상하이, 중국

파크원, 서울, 한국

현대중공업, 울산, 한국

CAD 인터내셔널, 마이애미, 미국

HJ 타워, 서울, 한국

Mulliez, Group Auchan, 프랑스

Schott Music GmbH&CO.KG, 마인츠, 독일

Musée Cernuschi, Paris,프랑스

Nam Tchun-Mo

Born in 1961, Yeongyang, Korea
Lives and works in Daegu, Seoul, Korea, and Cologne, Germany

Education

1982–1986 B.F.A. in Western Painting, Keimyung University, Daegu, Korea
1986–1988 M.F.A. in Western Painting, Keimyung University, Daegu, Korea

Nam Tchun-Mo (b. 1961) has established a distinctive pictorial language through the repetition and structuring of lines. Since the 1990s, he has presented his work in numerous solo and group exhibitions at major galleries and museums in Korea and abroad. As a leading figure of the post-Dansaekhwa generation, Nam explores new possibilities for painting—extending beyond the meditative discipline of Dansaekhwa through tangible, repetitive labor and the physical engagement of the hand.

The memory of the furrows he observed as a child in his hometown of Yeongyang, Gyeongsangbuk-do, forms the origin that permeates his entire oeuvre. The rhythm of a farming body, the tactile sense of soil, and the geometric order of hanok lattice windows and rafters—these formative memories are reinterpreted through the contemporary material of plastic resin Polycoat.

Nam's work traverses the boundaries between tradition and modernity, East and West. By transforming the H-beam of Western architecture into a 'ㄩ'-shaped module, and linking the hanok's '井(well)' structure to the contemporary '#(hashtag)' symbol, he articulates a spatial language that bridges cultures and eras. Even without the use of traditional materials such as hanji or ink, Nam embodies a contemporary sense of Koreanness rooted in spatial memory and bodily rhythm. Through the repetition of hand-drawn gestures where life and art converge, his painting ultimately affirms that to paint is to live.

Selected Solo Exhibitions

2025 From the lines, , Leeahn Gallery, Seoul, Korea
2024 Strokes and Rhythms, Ceysson & Bénétière, Luxembourg
From the Earth, Leeahn Gallery, Daegu, Korea
2023 From Lines, Indang Museum of Daegu Health College, Daegu, Korea
2022 Spring, Ceysson & Bénétière, Saint-Étienne, France
Gesture in Lines, Gallery Dorothea van der Koelen, Mainz, Germany
Lines from Gesture, Powerlong Museum, Shanghai, China
Gesture in Lines, Ceysson & Bénétière, New York, USA
2020 Line in Space, Leeahn Gallery, Daegu, Korea
Master of Lines, Ceysson & Bénétière, Paris, France
2019 Gesture in Space, Ludwig Museum, Koblenz, Germany
Nam Tchun-Mo, Leeahn Gallery, Seoul, Korea
2018 From Lines to Landscape, Daegu Art Museum, Daegu, Korea
Collision and Respreading of Lines, Gyeongnam Art Museum, Changwon, Korea
2017 Blackcolor, AAando Fine Art, Berlin, Germany
2016 Nam Tchun-Mo, Leeahn Gallery, Daegu, Korea
Art'Loft, Brussel, Belgium
2015 Nam Tchun-Mo, Leeahn Gallery, Seoul, Korea
Where Light and Dark Collide, AAando Fine Art, Berlin, Germany
Beam 2015, Kunstraum21, Bonn, Germany
2014 Gallery 604, Busan, Korea
Gallery Yedong, Busan, Korea
2013 Holly Hunt & Nam Tchun-Mo, Holly Hunt, New York, USA
IBU Gallery, Paris, France
Space Hongjee, Seoul, Korea
2012 Gallery M, Daegu, Korea
BIBI Space, Daejeon, Korea
Galerie Landskron Schneidzik, Nurnberg, Germany
2011 IBU Gallery, Paris, France
2010 Atelier24, Gelterkinden, Switzerland
Date Gallery, Busan, Korea
2009 IBU Gallery, Paris, France
Seok Gallery, Daegu, Korea
2008 Gallery Uwe Sacksofsky, Heidelberg, Germany
Gallery F5, Beijing, China
2007 CAIS Gallery, Seoul, Korea
2005 Atelier24, Gelterkinden, Switzerland
Lee Hyun Gallery, Daegu, Korea
2004 Johyun Gallery, Busan, Korea

2003	CAIS Gallery, Seoul, Korea
2002	Lee Hyun Gallery, Daegu, Korea
2001	Park Ryu Sook Gallery, Seoul, Korea
	Kumho Museum, Seoul, Korea
	Hyundai Arts Center, Ulsan, Korea
	Gallery M, Daegu, Korea
2000	Ci Gong Gallery, Daegu, Korea
	Johyun Gallery, Busan, Korea
1998	Ci Gong Gallery, Daegu, Korea
1996	Ci Gong Gallery, Daegu, Korea
1994	Galerie Epikur, Wuppertal, Germany
1993	Gallery XAS-multikult, Frankfurt, Germany
1992	Dubitz Gallery, Daegu, Korea
1989	Yemak Gallery, Daegu, Korea

Selected Group Exhibitions

2025	Experience Pommery #18 Meodies en Sous-Sol, Domaine-Vranken Pommery, Reims, France
	Fire, Boghossian Foundation- Villa Empain, Brussels, Belgium
	Highlights of Korean Abstract Art,Daegu Arts Center,Daegu Korea
2024	Shapes, Lines & Colors, Lee-Bauwens Gallery, Brussels, Belgium
	Wave of connection, Nakseonjae Changdeokgung, Korea
	Dansaekhwa the Attitudes : Not Settled in Completion, Seobo art space, Jeju, South Korea
	Visions of Beauty, La Gallery, Venezia(In parallel to the Bienniale), Italy
	HERE & MORE : HERE & MORE, Leeahn gallery Daegu, South Korea
	The House of Editor Gab, Ochoryang, Busan, South Korea
2023	HERE & MORE, , Leeahn Gallery, Daegu, Korea
	Blue-The Colour of the Place, La Galleria, Venice, Italy
	Find the Light, Suseong Artpia, Daegu, Korea
2021	Claudia Fährenkemper/Nam Tchun-Mo/Herbert Mehler, Kunstraum Villa Friede, Bonn, Germany
	Lines of Perfection, Kunstmuseum Den Haag, Hague, Netherlands
	ManHyang_brimming scent of art, Indang Museum of Daegu Health College, Daegu, Korea
2020	The Empty of Fullness, Park Ryu Sook Gallery, Seoul, Korea
2018	The Post Dansaekhwa of Korea, Leeahn Gallery, Seoul, Korea
	Absence, Art'Loft, Brussel, Belgium,
2017	Beautiful Black, Leeahn Gallery, Daegu, Korea
2016	Made in the EAST, MDZ Art Gallery, Knokke, Belgium
	Kunsttage Winningen, Winningen, Germany
	Changing Time, Kunstraum21, Bonn, Germany
2015	Korea Tomorrow 2015, Sungkok Art Museum, Seoul, Korea

Leading Artists 2015, Daegu Art Center, Daegu, Korea
Korean Contemporary Art, Ulsan Culture Art Center, Ulsan, Korea

2014 AHA, Kunstraum21, Bonn, Germany
Painting not Painting, Park Ryu Sook Gallery, Seoul, Korea

2013 10th Anniversary of Gallery Bernd A. Lausberg, Dusseldorf, Germany
Trois Accords, Dongwon Gallery, Daegu, Korea
Reconfiguring Contemporary Art : From a Korea Perspective, ICAS, Singapore
Color : Sentiment Whisper, ilwoo SPACE, Seoul, Korea

2012 Monochrom in Korea, Gallery Dorothea van der Koelen, Manz, Germany
Dansaekhwa, National Museum of Modern and Contemporary Art, Gwacheon, Korea
Light & Color, Space BBK, Cologne, Germany

2011 Made in Daegu, Daegu Art Museum, Daegu, Korea
Konkrete Abstraktion, Gallery Bernd A. Lausberg, Dusseldorf, Germany
Minimal Esthetics, Tong-In Auction Gallery, Seoul, Korea

2010 Iwami International Exhibition of Contemporary Art, Iwami, Japan
In Side Out, Bongsan Cultural Center, Daegu, Korea
The Young Artists of Today, Daegu Arts Center, Daegu, Korea

2009 Rhythm, Forms, and Intimacy : Spectrum, Sejong Center, Seoul, Korea
The Exhibition of 8 Artists, New painting, Gallery yfo, Daegu, Korea
Painted Painting, Art Park, Seoul, Korea

2008 Vacuum Space, Gallery Ssamzie, Seoul, Korea
Color, Face, Space, Gallery Mokkumto, Seoul, Korea

2007 Art in Life, Molteni&C, Seoul, Korea

2006 Light & Mind, Shin Museum of Art, Cheongju, Korea
Sea Art Festival, Busan Biennale2006, Busan, Korea
Quadrangle's Colors, Gallery M, Daegu, Korea

2004 Monochrome Paintings of Korea, Past and Present, Seoul Museum of Art, Seoul, Korea
15th Anniversary Special Exhibition, Kumho Museum of Art, Seoul, Korea
Nam Tchun-Mo-Bitzigeio, Landtag Rheinland-Pfalz, Mainz, Germany
SUM of the Contemporary, Daegu Art Center, Daegu, Korea
Nagasaki Contemporary Art Show, Nagasaki, Japan

2003 Extreme Beauty, Sungkok Art Museum, Seoul, Korea
A Pleasant Workshop, Seoul Museum of Art, Seoul, Korea
Happiness, Art Space M-POST, Seoul, Korea
20th Anniversary Special Exhibition, Park Ryu Sook Gallery, Seoul, Korea

2002 Aesthetic Meeting, Nine Gallery, Gwangju, Korea
2002 Daegu Contemporary Art Show, Daegu Art Center, Daegu, Korea
Korean Contemporary Art, Daegu Art Center, Daegu, Korea
September 9 Artists, BIBI Space, Daejeon, Korea
Share Living and Joy, Park Ryu Sook Gallery, Seoul, Korea

2001 Korea Art 2001 : Return to Painting, National Museum of Modern and Contemporary Art, Gwacheon, Korea
Refreshment, Sungkok Art Museum, Seoul, Korea

Selected Public Collections

Art Bank, Gwacheon, Korea
Busan Art Museum, Busan, Korea
CAD International, Miami, USA
Daegu Art Center, Daegu, Korea
Daegu Art Museum, Daegu, Koera
Daegu World Cup Stadium, Daegu, Korea
Embassy of the Republic of Korea in the Kingdom of Sweden, Stockholm, Sweden
Galila Barzilai Hollander Collection, Brussel, Belgium
Gyeongnam Art Museum, Changwon, Korea
HJ Tower, Seoul, Korea
Hyundai Heavy Industries Co. Ltd, Ulsan, Korea
Indang Museum of Daegu Health College, Daegu, Korea
Kolon, Seoul, Korea
Kumho Museum, Seoul, Korea
Kyungbook National University, Daegu, Korea
Leeum, Samsung Museum of Art, Seoul, Korea
Ludwig Museum, Koblenz, Germany
Mulliez, Group Auchan, France
Musée Cernuschi, Paris,France
National Museum of Modern and Contemporary Art, Gwacheon, Korea
Parc.1, Seoul, Korea
Powerlong Museum, Shanghai, China
Schott Music GmbH & Co. KG, Mainz, Germany
Seoul Museum of Art, Seoul, Korea

배원정 裵原正

1981년 서울 출생
국립현대미술관 학예연구사
홍익대학교 미술대학원 겸임교수

홍익대학교 대학원 미술사학과에서 「20세기 중국의 공필화조화 연구」로 박사학위(Ph.D)를 받았다. 20세기 동아시아의 수묵채색화와 서예를 중심으로 한국미술의 정체성과 동시대성을 탐구하고 있다. 전통이 근대와 현대를 거쳐 변모하고 재창조되는 과정과, 그 과정에서 주변부로 밀려났던 작가와 장르를 새롭게 조명하며 미술사 서사의 균형을 회복하는 데 관심을 두고 있다. 주요 논문으로 「20세기 중국의 工筆花鳥畵와 일본미술」, 「모던의 상징: 한국 근현대 장미화」, 「신예화가 박수근의 등단」, 「김관호 행적의 새로운 고증과 제 문제」 등이 있다.

국립현대미술관에서 동아시아 근대미술을 담당하며, 이론적 연구를 전시로 구현하고 있다. 그동안 제대로 조명받지 못했던 대한제국기 미술을 재발굴한 《대한제국의 미술-빛의 길을 꿈꾸다》, 서예와 회화의 경계를 조형적으로 확장한 《미술관에 書: 한국 근현대 서예전》, 한국미술의 계보를 통시적으로 추적한 《DNA: 한국미술 어제와 오늘》 등을 기획했다. 특히 《가장 진지한 고백: 장욱진 회고전》을 준비하는 과정에서, 60년간 행방이 묘연했던 한국 근대미술 대표작가 장욱진의 <가족>(1955)을 일본 소장가의 아틀리에 벽장에서 극적으로 발견했다. 이 발견은 학계와 대중의 큰 주목을 받았으며, 작품을 국립현대미술관 소장품으로 확보함으로써 작가론 연구를 한층 심화시켰다.

동아시아 미술사 연구를 바탕으로 《수묵별미(水墨別美): 한·중 근현대 회화》를 국립 중국미술관에서, 《미술관에 書: 한국 근현대 서예전》을 대만 타오위엔시립미술관에서 순회 전시하며 한국 근현대 미술의 국제적 위상을 높이는데 기여했다. 문헌과 현장 조사를 병행하며 미술사의 공백을 실증적으로 채워나가는 연구를 이어가고 있다.

Bae Wonjung

Born in Seoul in 1981
Curator at the National Museum of Modern and Contemporary Art, Korea (MMCA)
Adjunct Professor at the Graduate School of Fine Arts, Hongik University

Bae Wonjung received her Ph.D. in Art History from the Graduate School of Hongik University with a dissertation titled "A Study on 20th Century Chinese Gongbi Bird-and-Flower Painting." Her research centers on ink and color painting and calligraphy in 20th-century East Asia, exploring the identity and contemporaneity of Korean art. She is particularly interested in how tradition transforms and is recreated through the modern and contemporary periods, and in recovering balance in art historical narratives by shedding new light on artists and genres that had been marginalized in this process. Her major publications include "The Influence of Japanese Paintings on the Fine-brush Bird-and-Flower Paintings in the 20th Century China", "A Symbol of Modernity: Contemporary Korean Rose Paintings", "The Debut of Emerging Artist Park Sookeun," and "New Historical Verification and Issues Concerning Kim Kwanho's Career."

As a curator specializing in East Asian modern art at MMCA, she translates theoretical research into exhibitions. Her curated exhibitions include Art of the Korean Empire-Seeking a New Path, which rediscovered the underappreciated art of the Korean Empire period; The Modern and Contemporary Korean Calligraphy, which expanded the formative boundaries between calligraphy and painting; and DNA: Dynamic & Alive Korean Art, which traced the genealogy of Korean art diachronically. During the preparation of The Most Honest Confession: Chang Ucchin Retrospective, she made the dramatic discovery of Chang Ucchin's Family (1955)—a masterwork by one of Korea's most representative modern artists that had been missing for 60 years—hidden in a closet of a Japanese collector's atelier. This discovery garnered significant attention from both academia and the public, and securing the work for MMCA's collection significantly deepened scholarly research on the artist.

Building on her East Asian art historical research, she has actively engaged in international exchange, contributing to elevating the global standing of Korean modern and contemporary art through traveling exhibitions such as The Modern and Contemporary Ink Art of the Republic of Korea and the People's Republic of China at the National Art Museum of China and The Modern and Contemporary Korean Calligraphy at the Taoyuan Museum of Fine Arts in Taiwan. She continues her research by combining documentary investigation with fieldwork, empirically filling gaps in art history.

마르지 않는 우물(井):남춘모론
NAM TCHUN-MO A Well That Never Dries

저자	배원정
번역(한국어-영어)	박명숙, 필립 마허
그래픽 디자인	애드갤러리 서진선
사진	안동일

설치 사진

루트비히 미술관 코블렌츠 독일	요스트 가브리엘
낙선재 창덕궁 서울	이준호
샹파뉴 포메리 프랑스	김정

색분해	라이프치히의 카스텐 험
용지	아틱 볼륨 화이트 130g
인쇄와 제책	구텐베르크 보이스, 랑엔하겐

초판	2026년 1월
발행처	하트만 북스
주소	Liststraße 28/1 70180 Stuttgart
웹사이트	hartmann-books.com
이메일	info@hartmannprojects.com

하트만 북스는 하트만 프로젝트의 출판 부문으로,
예술가 지원, 전시 기획·큐레이션, 도서 출판을 수행하는 회사입니다.

인쇄	**독일, EU**

Author	Bae Wonjung
Translations Korean – English:	Myoungsook Park, Phillip Maher
Graphic design	adgallery Jin-Sun Seo
Photography	Dong Il An

Installation Photography

Ludwig Museum Koblenz Germany	Jost Gabriel
Nakseonjae Changdeokgung Seoul	Jun-Ho Lee
Domaine-Vranken Pommery France	Jung Kim

Color separation	Carsten Humme, Leipzig
Stock	130g Arctic Volume White
Printing and Binding	Gutenberg Beuys, Langenhagen

First edition	January 2026
Published by	Hartmann Books Liststraße 28/1 70180 Stuttgart hartmann-books.com email: info@hartmannprojects.com

Hartmann Books is the publishing arm of Hartmann Projects,
a company promoting artists, curating and organizing exhibitions,
and publishing books.

Printed in Germany, EU

ISBN 978-3-96070-140-8